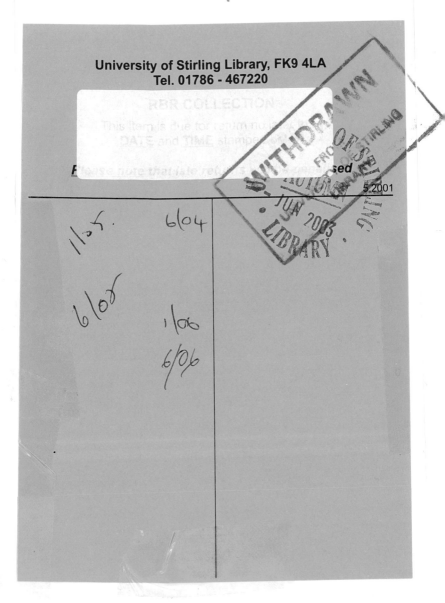

Nationalism, Devolution and the Challenge to the United Kingdom State

Arthur Aughey

Pluto Press

LONDON • STERLING, VIRGINIA

First published 2001 by Pluto Press
345 Archway Road, London N6 5AA
and 22883 Quicksilver Drive,
Sterling, VA 20166–2012, USA

www.plutobooks.com

British Library Cataloguing in Publication Data
A catalogue record for this book is available from the British Library

Library of Congress Cataloging in Publication Data
Aughey, Arthur.
  Nationalism, devolution, and the challenge to the United Kingdom state
/ Arthur Aughey.
     p. cm.
  ISBN 0–7453–1526–7 — ISBN 0–7453–1521–6 (pbk.)
   1. Regionalism—Great Britain. 2. Decentralization in government—Great
Britain. 3. Nationalism—Great Britain. 4. European Union—Great Britain.
I. Title.
   JN297.R44 A84 2001
   320.941—dc21

                                                      00–012146

ISBN 0 7453 1526 7 hardback
ISBN 0 7453 1521 6 paperback

10   09   08   07   06   05   04   03   02   01
10   9   8   7   6   5   4   3   2   1

Designed and produced for Pluto Press by
Chase Publishing Services, Fortescue, Sidmouth EX10 9QG
Typeset by Stanford DTP Services, Northampton
Printed in the European Union by TJ International, Padstow, England

Contents

Preface

Virginia Woolf wrote that, in 1910, human nature changed. That was poetic licence of course. Yet it did capture a mood, a definite sense that major transformations were taking place in British life. The issue that dominated public affairs then was the Irish Question. If the Irish Question was the central question at the beginning of the twentieth century, then it is the British question that is the central question at the start of the twenty-first. Those familiar with the debates on the Irish Question may find much that is recognisable in the debates on the current British question. This time, though, the Gladstonians in the shape of the New Labour government have won the argument. A radical reform of the constitution has been undertaken which will affect radically the future of British politics. Whether the Gladstonian premise, which New Labour shares, that devolution of power to the nations of Britain is the best means to secure the unity of the state remains to be proved. Despite the relentless optimism of New Labour, there are insistent voices enough prophesying doom. These have helped to create a mood of uncertainty about the future of the British state.

One might be forgiven for thinking – in this case with some political licence – that in 1997 the nature of Britain changed. This time the intimation is one of political mortality, a vague but insistent sense that Britain and Britishness are in terminal decline. A brief consideration of some recent literature would confirm that impression. The title of Tom Nairn's book *After Britain* (2000a) has an obvious Woolfian quality to it. The suggestion is that much of British politics may appear to go on as normal, but at a subterranean, cultural level the nature of political life has changed and changed for good. Britain has already broken up in spirit and the fact will soon follow. In that same sense, Christopher Harvie (2000) believes that one can now with some historical accuracy pinpoint the precise era of British nationalism: it was between 1939 and 1970. Today, it is dead and gone. Nationalism can no longer be British – it has returned to Ireland, Scotland, Wales and England after its brief British sabbatical. In similar vein, Andrew Marr (2000) has performed a critical pathology and suggested a number of recent dates for *The Day Britain*

Died. Conservatives have been equally pessimistic. Peter Hitchens has written of New Labour being responsible for a cultural revolution which will end in *The Abolition of Britain* (1999). Even the former Conservative Cabinet Minister, John Redwood, has written of *The Death of Britain?* (1999) – the question mark representing the possibility of the Conservative Party resuscitating the country. However, the evidence is that even some traditional Conservatives no longer believe that Britain can be saved or, indeed, that it is worth saving (Heffer 1999). What informs this dismal vision of the end of Britain? The answer is a number of interrelated assumptions.

The first is a theory of history which proposes that those conditions of Britain's world-historical significance that contributed to its integration as a state – its empire, its military reach, its industrial power – have now gone. By contrast, the world-historical tendencies of the modern age – globalisation, interdependence and national resurgence – now contribute to Britain's disintegration as a state. Historians can paint this picture of decay, the grey on grey of decrepitude, because the owl of Minerva has spread its wings at the dusk of Britishness. That Hegelianism is clichéd and overused. Nevertheless, it sums up well the historicism of the argument. This reading of history informs, in turn, a view that the political ideal once embodied by Britain – in its constitution, its culture, its civility – and that gave self-confidence to national identity is now exhausted. It can no longer inspire respect or interest abroad; it can no longer secure and sustain popular legitimacy at home. The Westminster model has crumbled and Britishness has all the appeal of the living dead. Historical and ideological judgement together issue in a political claim that the utility of Britain and Britishness has therefore ceased. The contract between the separate nations which once shaped them into a United Kingdom no longer satisfies the respective partners. It must now be laid to rest. This is, one might say, the four nations and a funeral conception of modern Britain. The four nations wholly or partly contained by the British state – England, Scotland, Wales and Ireland – must resume responsibility for their own futures. This can best be done within a new Union of world-historical significance, a Union that embodies an inspiring ideal, a Union whose contract is functional to real national interests. That Union is the European Union. Alternatively, as some Conservative English nationalists suggest, it can best be done by independent states living freely on their native abilities in the global market. But the conclusion is the same. There is no future in Britishness. Its narrative has ended. It is time to bury the United Kingdom.

These are the postulates that can be found in the literature suggesting the imminent or actual death of Britain. The purpose of this book is to examine these postulates and to consider their validity. The way in which the distinctive levels of the argument, historical, ideological and political, are deployed in this literature has guided the way in which this book itself has been organised. It is divided into three parts. The first, *Questions*, addresses the broad historical and conceptual issues of the British question. Chapter 1, 'When Was Britain?', considers the question of British history and the formation of its discreet identity. It examines the nature of historical thinking about Britain and how changes in historical thinking have affected the identity of Britain. An understanding of the meanings of Britishness in history is essential to understanding the debate about its meaning today.

Chapter 2, 'What Was Britain?', considers the political ideal of Britishness, the ideology of what is here termed 'the genteel tradition'. It reflects on what was thought (positively) to distinguish the British constitution from its continental European rivals and what were taken to be the instructive values it embodied. Understanding that ideal is a way of grasping a whole tradition of political behaviour, a tradition of behaviour which, its critics on both the Left and the Right argue, is no longer relevant to present needs and is the cause of the decline of Britain.

Chapter 3, 'Why Is Britain?', brings together historical and ideological reflection and considers the contemporary relevance of the ideal of Britishness in the light of recent political changes. These changes have challenged Britain's sense of itself historically and ideologically. In doing so they have brought forth the subversively nationalist question why? – subversive because the stability and security of Britain assumes that the why? of the state is a question which has already been answered. That it has become an open question today is a measure of Britain's political uncertainty.

Part II, *Narratives*, explores the two major ideological forms of integrative Britishness since the nineteenth century. It also considers the newly confident narrative of nationalism which aims to disintegrate Britishness. Chapter 4 looks at the components of the Conservative nation, that political community of interest which was astonishingly successful for most of the twentieth century. So successful was it that it was easy to confuse the particular attributes of the Conservative

nation with the entire character of Britishness. The crisis of contemporary Conservatism, therefore, may equally be taken as a
metaphor for a distinctively acute crisis of Britishness.

Chapter 5 assesses the changing profile of Conservatism's major
competitor for ideological hegemony, the Labour nation. Labour's
patriotism was, and remains, just as fervent as the Conservative
version and both have much in common. Labour's notion of the
people, however, has been quite distinct. Its stress on solidarity
rather than nationality as the basis of political community may be
taken as a distinction without real substance. This book argues that
it has had and continues to have practical significance. Indeed, it
can be argued that the fate of modern Britain is now indistinguish-
able from the fate of New Labour. That is a thought which may
inspire either confidence or the deepest despair.

Chapter 6 examines how the idea of nationalism, especially in
Scotland, challenges the British perspective of the former two
narratives. That challenge has changed. Hitherto, nationalism
presented itself as a movement of cultural or political defence against
Englishness or, as Eric Hobsbawm once put it, the exclusive vector
of historical development in a world made up exclusively of nation-
states. Or it presented itself as both these things. Today the appeal
of nationalism is less cultural defence than cultural chic. It talks not
of separatism but of reconnection with the wider community of
Europe. Nationalism, in other words, claims that it can give
democratic political shape to forces encouraged by the impact of
globalisation in a way the British state cannot possibly do.

Part III, *Futures*, essays an appraisal of the consequences of recent
constitutional changes on the nations and regions of Britain.
Chapter 7 is devoted to New Labour's asymmetrical devolution and
what that now reveals about politics in Northern Ireland, Scotland
and Wales. The major intellectual divide in modern British politics
is taken to be between an expectation that the disintegrative
potential of nationalism can be contained within a reformed British
constitution; and an expectation that these are two truths which
cannot be contained. This, of course, repeats the divide at the time
of the Irish Home Rule debate, but does so in very different historical
circumstances.

Chapter 8 looks at the peculiarity of England within the new
asymmetrical arrangements. It examines the spectral presence of
both Conservative and radical forms of English nationalism. Though
as yet without organised political articulation, these are considered

possibly the greatest, and self-fulfilling, threats to the integrity of the British state.

Finally, Chapter 9 investigates the manner in which the European Union has transformed and has become integral to the British question. This chapter reviews debates about the British question in the light of contemporary European influences and ends with a brief and tentative assessment of what the future may hold for Britain and Britishness.

The book does not claim to be a comprehensive study of these complex matters; no book can ever honestly make that claim. Though it draws substantially upon it, this book is not a substitute for the important research currently being done on constitutional change and on the nations of Britain. One thinks in particular of the scholars associated with the journal *Scottish Affairs*, the Institute of Welsh Affairs and the Constitution Unit. What it tries to do is complement that research by integrating it into a systematic survey of the identity of modern Britain. It is not intended to answer the British question. Rather it is intended as a contribution towards clarification of that question. The book is, in short, a meditation on British identity: what it once was, what it now is and what may become of it.

The book began its life as a short paper read to the joint British-Irish Association/Encounter conference for Young Politicians in Oxford in the spring of 1998. Some of the participants at the conference suggested that the ideas sketchily outlined there could be profitably extended into a book-length study. In particular, Professor Paul Bew was very supportive, as was Dr Peter Shirlow, the series editor of Pluto Press's Contemporary Irish Studies catalogue. The argument was given a more public outing as a brief contribution to the book *Cool Britannia: What Britishness Means To Me*, which was published in 1999 by The Ulster Society. I would like to thank the editors, Gordon Lucy and Elaine McClure, for encouraging a wide-ranging debate on the subject. Conversations with Professor Henry Patterson later helped to sharpen some of those ideas. In the spring of 2000, another joint British-Irish Association/Encounter conference for Young Politicians held at Stranmillis College, Belfast enabled me to present a more considered paper which tested some of the arguments presented in this book. I appreciated the kind responses of the delegates. In particular, I am much obliged for conversations about aspects of contemporary Scotland with the Scottish National Party participants, especially Shona Robison MSP. The insights provided by George Lyon MSP of the Liberal Democrats were very enlightening. Dr Jennifer Welsh's paper to the same conference encouraged a reassessment of the politics of European integration. I appreciate the opportunity both these conferences provided for the development of this book. In this case thanks go to Mary Keen, Sir Nicholas Fenn, Sir David Goodall, Professor Terence Brown and also to Peter Lyner and Phyllis Shaw of the British Council Office in Belfast. Part of the argument in Chapter 7 appeared first in an article published in the *Brown Journal of World Affairs*, Vol. VII, Issue 1, Winter/Spring 2000. I would like to thank the editor in chief, Jennifer Schwartzman, for her permission to reproduce parts of that article. I would also like to thank Roger van Zwanenberg of Pluto Press and Peter Shirlow for their comments on the original typescript, which significantly improved the final text. All the faults, of course, are entirely my own.

No book would ever be written if there was not enough time in which to write it. Most of this book was written during a sabbatical in the second semester of the academic year 1999–2000. I would like to express my thanks to the University of Ulster for granting me that sabbatical and to the former Dean of the Faculty of Humanities, Professor Terry O'Keeffe, for supporting my application. In particular Professor Alan Sharp, Head of the School of History, Philosophy and Politics, has been consistently supportive. A period of academic leave increases the pressure on one's colleagues. I am grateful for their willingness to shoulder the extra demands caused by my absence, especially at a time when everyone was in the midst of preparing our Self-Assessment Document for the Teaching Quality Assessment.

Equally, no book would ever get written to deadline without supportive family. Kathleen and Sky have had to endure the process, and they did so with good grace and understanding. In the school summer holidays Sky even sacrificed her mornings to help me track down obscure references in even obscurer journals. Kola was a constant guard and companion. Kathleen, as ever, has been my inspiration.

Questions

1   When Was Britain?

Shortly after the election of the New Labour government, a leader in *The Times* proclaimed that 'History has become the battlefield for Britishness' (cited in Weir 1999, p. 56). History always has been that battlefield. What *The Times* meant was that the battle for Britishness had intensified and that the outcome seemed more in doubt today than ever before. The prospect of disintegration was now imaginable. Some, indeed, believed it was already happening. Of course, how British history is understood has always had significant implications for the stability of the state. Historical reflection can never avoid being called upon to explain the present and all such explanations are, by their very nature, politically contentious. Michael Oakeshott famously took a very severe position on such activity, believing that the stronger the influence of the present the more history became an occasion for the exercise of political opinions 'like whippets in a meadow on a Sunday afternoon' (Oakeshott 1991, p. 81). The point is an important one. Yet what interest would history have if it were not in some way meaningful to us today? Historical argument forces us to ask questions about Britain and Britishness because it is constantly revising what they once meant and now mean. It may lead us to ask whether the story of Britain itself is coming to an end, such that the question 'When was Britain?' does not appear illogical. It becomes a rational measure of the present crisis of Britishness (Taylor 1997a).

A brilliant example of a critical politico-historical exploration of these matters is found in Gwyn Williams' history of the Welsh in which he sought to answer the question 'When was Wales?' The question itself offends common sense by its apparent confusion of time with place. This is precisely where its genius lies. What Williams intended was to make transparent what common sense occludes. He wanted to show the creative intimacy of history, the imagination and a political sense of place. These things are not fixed or self-evident or timeless, as solid as solid earth. Once there 'was no such place as "Wales". How could there be?' (Williams 1991, p. 2).

In a sustained exploration of what Benedict Anderson (1983) has called 'imagined communities', Williams proposed that Wales was an invention of the Welsh, and the Welsh had invented themselves:

'They had no choice' (1991, pp. 2–3). Perhaps they had no choice either than to become part of that 'human reality rather than a ritual title' of British, that historical people which Williams dates from the Union of England and Wales and Scotland in 1707, a Britain taking shape 'nowhere more visibly than in the land of the original Britons'. Williams recounted how Lord Nelson visited the Cyfartha ironworks at Merthyr Tydfil to meet the men who were making his ships' cannon. 'Richard Crawshay, a shirt-sleeves-to-the-peerage entrepreneur if there ever was one, took the hero's arm and shouted, "Here's Nelson, boys! Cheer, you buggers!".' Cheer they did, wrote Williams, 'and the buggers have gone on cheering ever since' (1991, pp. 141–2), yet perhaps with muted enthusiasm and diminished conviction. For that too is a Wales which is only vestigially or nostalgically now. Modern Wales has been emerging from the wreck of that imperial Britain, a 'morning after a night before which lasted over four generations' (1991, p. 181).

It was not quite 'glad confident morning' either. Writing his history during the early years of Margaret Thatcher's period in office, Williams' tone had become darkly apocalyptic. He believed that Welsh identity was under threat. There might once again be no such place called Wales. The irony rather appealed to Williams. For the new Conservative identity of the 1980s was also intent on getting rid of the old Britain. 'This history of the Welsh may close with the intriguing thought that the Welsh, First of the British, look like being the Last' (1991, p. 303). Such a conclusion might be dismissed as the exaggeration of a tormented romanticism, an example of traditional Welsh pathos. It might also be taken as the predictable lament of a marginalised culture, a lament which also delights in proclaiming the doom of that which has marginalised it. The question, 'When was Wales?', some might argue, is the sort of question which agitates only those whose future is behind them or those Gramscians, like Williams, seeking in vain to subvert Thatcher's English hegemony. But it is not the sort of question for a metropolitan culture confident of making its way in the world – precisely the message Thatcher's government liked to convey about Britain.

Since the publication of Williams' book, things look rather different. His proposition – that Britain is nearing the end of its long march out of history – is what animates keen academic debate. As the discourse of class politics has atrophied and fallen from favour, the discourse of national identity has asserted a new prominence. The question Williams asked is no longer marginal, no longer just what you would expect to hear in Wales (or Scotland or Northern Ireland). It is the question you would expect any intelligent engagement with contemporary British politics to address. The question 'When was Britain?' is now a very live one, and not, as Williams has shown us, a question of exclusively historical interest. It is a deeply political question, and there is no simple or single answer.

Even in the terms of Williams' own approach one might be sceptical about jumping to large conclusions. Did not Williams tell us that the presiding spirit of Welsh history is Gwydion the Magician who always changed his shape and always stayed the same? And might this not also be the presiding spirit of British history? However, large conclusions *are* being made about the fate of Britain as we have known it. In one case, nationalist hope and history rhyme in a world after Britain (Nairn 2000a) and in another, night is already falling on the day Britain died (Marr 2000). In 1992 one of the most influential historians of this generation recommended that anyone who wanted a sense of how critical this question had become in British politics had only to glance at the daily newspapers (Colley 1992, p. 413 fn. 22). They would probably get a clearer understanding if what they read had been published in Edinburgh, Cardiff or Belfast rather than London.

Williams believed that in the making and remaking of Wales history had been crucial. History, he thought, had been employed to make a 'usable past'. In short, it had been employed to 'turn a past into an instrument with which a present can build a future'. It used to be done in terms of myth told by storytellers. Now it had to be done in terms of history told by historians (1991, p. 304). Whatever line we draw to demarcate history from myth, the political significance of history and its contribution to national self-understanding are beyond doubt. In a sophisticated study of nationhood, Adrian Hastings, like Williams, concluded that it can 'survive only through an exercise in imagination, both collective and personal, and imagined things can prove very impermanent. Yet some of them can be toughly enduring as well' (Hastings 1997, p. 27).

A QUESTION OF NOMENCLATURE

That reflection is an appropriate starting point for an assessment of Norman Davies' massive study *The Isles: A History* (1999). The political crisis facing modern Britain, argued Davies, is also a crisis of historical understanding. If the reports coming from the schools were accurate, then the crisis was well advanced. The present generation had little historical awareness, '[a]nd a society unaware of its history is like a person suffering from amnesia. It simply cannot function efficiently' (1999, p. xxvi). This lack of historical awareness was illustrated by the public's ignorance of the basic parameters of the state. Crucial historical and political distinctions fail to register. 'They often do not know what it is called; they do not distinguish between the whole and the constituent parts; and they have never grasped the most elementary facts of its development. Confusion reigns on every hand' (1999, pp. xxvi–xxvii). From the common examples which Davies cites – using England when the United Kingdom is meant or believing one holds an English rather than a British passport – the problem would appear to be an exclusively English one. This does not diminish the extent of the confusion. Rather, it indicates its breadth, since the English constitute over 80 per cent of British citizens. In truth, this does not apply to the English alone, though it is convenient, from Davies' point of view, to suggest that it does. Malcolm Rifkind, Secretary of State for Scotland from 1986 to 1990, once told Gerry Hassan that Scotland was a country with a proud national identity in a union with the other nations in the British Isles. Yet as Hassan pointed out, the British Isles includes the Republic of Ireland, even if the Republic of Ireland no longer employs that term (1994, p. 14). These common-place lapses would not be so serious, argued Davies, if it were not for the fact that they are not confined to popular usage: 'The scale of the problem only begins to emerge when one observes the inability of prominent authorities to present the history of our Isles in accurate and unambiguous terms' (1999, pp. xxvii).

In an extended survey of the work of popular historians, versions of the *Oxford English Dictionary*, *The Oxford History of Britain*, BBC Radio's *This Sceptred Isle* and on-line library classifications, Davies systematically catalogued the problem. He could imagine only one other parallel and that was the former Soviet Union, a point made much earlier by Raphael Samuel. Whether that is true or not, the moral is clear enough: Soviet historians had no incentive to make any distinction between myth and history. Their ideological task was to manufacture a politically useful history, but ultimately, they failed to prevent the dissolution of the Soviet Union. British historians have no such excuse. Their different sort of failure coincides with the same sort of outcome – the dissolution of the United Kingdom. Indeed, Davies' history presents itself as the history of that dissolution. His is an exercise in clarity because the future of Britishness is now past.

It is too late to save Britain by the proper use of nomenclature. However, that is only one rather limited way of looking at the question of Britishness. It ignores what has been distinctive about multinational Britain mainly because its model of nationhood is European. If for Renan getting its history wrong was a condition of nationhood, then one could argue that getting its name wrong was a condition of Britishness. That this implied a relatively benign political culture has been attested to by writers such as Bernard Crick. For Crick, the confusion was functional. It helped to reconcile Englishness with Britishness; it also permitted a useful vagueness which served to accommodate the different legal and religious establishments in Scotland and England to a common Britishness (Crick 1989, pp. 23–34). It may be argued that this is no longer sufficient to reconcile the English or to accommodate the Scots. This does not mean that it is impossible to achieve that reconciliation or accommodation. It is true that the question of nomenclature is bound up in a wider political struggle to transform Britain, and for some to end it altogether. 'When was Britain?' is a question of mastery and goes to the very heart of the state. Nationalists who want to dissolve Britishness recognise this. So too do those who want to preserve it. The important point is that the question is not closed.

Those Parisian radicals who proclaimed in 1968 that history never repeats itself, it only stutters, were right – up to a point. What often appears to be repetition is invariably something rather different. Times do change and so also do the players. But there are always fascinating similarities. In 1913, during the debates on the Home Rule Bill, the Conservative MP Leo Amery felt that the difficulties between Ireland and the rest of the United Kingdom had a particular source. It was a problem of nomenclature. His view was that if only a single name had been coined for the United Kingdom a century earlier, then the whole question of Home Rule would never have arisen (Robbins 1984, p. 290). While one may concede that the power to name is also a part of the power to control, one may doubt Amery's conclusion. His ruminations revealed that the significance of how the state is described has never been far from the surface of British politics. Political scientists have been discussing this for some time

(Jones and Keating 1985, pp. 11–13). It breaks the surface to become a pressing issue at times of chronic or acute constitutional crisis.

Amery's remarks were used to good purpose by Keith Robbins in his own imaginative enterprise to construct a comprehensively British (rather than a merely English) history. Writing over 15 years before Davies, he noted: 'United Kingdoms are sufficiently rare in the contemporary world for there to be little doubt about *the* United Kingdom.' For Robbins, however, the lack of a usable, convenient and accurate adjectival form had been crippling. He concluded, like Davies, that this lack has left 'most citizens with a very imperfect grasp of the complexity and diversity of the state to which they belong' (Robbins 1983, p. 3). It left historians reluctant to deal with the problem of 'writing' the United Kingdom. In the nineteenth century it was something of a convention, and not an example of political incorrectness, to substitute England for Britain. Even Gladstone (of Scottish descent) and Lord Rosebery (of Scottish birth) did so. Some historians would continue to defend that bias in historical writing. Thus, Geoffrey Wheatcroft believed that we read more about English history than about Welsh history, for example, not because the English are patronising but because English history is much more central to world developments: 'That is a fact, as it is also a historical fact that England – especially southern England – has politically, economically and culturally dominated the rest of the British isles for more than 1,000 years' (Wheatcroft 1999, p. 58).

Wheatcroft's bluntness serves only to restate the very problem he seeks to answer. To what extent is it legitimate to argue that it was England alone and not Wales that carried the burden of world-historical significance given the long union of the two countries? Indeed, does this view not ignore the role played by Welsh iron and coal and Welsh sacrifices in the making of British greatness? Lord Nelson fully acknowledged its vital contribution: why else was he visiting Merthyr Tydfil? Furthermore, to what extent should that dominant history acknowledge, by redescribing itself, those who were politically, economically and culturally dominated? It is that sort of redescription which has been the objective set by historians such as Robbins and others and towards which they have been labouring (Morrill and Bradshaw 1996). These historians have been seeking a balance between the claims of a national and of a homogeneous British history: 'If a history of the United Kingdom were to be written it would need to move beyond ethnically driven narrative (à la *Braveheart* or *1066 and All That*) towards a comparative dimension in which "our" response to "our" problems could be judged more dispassionately' (Kearney 2000, p. 24). Kearney, however, was not oblivious to the possibility that the *Braveheart* style of ideological history might prevail, encouraging political disaffection and ultimately separatism. The British response to Wheatcroft would be as follows. Though considerable, English influence in the British Isles has fluctuated. Conversely, the so-called Celtic fringe has exerted a fluctuating influence on England. In sum, the question of British history is a question of balance.

A QUESTION OF BRITISH HISTORY

The attempt to remedy these deficiencies of interpretation is scholarly and professional. It is possible to detect a broadly political objective as well. The focus upon the 'Britishness' of relationships is an act of recovery and remembering. It draws an intellectual map of a very distinctive 'community of fate' (to use Bruno Bauer's expression). It answers the question 'When was Britain?' in a manner which tries to salvage the worth of the subject matter. It also helps to preserve the consciousness of Britishness. As Robbins put it in an address to the Historical Association some 20 years ago: 'In recent decades, we have been frequently told that we have lost an Empire and not yet found a role and part of that process may entail a reconsideration, in a fundamental way, of the history of the British isles as a whole' (Robbins 1981, pp. 413–14). It had become unfashionable to speak favourably of Britain, and though securing it had never been easy in the past, that was no reason to accept the fashionable assumption that it could not be done in the future (Crozier 1990, p. 15).

Raphael Samuel did not mention Robbins in his sweeping survey of what he termed the concern with 'British dimensions', but Robbins clearly falls within the sort of four nations history to which he was drawing attention. For Samuel, the 'when?' of this idea of British history was quite specific: it 'crystallised at a time when the nationality question was becoming a storm-centre of domestic politics, and when the legitimacy of the British state was increasingly called into question'. In the 1990s, this historical approach was experiencing once again a 'current small vogue'. Samuel clearly thought that it suffered from historical, by which he meant political, futility. It might be magnificent, but it was also misconceived.

'History notoriously takes wing at dusk', he wrote. It is then that ghostly presences, like Britishness, make themselves felt. It is only 'a vertiginous sense of impending loss' which conjures up these ghosts (Samuel 1995, p. iii). They make their presence felt only when living history is to be found elsewhere. Samuel's list of the problematic qualities of sustaining this idea of Britain were numerous, amongst them the redundancy of the post-imperial state, the recognition of the contingency of Britishness in the face of nationalist challenges, and the general drift towards a European identity. 'When was Britain?', and the sort of answer that Robbins would present, here becomes a sophisticated exercise in nostalgia, sophisticated in its historical scholarship but nostalgic none the less. The suggestion that an historian has been wrong-footed by history would be amusing if it were not so serious. There is no refuge in the past – at least, there is no refuge in that sort of *British* past.

For Samuel, the condition of 'having been' is increasingly that of Britain. The integration and completeness which Britain lacks in the present are to be found in European unity and ethnic nationalism. His prediction was that a very different four nations history might soon emerge, 'one which focuses on the tenacity of our island ethnicities, and allows more conceptual space for schisms and secessions' (1995, p. xiii). The unity appreciated by Robbins will not be Britishness whose time has gone, but popular republicanism of the nationalist variety, whose time, with the break-up of Britain, is coming. The implied formula is this: problematic constructions of multinational Britishness can no longer withstand the unproblematic assertiveness of ethnic identity. At the other pole is the attraction of European integration, a new Union which will provide a political home for the nations of the unravelling United Kingdom. 'Can historians, then,' asked Samuel, 'fly in the face of politics, pursuing their scholarly agenda in defiance of the spirit of the age?' This question, prompted by Hegelian Idealism, is rhetorically answered by the claims of material self-interest. There would be little future for historians if they persevered with British history since all the lucrative opportunities for advancement are gravitating towards Europe. The recommendation was implicit. British history should be history with a European vocation, a history written with Europe as the milieu, with Europe as the destination. And since the Scots and the Welsh, exercising their self-determination, were more comfortable with this destiny their distinctive histories had become newly significant. Certainly, Samuel's 'problematic' of British history was not without its own problems, none more so than the constructions of 'Europe' and 'island ethnicities'.

That same owl had made its appearance earlier in what became the seminal essay of 'new' British history: J.G.A. Pocock's 'British History: A Plea for a New Subject', published in 1975. In making his plea, Pocock was conscious that he seemed 'to be drawing up flight paths for Minerva's owl'. Like Robbins, he sensed that traditional British history seemed to be drawing to an end. This was the closure of a distinctive 'when was Britain?'. It was an idea of Britain characterised by an imperial and oceanic role, a unitary government and a certain distance from European affairs. As Pocock noted, 'the first and third of these have come decisively to an end, and the second is not yet at the end of its modifications' (1975, p. 628). This was not, however, something to be greeted with lamentation (an unhistorical response). Rather, it was an opportunity to look again at British historical experience, to shift from an Anglocentric focus to the wider scheme of what Pocock called 'the Atlantic archipelago'. It was this enterprise, energetically initiated by Pocock, which was really the subject of Samuel's criticism. He could detect in it a repressed nostalgia and a reactive pessimism, the superficial self-confidence of the approach masking a deeper political melancholy (Samuel 1995, p. vii). And, given Samuel's own vision of the trends of historical research, he suggested that Pocock's history had an unconscious bias against Europe, that it was history for the intelligent Eurosceptic. Pocock, of course, has been alive to the charge.

Pocock attributed a large part of the problem to an unlikely source – the postmodernist's lack of imagination. British history's plurality of nations demands imagination to make sense of it. Confronted with a multinational state such as Britain, the postmodern political mind 'seeks first to dissolve it into its constituent nations, after which it pronounces that the "nation state" is obsolete'. At this point the new British history, which Pocock has championed, takes on a particular conjunctural significance. What he has detected is an ideological pincer movement, which would, in writing a different sort of history, remove the consciousness of Britain altogether. 'Britishness' would dissolve into the mere interaction of national histories – Scottish, Welsh, Irish, English – while 'British' history would be reconstructed to reveal its true – continental – European pedigree. This historical move corresponds to a political fashion. It has become fashionable to propose that the traditional nation-state is both too large for many purposes – hence the need for devolution or even separatism – and too small for most others – hence the need for further European integration. Pocock's conclusion was that to achieve the radical project of evaporating the United Kingdom upwards into 'Europe' and distilling it downwards into its constituent parts requires its own appropriate historical transformation. That transformation may best be described as the dissolution of the imagination of 'Britishness'. To that extent, Pocock is open about the political setting for the trajectory of new British history. Samuel is one of his targets.

In so far as this 'end of British history' fashion had become adopted by the Left, Pocock was keen to point to its ironies. It was a curious objective for the Left, he thought, to dissolve an historic state such as Britain into the market of Europe; curious, that is, 'if one did not know the strategic convolutions of the Leninist mind' (1999a, p. 494). That 'Leninist mind' had taken up residence in the work of Nairn and Samuel. Considering their project on another occasion, Pocock felt that ideological history was repeating itself. In the prophesy of the break-up of Britain (Nairn) or the unravelling of Britain (Samuel) Pocock detected the old Marxist strategy of pushing the capitalist revolution to the limit in the hope of socialist revolution (1999b, p. 138), which is not to say that the project is without its attractions or that it is fated not to succeed.

A QUESTION OF AMNESIA

Pocock's argument is with those who would claim to have history on their side and, on that basis, to speak confidently of a future in which Britishness dissolves. While he would not share the politics of those he criticises nor their hopes, like them he does object to Anglocentric history. Pocock seems to find in it the threatening qualities of laughter and forgetting. Gore Vidal once advised the defeated presidential candidate Hubert Humphrey, who complained that he could not get on the lucrative university lecture circuit because he was seen as a loser, simply to tell people that he had won. After all, Vidal told him, we now live in The United States of Amnesia. Possibly Pocock's sense is that this is becoming true of the United Kingdom. It wasn't all that funny. The main reason was English political forgetfulness. It had happened once already with Ireland (though it was to return bloodily in the shape of the Ulster crisis in 1969).

From Pocock's historical vantage point, the memory loss looks even starker. Within short order the governing class in Britain had declared that neither empire nor Commonwealth ever meant much to them. And some have begun to proclaim that Britain was 'European' all along. Where would it end? If it was possible psychologically to annihilate the idea of the Commonwealth, it was not 'altogether beyond the bounds of possibility that "United Kingdom" and even "Britain" may some day become similarly inconvenient and be annihilated, or annihilate themselves, in their turn' (1975, p. 602). 'When was Britain?', a question which invites serious reflection on historical identity, might soon become a laughable non-question. Or it might become a question of merely defining a distinct historical period, only tangentially related to modern political concerns. It was not inconceivable that future historians would find themselves writing of a 'British' period of history in the same way in which they would write of Angevin kingship or the Holy Roman Empire. The Scot Christopher Harvie (2000) has put the moment of British nationalism between the years 1939 and 1970. English lack of interest, possibly more than nationalist secession or European ambition, could be the cause of this historical closure. One might sum up Pocock's purpose thus. If the British empire was, as the saying goes, composed in a fit of absentmindedness, then the dissolution of the United Kingdom might equally be the result of popular, especially English, absentmindedness. Dissolution may happen, but in the meantime it is worth the effort to be mindful of what could be dissolved. And if, at the same time, it encourages a history that critically explores the meaning of Europe, then that would be a bonus.

Since 1975, the possibilities outlined by Pocock have intensified. Some historians – Davies is an example – do argue that Britain was European all along. There also exists a presumption, again found in Davies, that the United Kingdom will fall apart. Equally, English chauvinism remains alive and well, sometimes in its Conservative denial of Europeanism, sometimes in the Left's hostility to Britishness. The sort of historical enlightenment that Pocock desired does not appear to have influenced matters significantly. Subtle and complex historical reasoning is usually no match for the simplicities of history required by political argument. This should not surprise us given that politics is not concerned about the past but about the present and the future. Historians always find themselves, whether they desire it or not, co-opted into the service of political necessity.

An historian conscious of that unavoidable public condition is David Cannadine. 'Historians,' he wrote, 'are the mediators between the past and the present.' Their intent, of course, is not to serve a political cause. The business of professional history is to remind the public of the error which lies in mistaking the values of the present for those of the past. Historians intend to be the 'enemies of temporal, territorial and cultural parochialism'. Yet history is what historians make of it and historians are bound by their own time and place. For Cannadine, the time and place of Britain at the end of the twentieth century meant 'that we are burdened by the simple and sombre fact that the future of the British past looks bleaker today than at any time during the last forty years' (1987, p. 169). His was a pessimistic meditation on the question 'When was Britain?'. The state of the subject matched the subject of the state and both were in obvious crisis.

'When was Britain?' for Cannadine was the Britain created by historians within living memory, a certain idea of Britain fashioned in the self-confidence of the postwar decades. That history was not only exciting, it was also usable and relevant to a Britain embarking on the enterprise of building the Welfare State. And not only usable but lucrative. It sold well in an expanding academic market both at home and abroad. Understanding British history was the means by which a worldwide readership could understand how the modern world had come into being. Britain's past was the workshop of world-historical significance. Its achievements had inaugurated the important ages of modernity. Britain was the first modern state-builder. It experienced the first bourgeois revolution, it generated the first industrial revolution and it was the first urbanised society. In the twentieth century, its parliamentary institutions had survived what Eric Hobsbawm called the age of extremes. In a striking phrase, Cannadine argued that 'Britain's past always seemed to be antici-pating the future' (1987, p. 174).

The contrast with its condition today could not be greater. British history, rather like the British motor car industry, no longer seemed capable of producing what the world market, or even the domestic market, wanted to buy. Britain was becoming again what it once was, a small off-shore island, a medium-sized power with limited ambitions and limited influence. There was no great reason for the world to be interested in British history and this realisation lowered popular self-esteem and undermined political confidence. The question haunting Cannadine bears comparison with Pocock's concern about the evaporation of Britishness: 'If British history no longer seems a success story, then why bother to make it a story at all?' (Cannadine 1987, p. 189), unless it becomes a story of political undoing which appeals to both *Schadenfreude* (one thinks of the Scottish nationalist) and self-pity (one thinks of a letter writer to the *Daily Telegraph*). But those appeals are limited and unlikely to sustain widespread interest. When Tony Blair laments the lack of a compelling political narrative, that is the British question he has in mind.

In a provocative manner, Cannadine was trying to alarm his profession into reflection. The response to his diagnosis showed alarm at the current political situation and some alarm at his analysis. His apparent nostalgia for a former rosy Whiggish/liberal consensus was seen as a significant part of the British problem. Was it really desirable that historians should mourn the loss of this consensus? The hold of the Whig interpretation, of Britain's uniquely favoured tradition of greatness, had been so strong that its confounding was always likely to produce a pathological response (Cross 1988). Yet the loss of the ideal of 'onwards, upwards' was no good reason to substitute its opposite, 'downwards, outwards'. Other options were available. Moreover, William Lamont thought the sub-text of Cannadine's article to be anxiety about the sort of British history Thatcher's government thought appropriate. The emancipation of historians from Victorian preconceptions of the subject had provoked the Thatcherite ideological backlash: 'The "tell-the-children-Wolfe-won-Quebec" philosophy' of history claimed its reinstatement as the official view of Britain. This was a political as much as a professional concern (Lamont 1988, p. 193). British history was indeed a public matter of some significance and the answer to the question 'When was Britain?' was possibly the key to finding answers to Britain's current troubles.

FORGING THE NATION?

This was obvious to J.C.D. Clark, whose thoughts on the matter provide a remarkably clear-sighted view of the problem. The debate about the teaching of history, which tended to be conducted professionally in terms of methods, was for some an excuse 'for marginalising the old *contents* of which they disapproved – the story of power, liberty, wealth creation, religion, empire' (Clark 1990a, p.

97). What was agitating historians in the 1980s was not so much methodology as Thatcher's attempt to prescribe the contents. Some complained that history was being hijacked by Thatcherism. Some argued that the problem with Thatcherism was that it had no new historical vision for Britain, but simply recycled nineteenth-century myths. The real question for school history was not the question agitating professional historians. It was 'What shall we celebrate?' That is why history would always remain a battlefield. The battle was a battle for cultural hegemony. 'When was Britain?' means 'What sort of Britain is worthy of our patriotism?'

In Clark's opinion, we cannot avoid making a judgement. The politics of the matter is about content. It is also about the 'we'. If Right/Left arguments used to focus on the contest of class or elite versus people, then the change over the last two decades revealed a subtle shift towards the contest of identity. Nationalism's challenge to Anglocentrism has brought with it a challenge to British patriotism. Reflecting on the period since Cannadine's article appeared, Clark concluded that British history had changed more than at any time in the last 150 years: 'It has reappraised the English experience by relocating it in its British and United Kingdom contexts.' Clark concluded that the British Isles 'were a valuable yardstick against which to measure continental European evidence exactly because Britain was related yet not identical' (1997, p. 806).

These positive professional revisions of British history, owing much to Pocock and Robbins, have brought with them a new intellectual vigour. But Clark questioned the impact of this research upon that particular history with which the British once seemed to have a special relationship. In an echo of Cannadine's despairing question, Clark noted that if British history was merely read as a story of decline and political decay then it would cease to have any relevance for the United States. Nor would it inspire its students at home (1997, p. 808). That was not very good news for Britain's political standing. In terms of world significance, British history would no longer be able to play the Greek to the American Roman. The intellectual connection with global power would be correspondingly diminished. The *political* role of British history would be equally diminished. That role has been an important contribution to helping Britain 'punch above its weight' in world affairs. Clark also observed the contrast between the United Kingdom and the United States in the way in which history contributed to national political debate. The question of identity had been at the heart of American politics for a generation. However, in Britain the debate was not really about inclusiveness within a secure constitutional identity, it has been about 'whether to undo the effects of early-modern state-building, and whether to find historically plausible the claims of some Welsh, Irish and Scots to what they allege is an historic mandate to pursue federalism or independence' (1997, p. 793). Yet, things are not that straightforward. The existence of nationalism has never predetermined its victory over multinational Britishness. The context of its challenge had certainly strengthened because of the development of the European Union. Thus Clark situated the most influential recent book seeking to answer the question 'When was Britain?' That book was Linda Colley's *Britons: Forging the Nation, 1707–1837* (1992).

Colley's richly textured work is an articulate expression of a mood as well as a superb intellectual achievement. The irony of Thatcherism was that its radicalism, which had effectively disposed of the power of Old Labour, also helped to dispose of the attractiveness of traditional Britishness. The apparent ease with which the Conservative Party halted and reversed the 'long march of Labour' weakened the grip of other supposed historical certainties. Colley's brilliant study of British identity illustrates the contingency and complexity of the subject. For Colley, the question 'When was Britain?' has a very definite answer. Britain had come into being with the Act of Union joining Scotland with England and Wales in 1707. Over the next century there developed a distinctive British nationalism. Colley felt obliged to justify this expression since she assumed that her readers would understand the term nation to mean cultural and ethnic homogeneity. Her definition, like Gwyn Williams', stressed imagination and political construction. The British nation – or Great Britain, for Colley excludes Ireland – was 'an invented nation super-imposed, if only for a while, onto much older alignments and loyalties' (1992, p. 5). It was an 'invention' and one mainly forged by war against a 'hostile Other', the French. The thesis was stated with clarity and subtlety, and the work itself charted a course between the two mis-descriptions of the state, one based on perfect harmony and the other on coercion. The growing sense of Britishness did not supplant and obliterate other identities. For Colley, identities are not like hats; it is possible to put on several at a time. The idea that Britain was a unitary state was a governing myth. Equally, the claim that it was a product of malevolent English domination was a radical myth.

Getting the question 'When was Britain?' right helps to explain the present difficulties of the British state. For the conditions that served to 'forge' British identity have now almost entirely disappeared. To put it crudely, Britain has lost its significant 'Others'. The imperial 'Other' has gone; so too has the European 'Other'. Inside the European Union it is hard (though not impossible) to define the nation against other European states. Therefore, it was not unusual in these circumstances to see 'the re-emergence of Welsh, Scottish and indeed English nationalism which has been so marked in recent decades'. This was not only the outcome of cultural diversity, 'but a response to a broader loss of national, in the sense of British, identity'. The decaying relevance of the making of Britain may intimate its unmaking in the future. The future of the state was more uncertain now than it had been for the previous 300 years. Colley was aware of the political conclusion which flowed from her historical study: 'What seems to be indisputable is that a substantial rethinking of what it means to be British can no longer be evaded' (1992, p. 375). It is a measure of its contribution that *Britons* became the critical reference point for whatever rethinking was to take place.

The lines of criticism were obvious. First, the stress upon the role of Otherness in creating a British identity seemed to have the effect of hollowing out any substance to that identity. If one's character is dictated exclusively by external forces, then one becomes characterless. Protestantism appeared to be the popular cement. The Protestantism of Great Britain and parts of Ireland may have been shared, but it also contributed to division; closer attention to Ireland would have shown this. Second, the identification of the Act of Union of 1707 as the beginning of *an* idea of Britishness seemed to transform itself into *the* idea of Britishness. This ignored the possibility that important continuities pre-dated the Union with Scotland. These continuities in turn mitigate the impression that, after *Britons*, the days of Britishness are numbered. Simon Partridge has argued that British identity existed well before 1707 and had been in the making since the tenth century. This does not guarantee its survival, but it does challenge the fatalistic assumption that the break-up of Britain is inevitable (Partridge 1999, p. 10). Third, the disappearance of those major factors of British identity noted by Colley did not necessarily mean that Britishness itself would disappear. As Wheatcroft argued, the decline of the foundations of historic Irishness – the Irish language and Catholic Church – did not seem to imply the disappearance of Irish identity (1999, p. 58).

The politics of this was referred to by Donald Dewar, who argued that Colley's description of Britain's historical identity was persuasive, but it became less plausible when it tried to deal with the contemporary era. The extrapolation of Colley's argument into this period implied an 'exhaustion of Britain' thesis and promoted the idea that what had bound Britain together no longer exists. However, Dewar believed this ignored one hugely important fact: the 'community of interest' or democratic solidarity which had evolved since 1707. 'Whatever the old logic to the union, there is a new and robust logic now.' As the factors identified by Colley fell away, other positive interests took their place from the National Health Service through inextricable economic linkages to international security (Dewar 1998, p. 18).

Finally, *Britons* stressed the construction and invention of identity (except, strangely enough, for those older nationalisms which supposedly pre-date the Union of 1707). If the Union of 1707 was new, 'this did not establish that national identity as such was new (it was very old), or that it was false consciousness (it was no more false than any other consciousness), or that it was weakly grounded (it arose in response to their perception of their situations and practical experiences of millions of men and women over centuries)' (Clark 1997, p. 802). Indeed, Clark thought that Colley might prove to be a sorcerer's apprentice, setting loose fashionable but false ideas about British history with disastrous public consequences (2000, p. 276). If these strictures do apply, they apply more directly to Davies' *The Isles*, where Britishness is held to be 'running against the contemporary tide', than they do to Colley's *Britons*, which is more properly ambivalent. This was made clear in Colley's sympathetic review of Davies' book, which also managed to be critical of its assumptions, historical blind spots and conclusions.

In particular, Colley was critical of Davies' conviction that fixed national identities were sufficent in politics; the uniqueness of the question of identity in Britain; and the uncritical looseness of his idea of Europe (Colley 2000, p. 7). If a political project of any sort may be detected in Colley's recommendations, it is the project of New Labour. The new Britain after *Britons* should be more inclusive, more democratic, have a modernised constitution and embrace more confidently the opportunities within the European Union. At the end of the 1990s, Colley wrote that she did not think the current changes in Britain's constitution would lead to the country breaking up. Rather, she was confident that it would have a positive effect.

New Labour's constitutional reforms would help the country adapt more imaginatively to changes in Europe. Wales and Scotland would now take their place as educators of the English. Their self-confidence about a European vocation would encourage England, and therefore Britain, to come to terms with, and play a leading role in, that larger Union. Coming to terms with a European vocation meant dispelling the confusion about the future of Britain. 'Just as our long paralysis over "Europe" derived in part from uncertainty over Britain itself, so these fresh solutions to our own internal diversity may create a new confidence in dealing with our Continental partners' (Colley 1999, p. 29). If these things seem banal, that is the price of political engagement. And the continued absence of Northern Ireland from her thoughts proved that, politically as well as historically, Colley's thesis could cope with only so much diversity at one time.

The complexity and diversity of British history always makes generalisation misleading. Its similarities may mask local differences and local differences may obscure broad similarities. Britain contains political worlds related but not quite on the same wavelength. What recent historical reflection confirms is easily stated. What was once taken for granted about Britain and Britishness must now be openly examined. As a youth in postwar England, Robbins remembered, no one thought about Britain; it was simply a given fact (1999, p. 186). Robbins' professional career is a testament to how far that 'fact' has changed. His concern that 'Britishness' might be an endangered species shows how widespread the sense of crisis has become. This entails another question. What was the Britain which was once a given fact? What was its ideological character?

2 What Was Britain?

Recent historical reflection provides evidence of the transience of political identities. Therefore, the stability of a political association may be measured by the longevity of the 'taken-for-grantedness' of which Keith Robbins wrote. This British taken-for-grantedness was selective in its historical assumptions. Recent generations who grew up on the textbook formula of Britain's constitutional durability and continuity found it hard to understand, for example, the passion of the Irish Home Rule debates. The Irish Question no longer fitted in with conventional political wisdom. As a consequence, the complexity of British national politics faded from public discourse and with it sustained reflection on the ideal and artifice of Britishness. That complexity became a subject of interest for political scientists once again in the 1970s with the return of the Irish Question and the rise of Scottish nationalism. Political theorists were much slower to reflect on what legitimised the identity of the British multinational state. The taken-for-grantedness of national solidarity was integral to the liberalism of academic philosophy. Traditional legitimation of Britishness had become invisible. In order to understand what threatens the survival of the British state today, it is important to understand that traditional legitimation.

One good example of the crisis of British taken-for-grantedness is related by the political philosopher Margaret Canovan. In 1988, she attended a conference where the keynote speaker was the Conservative thinker Roger Scruton. Canovan recounted how Scruton's paper on the subject of national community caused quite a stir amongst the audience. 'Like most British university teachers,' she admitted, 'the academics at that conference were more or less liberal in outlook; not in the sense of belonging to any party or group of that name but in sharing a well-established consensus that takes for granted some vision of traditional liberal ideas like human rights or toleration of diversity.' Scruton's argument – a criticism of multiculturalism – presented a threat to the assumptions underlying that liberal British consensus. His defence of the (Conservative) nation appeared ominously persuasive compared with alternative visions (Canovan 1990, p. 7).

Scruton's arguments had the effect of profitably disordering Canovan's political senses. One consequence was the excellent study of national identity, *Nationhood and Political Theory* (Canovan 1996). Her book was a critical revision of much of contemporary British political thought. Its preoccupations were re-examined in the light of what she felt they already assumed. Questions of nationhood, in her opinion, could no longer be an optional extra for political theory; they should be at the heart of the discipline. The reason for this was simple. Nationhood was the tacit premise in almost all contemporary political thinking and upon which political theorists relied 'to supply the power and solidarity taken for granted in their theories' (1996, pp. 1–2). What Canovan asserts here would seem to have some affinity with Michael Billig's term 'banal nationalism', the ideological means by which established states in the West, like the United Kingdom, are reproduced. In these states there is a 'flagging' of nationhood which is as pervasive and suggestive as modern advertising. However, 'banal nationalism is not a flag which is being consciously waved with fervent passion; it is the flag hanging unnoticed on the public building' (Billig 1995, p. 8). Billig's imagery suggests that it is no longer recognised for what it is.

Canovan concluded that political theorists had to be more willing than hitherto to think seriously about nationhood. The connection between nationhood and power, legitimacy and solidarity required greater attention. This did not mean that theorists should not be concerned with ideals of human rights. Rather it meant that in reflecting upon these matters attention should also be devoted to 'the stability and preservation of those nation-states that have in some imperfect degree given civilized politics an earthly home' (1996, p. 140). Here theoretical assessment intersects with the historical concerns of Chapter 1. The difficulties of nomenclature may well have something to do with that taken-for-grantedness of British nationhood. That distinctive mix of reformed religion, constitutional liberty and imperial mission, which Colley identified as the historic idea of Britishness, once claimed to have given civilised politics an earthly home as well as having bequeathed humane ideals to the world. The historian's sense of the transience of earthly power has intimated the possible demise and certain transformation of Britishness such that the stability and preservation of the United Kingdom is now, as Canovan argued nationhood should be, at the heart of the study of politics. It is interesting, then, to consider her understanding of the Davies problem.

Canovan's solution was neat if problematic. Like some before her, she substituted the expression English/British for either English or British. It was neat, in that it alerted the English to the distinction as well as the relationship between the two identities. It was problematic, in that it raised doubts about the inclusiveness which Canovan claimed for it. It also suggested that Britishness might be a collectively adequate identity for all who were not English. However, she was insistent on one point: those who deny any such thing as a British nation and who claim that there are simply four nations within the United Kingdom bound only by a constitutional contract are misguided. It was far too simplistic to claim that Britain consisted of four nations and one state. For Canovan, the crucial aspect of Britishness is not so much that the Scots or Welsh feel British as that the *English* do. Unlike Davies, she thought that the confusion of English with British is not a sign of arrogance. Rather, it reflects a sense of kinship, 'at any rate with the Scots and Welsh' (1996, p. 79).

Setting such difficulties to one side, it is possible to detect in Canovan's observation the outline of an ideal, which, for a century or more, became part of a 'banal' official self-understanding of Britishness. One may approach it by indicating two misrepresentations. First, Britain is misrepresented if attention is focused exclusively on what distinguishes its component national parts. Second, it is misrepresented if one ignores those things that do distinguish its component national parts. What one calls the place is part of the problem of getting this particular balance right. Unreflective use of the term 'British' can suggest a cultural and political homogeneity which does not exist. Equally, the notion that there is no commonality between the parts of the United Kingdom is unsustainable. Doing justice to what is strange and to what is familiar required some effort on the part of those who helped to fashion the ideal of what was Britain and who helped to forge, in Colley's ambiguous use of that term, a British identity. The question of identity, of course, is a tricky one and the question of British identity is possibly trickier than most. How might one express the ideal of popular Britishness? What was the political balance struck between the claims of four nations and the claim of an encompassing national integrity? One may approach this question of British identity by way of a political paradox.

THE PARADOX OF BRITISH POLITICS

That paradox is the paradox of democratic politics explored at the turn of the twentieth century by the English philosopher Bernard Bosanquet (1910). He called it 'the paradox of self-government'. The paradox starts with the existence of political authority and social coercion and asks how these can be reconciled with modern freedom and self-determination. It is, in other words, a question of political obligation and its obverse, political legitimacy. Why should a community obey laws and rules which, at first glance, might not be those of its own choosing? How can the term 'self-government' apply to those making the laws and also to those obliged to obey them? The question was: 'under what conditions can we say of a community that when its members obey the government and the law, they nevertheless obey only themselves and, in obeying, remain free?' (Primoratz 1994, p. 255). The press of this question intensified as, in the course of the nineteenth century, the *people* jostled for their place on the political stage. Political legitimation demanded some acknowledgement that the state was an expression of the people (Canovan 1999, p 13). The modern world, emerging as a result of these political forces, was redefining the nation in terms of the people. The historical confluence of national and democratic demands generated one way of solving the paradox of self-government. That solution was nationalism.

Nationalists addressed the paradox of self-government by asserting the necessary identity of ruler and ruled. It did so by way of the logical equation: *the national people is the sovereign people*. The collective self (the nation) is only obliged to obey the law because its identity is reflected back to it by the personnel of its government (one's own kind) and by the purpose of state power (advancing the national interest). Identity and loyalty are thus one and the same. This seemed so self-evidently natural a solution to the paradox that any alternative began to appear illogical, unnatural or 'forged'. Its origins were French. As Ernest Barker put it, France said to the Bourbons 'You are wrong in proclaiming, "L'Etat c'est moi"; she said to herself, and she said to the world, henceforth we proclaim, "L'Etat c'est la nation"' (1945, p. 53). This was revolutionary stuff. For Barker, the self-governing nation had become the unit of modern life. No longer was the nation controlled by a single dominant person; it was now the national people.

Despite all the attempts to provide a venerable identity for political nationalism one has to look no further than the eighteenth century for its central idea. Tom Nairn (1981) has proposed, with admirable clarity and insight, 'that a mobilizable nationalism is not only a matter of having common traditions, revered institutions, or a rich community of customs and reflexes'. For him, nationalism is not a question of cultural identity. Rather, the 'mobilizing myth of nationalism is an idea of the people' (Nairn 1981, pp. 294–5). Nairn's view was that Britain lacked a coherent nationalism precisely because it had not absorbed the democratic ideal of French popular sovereignty. Indeed, much of its official identity developed in opposition to it. Colley's 'Other' was France as the embodiment of this alien principle. Britain, according to Nairn, experienced a form of arrested political development because of its archaic monarchy and aristocratic constitution. The Union was a political form dedicated to the frustration of the egalitarian 'idea of the people'. It is an idea which can find expression only in the mode of national and republican self-assertion. Like the old Habsburg empire, the United Kingdom is held to be a prisonhouse of the nations (Nairn 2000a).

Though many of Nairn's assertions drew justified criticism from E.P. Thompson and Eric Hobsbawm, there is some truth in the thesis, a truth that must not be confused with the whole truth. A.D. Smith has argued that a sense of social commonality is essential for nationhood. For Smith, its requirements are a myth of common ethnic descent; an ethnic core from which elites can be drawn; a public emphasis on the uniqueness of the ethnie's cultural values; and, finally, the central role of the people in the political life of the nation (Smith 1996, p. 458). Britishness had fulfilled these requirements, if at all, in a rather muddled way. The pull of distinctive nationalities denied a common ethnic descent, though the power of the south of England provided a ready source of elites. These elites were readily permeated by those from outside the south of England. The unique and irreplaceable values were established constitutional ones and, as a consequence, the people did not participate *as sovereign* in political life. Britain was not a democracy but a constitutional monarchy. The difference might appear to be one of perspective. In his survey of the history of states and nationalism in Europe, Charles Tilly distinguished between what he called state-seeking nationalism and state-led nationalism. The former meant representatives of a population claiming 'an autonomous political status, or even a separate state, on the ground that the population had a distinct, coherent cultural identity'. The latter meant established power adopting the rhetoric of nationhood and demanding 'that citizens identify themselves with that nation and subordinate other interests to those of the state' (Tilly 1994, p. 135). This might go some way towards complementing Nairn's view that, in Britain, established power colonised national sentiment in order to deprive it of radical democratic effect. But it can go only so far in identifying what was distinctive about British identity; it fails to acknowledge its genuine popular support.

The idea of Britishness presented an alternative to the French idea of popular sovereignty. It attempted to distinguish two ideas, which the formula 'the nationalist people is the sovereign people' collapsed. These ideas are nationalism and nationality. Of course for the nationalist, as Nairn correctly pointed out, nationality alone is insufficient. It is an identity arrested only at the level of culture, *in itself* but not *for itself.* Yet, as the Spanish-American philosopher George Santayana once put it, nationality is too deep to be changed honourably and too accidental to be worth changing. This was the insight which the ideal of Britishness claimed to acknowledge and its practical acknowledgement by government has been one important aspect of the survival of the United Kingdom. The claim was that Britishness did not promote a single cultural identity. Nor was it committed to homogeneous political forms. As a consequence, a benign governing tradition protected the honour of its constituent nations and the accidental aspect of nationality was complemented by the extension of common rights of citizenship. The argument further proposed – and without prejudice to the existing traditions of nationality – that a new sovereign people had been brought into existence by the creation of the United Kingdom (Malcolm 1996, p. 359).

The identity of this sovereign people was not to be found alone, as nationalists would have it, in the genealogy of nationhood. Nor was it to be found alone in the formal arrangements of statehood, as utilitarians would have it. Rather, it was to be found in a distinctive British reconciliation of the two. How might this be characterised? In a number of essays published in the journal *The Public Interest,* Harvey Mansfield Jr tried to define the forms and limits of constitutionalism and popular democracy. Constitutionalism, he argued, involved restraining the confidence of democratic majorities in their own sovereignty. For Mansfield Jr the purpose of a constitution was to make political reason paramount over the popular passions.

Ultimately, constitutionalism 'demands a people that is independent, but not so much as to think itself capable of governing without a constitution; it needs a sense of responsibility that is aware of the limits of responsibility'. If it is to be viable, constitutionalism must mean that 'the sovereign people has been replaced by the constitutional people' (1987, pp. 55–7). These American reflections have relevance for identifying the distinctive claim of Britishness.

Britishness involved an idea of the people and of its identity rather different from that of nationalism. It proposed that *the constitutional people is the sovereign people*. It was not Britishness as some peculiar spiritual substance which defined the United Kingdom. Nor was it the acknowledgement of the legitimacy of the constitutional relationship. Rather, the experience of a common loyalty to the constitution had created a new political *persona*. And it was in this 'artificial' persona – the constitutional people – that the identity of ruler and ruled was to be found and with it the resolution of the paradox of self-government. There was union in difference, or what today would be called 'duality'. It was an arrangement certainly grounded in the contingencies of history (Acts of Union), but this did not mean that it was without solidarity. And this appeared to be a thin identity only because 'state-seeking' nationalism suggested that solidarity and community must be grounded in something beyond contingency and beyond history. Nationalists sometimes appear to propose an identity which is at one and the same time above history – the nation is the natural and eternal form of political association – and in history – that Scottishness or Irishness or Welshness is something which can be fully attained only by political activity. To propose an identity which is both above history and yet working itself out in history is to transfer to the nation the sort of reverence formerly accorded to God. As Smith put it, by rehearsing the rites of fraternity, 'the nation communes with and worships itself, making its citizens feel the power and warmth of their collective identification' (A.D. Smith 1995, p. 155). This is also true of Britishness, but it is expressed in a much more formalistic manner.

Britishness was unitary only in a limited sense, partly because of the unifying symbolism of the Crown, partly because of shared political experience. Otherwise, it claimed to accommodate diverse and distinctive institutions, practices and cultures. This subtle ideal often worked in a fit of absentmindedness – so absentminded that most people, especially the English, had difficulty describing it properly (a variant of the Davies problem); and so subtle that those governing the country, especially the English, often failed to understand properly what they had helped to bring into existence. Whatever the reservations – and they were commonly held and frequently voiced – the British solution to the paradox of self-government in a multinational state proved to be distinctive and relatively enduring. The character of the constitutional people attracted international interest (Buruma 1999). That it did have a distinctive character is detectable in the commentary of foreign critics.

The French academician Emile Boutmy, for instance, enjoyed attacking the self-satisfaction he found in British political life. His comments were quite revealing. Boutmy noted that it had been said that Britain is no more than a geographical expression. This, he argued, 'is true of the United Kingdom as a whole: it does not constitute a political unity, and still less a moral unity. Each of its four parts feels its own individuality, and is conscious of a distinct life.' This untidy and irrational arrangement Boutmy found difficult to understand. They would certainly have ordered things better in France. 'Is it possible,' he asked, 'to imagine France occupying the position towards one of her dependencies which England has adopted towards these three Celtic countries: certainly she would not have taken a century to merge their individuality in her own and efface the differences which might hinder the establishment of a general system of government' (Boutmy 1904, p. 98). Things were very different in Britain. Boutmy's criticism revealed much of the difference between the French republican idea of the sovereign people (uniformity) and the British monarchical idea of the constitutional people (duality). This is something which was picked up by R.W. Johnson, who noted that the idea of the 'sovereign people' in Britain was undermined linguistically by the fact that the terms 'people' and 'popular' are not often found in their European sense; the word 'public' was used instead. For Johnson, the British idea of the public had a more reserved and restricted political meaning than the French idea of the people (1985, pp. 230–4), and in his view that was a failing. For most of recent British history the intellectual consensus was very different (Laborde 2000).

These matters had been rehearsed in Lord Acton's famous article, 'Nationality', published in 1862. In the old European system, argued Acton, the rights of nationalities were neither recognised by governments nor asserted by the people. 'Beginning by a protest against the dominion of race over race, its mildest and least developed form, it grew into a condemnation of every State that included different races, and finally became the complete and consistent theory, that the State and the nation must be co-extensive' (Acton 1909, p. 385). In the history of national theory, two distinctive political forms emerged. First, there developed the 'right of national unity which is a product of democracy'. Second, there developed 'that claim of national liberty which belongs to the theory of freedom' (1909, p. 288). For Acton, these two views of nationality were connected in name only and in reality stood at the opposite ends of political thought. They corresponded to the French and the British systems respectively. The latter was distinguished from the former because 'it tends to diversity and not to uniformity, to harmony and not to unity; because it aims not at arbitrary change, but at careful respect for the existing conditions of political life, and because it obeys the laws and the results of history, not the aspirations of an ideal future' (1909, p. 289). This was Burkean constitutionalism, that powerful stream of nineteenth-century English thought, revised and reapplied to the theory of nationalism. Moreover, the coexistence of several nations in the same state indicated a more progressive idea of nationhood than the unity which was the ideal of modern nationalism. Coping with the challenge of nationalism was a test for all states, but Acton was convinced that it was a test which had been solved in Britain (1909, p. 296). As we shall see, British liberals, especially of the Dissenting tradition, did not agree wholeheartedly with Acton. But what they did agree on was the beneficence of the British 'solution', a solution postmodern before postmodernism.

This idea of Britishness, of course, did not completely displace a different idea of the people. That was an idea of the people conceived apart from conventional constitutionalism. As such it had a radical potential, a capacity to challenge fundamentally the procedural conservatism of the dominant perspective. In other words, if the policy of the British state appeared to undermine the rights of the constitutional people, then an uncivil state of popular action could be the way to reassert those rights. This has been an important contribution to the leftwing tradition in Britain. Its most recent demonstration was the revolt against Thatcher's poll tax. Some would even point to the funeral of Princess Diana.

Indeed, the neglect of this popular tradition was the basis of E.P. Thompson's criticism of Colley's British patriotism. Hers was, he argued, a top-down history which flattered 'the conservative self-image' of Britain. Thompson's opinion was that she had done a good job on the making of the British ruling class, but had failed to do such a good job on incorporating the people into the same story. Thompson's own *The Making of the English Working Class* (1963) had shown how 'a significant part of the British experience in these years was the formation of the structures, oppositions, and contradictory cultures of "class"'. Thompson was honest enough to acknowledge that such class analysis was no longer in vogue. However, it was best not to forget its influence entirely. While the radical potential of British society was limited by the extent of constitutional patriotism, it was important to remember that it always existed as a possibility. The British were sometimes 'highly loyalist and sometimes decidedly not so'. There are times, thought Thompson, 'when the patriot must also be a revolutionary' (1993, pp. 377–82). These qualifications and caveats are necessary, but noting them actually illustrates the historic efficacy of the idea of the constitutional people (Brown et al. 1996, p. 42). Influential expressions of its character are deeply laid in the politics of the nineteenth and twentieth centuries.

Take, for example, Dicey and Rait's *Thoughts on the Union between England and Scotland*, the first consideration of which, interestingly, was the Davies problem: the ignorance, even of educated Englishmen, with regard to the Act of Union 1707 (Dicey and Rait 1920, p. 1). Their concern was that the political success of the Union now concealed from many people the problems which had attended its creation and, therefore, the political intelligence needed to sustain it. The judgement of Dicey and Rait was that the Union of England and Scotland had conferred great benefits upon both nations and that their unity was 'the unshakable foundation of British power and liberty' (1920, p. 320). At the same time, the Union preserved what they called the 'nationalism' of England and Scotland. Both acknowledged that in the English case the Union had caused no problem, for its identity had achieved 'perfect security' in the new dispensation. England remained the dominant partner. The case of Scotland was different. The preservation of its identity was a more difficult and serious matter, and Dicey and Rait accepted that the sacrifice made by Scotland in accepting a British fate should never be underestimated. They argued, in a variation on the Santayana aphorism, that if two nations really wished to unite into one state they would 'preserve as much of the noble spirit and traditions of their separate nationality as may be compatible with the wider sense and the extended patriotism which ought to bind together all the citizens of the one politically united country' (1920, p. 326). This, they claimed, had been achieved within the Union.

Their conclusion was an exposition of the ideal of the constitutional people. The extraordinary success of the Act was that it had 'destroyed everything which kept the Scottish and the English people apart; it destroyed nothing which did not threaten the essential unity of the whole people; and hence, lastly, the supreme glory of the Act, that while creating the political unity it kept alive the nationalism both of England and Scotland' (1920, p. 362). That this was more than mere rhetoric has been confirmed by some recent detailed and sophisticated historical research on eighteenth-century Scotland (see Kidd 1993). Today, it has become fashionable to attack Dicey as an unreconstructed English supremacist who dressed up his nationalism in the dignity of parliamentary sovereignty. That is too harsh. Dicey did not favour Home Rule, certainly; nor did he think it was capable of delivering the results its advocates believed it would, namely justice, stability and the integrity of the state (Boyce 1975). This does not mean, however, that he was a state authoritarian. And his collaboration with Rait on Scotland shows that it is inappropriate to claim that he had no respect for cultural diversity either.

The idea of the constitutional people could be used as a practical claim rather than, as in the Dicey and Rait example, a cause for celebration. It informed the Ulster Unionist opposition to Home Rule. What was defended tenaciously was the proposition that the Union had brought into existence a new identity which could not be decomposed without consent into its component parts. In 1912, Thomas Sinclair argued that a minority within the United Kingdom should not be measured by mere numbers alone. Rather, its place in the constitution was to be tested by 'its association with the upbuilding of national character, by its fidelity to law and order, and by its sympathy with the world mission of the British Empire in the interests of civil and religious freedom'. There was no doubt in Sinclair's mind that, albeit a minority in Ireland, Ulster Unionists were an integral part of the British constitutional people. 'Tried by all these tests,' he concluded, 'Ulster is entitled to retain her full share in every privilege of the whole realm' (Sinclair 1972, p. 173). The demand was that they should not be deprived of the protection of British law and the rights of British citizenship. Ironically, the significance of this argument today goes beyond the interpretation made of it by anti-Home Rule Unionists. Shorn of its particular historical circumstance and affiliation, it is an argument appropriate to those campaigning for the rights of racial minorities in Britain today. Indeed, shorn of the imperial claims of Sinclair, it now returns to provide a barrier against the racist ambitions of those who speak of 'repatriation'.

In the Welsh case, there was less clarity than in the Scottish–English relationship though less conflict than in the Irish–British relationship. The national political claim, articulated by Welsh liberalism, was for cultural recognition too frequently denied them by London. 'The ideal of Wales was to be recognised as a part of the British political and social structure: the ideal of Ireland was to be severed from it. The object of the one was equality: the aim of the other was exclusion' (Morgan 1970, pp. 306–7). The Welsh problem, as ever, was its politically indeterminate position as part of England *and* Wales. The Welsh problem, in part, was also a product of its cultural divisions. These examples do illustrate the lineage of a certain idea of Britain, the idea of the constitutional people. As the official self-image of the state, it encouraged a certain style of political writing about Britain. This may be called 'the genteel tradition' in British political thought.

THE GENTEEL TRADITION

The term 'the genteel tradition' is borrowed from Santayana's famous essay *The Genteel Tradition*, though it is not used here in exactly the same way that Santayana used it in his criticism of the smugness, complacency and lack of vigour he detected in the American academic establishment (Santayana 1998, pp. 37–65). The purpose, rather, is to illustrate what was taken to be the security of the British state and the truths it was held to embody. Its self-confidence has already been subverted by events. That tradition can be traced in the work of one of its most outstanding exponents, Ernest Barker. Barker was neither a simple apologist nor a patriotic hack. He was a serious thinker and an influential figure in the public life of twentieth-century Britain. Barker's reputation has suffered partly because the genteel tradition itself has decayed. As Stapleton argues, Barker's difficulty in making the transition to contemporary relevance is that 'his complacency and sanguinity often represented a triumph of faith over considerable anxiety about modern social and political life. That anxiety is not so easily dismissed as his now rare optimism' (Stapleton 1994, pp. 202–3). The faith, however, is still worth examining.

In *National Character and the Factors in its Formation*, Barker argued that nationhood was a function of nurture not of nature. It was made, and as such was also modifiable (Barker 1928, p. 7). A nation was not the physical fact of one blood; it was an effort of the imagination which had created a common tradition. And it was out of such a common tradition that one could speak of the British nation. It was here that the liberal Dissenter took issue with the Catholic Lord Acton. While acknowledging the intellectual force of Acton's essay on nationality, Barker took issue with him on the character of the multinational state. This was, in effect, a surrogate criticism of the old Austro-Hungarian Empire for which Acton (naturally enough) expressed some sympathy. It is vital to follow Barker's argument in some detail here for it highlights concisely the character of the constitutional people.

Barker thought Acton's understanding was defective for a number of reasons. First, the sort of multinationalism with which he seemed content – the Habsburg model – 'either pits each nation against the rest to secure its own absolutism, or allows itself to become the organ of one of the nations for the suppression of the others' (1927, p. 16). Second, Acton assumed that nationality existed in two different forms: there was nationality as only a social fact which revealed itself 'in common thoughts and feelings, custom and dress, language and possibly literature'; and, there was nationality as a political as well as a social fact where 'it issues in a common organization, possessed of authority, which expresses a common and independent will'. This was true, argued Barker, but only up to a point. It was too neat. It showed its limitations clearly when applied to the British case. 'There is a sense', he thought, 'in which the Scottish and the Welsh peoples are nations of the first degree, content with the social expression of their quality.' But this was only the half of it. 'On the other hand, the members of these peoples are also members of a nation – the British nation – which is a nation of the second degree.' The Scots and the Welsh would not be content with a social expression of their identity, he thought, if they did not possess a political expression for it in the British state.

It was democracy which had transformed the fate of British multinationalism. An autocratic state might have united under the single will of the monarch a number of nations that were required to remain in the first degree, that is as mere social groups. This was no longer possible in the era of popular politics. In stating his reasons, Barker expressed the key notion of Britishness. A state which is multinational would fall apart into as many democracies as there are nationalities by the dynamic of democratic will unless there was a countervailing democratic will securing the state. This had indeed been achieved in Britain. The British 'can be both multi-national and a single nation, and teach its citizens at one and the same time to glory both in the name of Scotsmen or Welshmen or Englishmen and in the name of Britons' (1927, p. 17). The assumption, quite clearly, was that of a problem solved. Yet once the rather rosy assumption came in for serious and sustained questioning, the political basis of that solution can appear rather fragile. Nevertheless, Barker had made his case with admirable clarity. He was not unaware of the difficulties which attended it.

Later in the same study Barker noted that the Scots had a distinct nationhood. If Scots remained satisfied with this duality, no question of divided allegiance arose. If they should ever resolve to decide otherwise, then they would have their way (1927, p. 130). There is no suggestion here of a British state, like the French, one and indivisible. The association which Barker believed secured national justice was also a free association. If the Scots should choose to leave, that was their right. No power could or should stand in their way. In his influential *Principles of Social and Political Theory* (1951b), Barker further acknowledged the special case of Scotland and, in anticipation of another of Nairn's arguments, accepted that it was 'seldom easy for a national minority to be content to exist simply as a *social group*'. There always existed pressures to push beyond that limit to full statehood. It was no good trying to make hard-and-fast rules about that limit, it all depended on the disposition of the nations in the United Kingdom. 'To distinguish between the "social" and "legal" sphere' is no solution unless the national minorities are 'willing to recognize and observe that distinction'. The same thing applied to the majority nation upon which the state was predominantly based (Barker 1951a, p. 57). This liberal lightness of touch in Barker's concept of Britishness explains his predisposition towards 'neighbourliness' as opposed to an integral, European form of nationalism. For him, true nationality was to be found in 'the sweet ties of neighbourliness' which were strengthened by common traditions, a perfect conception of gentility if there ever was one, conjuring up as it does the privet hedge of privacy and the village green of conviviality. Even after the slaughter of the First World War, the practical wisdom of the liberal, Burkean Englishman remained assured. 'Neighbourliness is a quiet virtue – quiet but deep and permeating. It is a virtue that pays' (1919, p. 144). The conception was also functional in that it identified the proper conditions for the management of Britain's empire.

In Barker's imperial imagination, neighbourliness had become zoned, and these zones were to fit concentrically into one another. The neatness of the conception did not dispel its genteel mystery. First, there was the broad and comprehensive zone of the empire. Second, there was the narrower zone of the United Kingdom. Third, within the United Kingdom there were the distinctive nations. Finally, there was the innermost zone of the counties and shires, each with their own particular loyalties. When the British spoke in terms of the nation and of national life, Barker did not wonder at its difficulty (1927, p. 130). The outward expansion of empire did not depend on uniformity but on what Barker called 'indirect rule' (1951b, p. 69). This precluded the creation of imperial federation. It also permitted the transformation of empire into Commonwealth without too much trauma. For Barker, this ease of transformation had to do with the distinctive political *modus operandi* of the British themselves, 'that tentative method of gradual experimentation which is rooted and grounded in its national temper'. This good fortune meant that the 'free expansion of English society overseas could create new nations of no less quality than the old'. Nor was there any good reason to feel a tragic sense about its changing character or even its loss. That would be a distinctly un-British thing. The genteel tradition, as Barker saw it, was not given to an 'indulgence in *Weltschmerz*' (1947, p. 558).

The ideology of Britishness had the sort of qualities found in Lord Reith's ideal of British broadcasting. It was deferential, serious of purpose, worthy in its ethos of public service, decent, restrained, confident of its values, certain of what was unacceptable and rather snobbish. In almost Barkerian tones, the *Listener* proclaimed in an editorial of 4 July 1940 that its 'patriotism is not of the kind that passionately protests its love'. It found this sort of raucous, popular patriotism rather indecent – much in the way in which Jack Straw believes that the patriotism of English football hooligans is a disgrace to the nation. The BBC, declared the *Listener*, had no intention of 'setting up standards of self-conscious nobility that are foreign to our nature as a people' (Nicholas 1998, p. 42). That sort of attitude, in the circumstances of war, was quite magnificent. Indeed, one could go so far as to say that the genteel tradition was what Britain believed it was fighting for in the war against Nazi Germany. It was precisely this tradition which came under such merciless attack in the 1960s. Gentility, especially of the superior sort, was an obvious target for satire. Demolishing its pretentions by rendering it absurd, begun by *That Was The Week That Was*, was continued until the job was completed by alternative comedy in the 1980s. That particular genteel *style* has disappeared almost entirely from British political discourse. Its spirit certainly has not. Albeit in a very different guise, it continues to inform much of British liberalism (as Canovan recognised).

For all its pomposity, it helped to transmit something of value – a habit of tolerance and decency – which has acted as a counter-vailing power to the more atavistic and chauvinistic instincts in British society. In a classic restatement of that tradition, Peter Scott has outlined its essential principles: a citizenship based on reciprocal rights and duties; reform without revolution; a belief in progress and self-improvement; an embrace of competing ideologies within a community of interest; a sense of public service; and the notion of the state and nation as ethical institutions. A statement of virtue perhaps, but not without some historical substance, nor without some future. Scott thought it was possible to fashion a new Britain from its contemporary vestiges, a Britain 'which values social welfare and devalues class antagonism, at home egalitarian to foster patriotism and abroad peaceable to secure a safer world, a nation austere in its material promises but devoted to the enlargement of democracy' (1990, pp. 193–4). That is not too distant from the ideal of New Labour. Therefore, for all its elitism and snobbery, for all its imperial association, the genteel tradition has been a progressive leavening element in British politics. Indeed, the post-1945 culture of the Welfare State owed much to it.

The influence of British Idealist thinkers such as Bosanquet, T.H. Green and Barker in the disciplines of political theory, social admin-istration and social philosophy has been pervasive and long-lasting. Much of the official mind in twentieth-century politics was deeply influenced by the notion of British national solidarity which it had inherited from that tradition (Harris 1994, p. 18). This muscular morality, which implied a common set of public values and a shared way of life, also valued the plurality of the nation and of its people. And a stimulating reassessment of Bosanquet's contribution has shown that far from his work being the last throw of laissez-faire capitalism, it now looks 'more like a part of a tradition which took on a more positive approach to state action and state reform – a tradition that was to live on long beyond the end of the Victorian era' (Carter 1999, p. 694). On both Left and Right in politics this approach was held to be an important quality of Britishness (Weight and Beach 1998, p. 6). It helped to foster a sense of commonality which was the cement of multinational political life.

CONTRACT AND SOLIDARITY

The commonality of the British 'constitutional people' can be understood as a distinctive compromise between the claims of contract and solidarity. Another way of making the same point is to say that it was a distinctive compromise between four (contracted) nations and a (solidaristic) Union. Jim Bulpitt has explored this territory and concluded that the English official mind was against the construction of a highly integrated unitary state (Bulpitt 1983, p. 97). This would be, as Barker might have said, too French. Bulpitt described Britain as a 'dual polity', that is 'a state of affairs in which national and local politics were largely divorced from one another' (1983, p. 235). The British state for most of its history remained an essentially contractual Union. It was 'a deal between celtic elites and the central authorities in London, in which both had rights and duties', but one which did not demand too much of the English centre. Its contractual nature was most obvious in Ireland but a similar sort of contract existed for the Scots and even the Welsh (1983, p. 98).

Bulpitt's was a perceptive and influential interpretation of the territorial dimension in British politics. However, as he himself admitted, it was an interpretation more appropriate to the 'making' of the United Kingdom than to its sustaining. And his description entailed a bias which, if left unqualified, would distort the picture. The bias towards the idea of contract is one in which the four nations loom much larger than the Union. However, this is not the whole truth. The idea of solidarity was given insufficient weight by Bulpitt in the territorial balance. What are the distinctive attributes of contract and solidarity when considered politically? What are their relevance to consideration of Britishness?

Contract supposes an engagement of limited extent. The commitments entered into by the contracting parties are reasonably precise. The nature of the enterprise may be calculated in terms of costs and benefits, though goodwill and trust are essential components of such a partnership. None the less, the partners in collaboration retain their separate identities. Interdependence may be acknowledged to constitute one of the necessities of the venture; but interdependence does not create any obligations other than those willingly entered into and subscribed to by all the partners. This association is limited in what can be expected in terms of friendship and sympathy. It is constitutional formality, not brotherly or sisterly love, that forms the crucial bond. Changing relations between the partners will take the form of contractual adjustments. No partner can be expected to do more than what they have 'bargained for'. If they feel unduly put upon they have the right to dissolve the contract.

Solidarity supposes a sense of belonging, a shared experience which brings with it ethical responsibilities. There falls a duty to the association as a whole to ensure a common good amongst all its members. To the extent that the 'good' is not commonly shared, the requirement is to redress the balance of opportunities between the partners. It implies a strong degree of mutual support and, on that basis, an equal degree of welfare. That need not mean only social welfare but also physical security. The citizens in the association are not just members of particular communities, they are also members of one community. Justice consists, as far as possible, in ensuring that a basic equality should subsist throughout the association because it goes beyond merely formal arrangements. It has a moral substance which might be difficult to define in precise terms but which exists in practical measures of mutual aid or even common sacrifice, and not just in time of war.

The categories of contract and solidarity are not, of course, exclusive. They are abstractions from a complex reality, a reality which is politically ambivalent and open to revision. They are part of the bag and baggage of ideas bound up in answering the question 'What is Britain?' Nationalists tend towards the idea of contract for it preserves the integrity of the contracting nations and attenuates the sense that Britishness has a transcendent quality. Unionists tend towards the idea of solidarity precisely because of its transcendent quality, precisely because it concentrates attention on the benefit of the whole as opposed to the claims of the parts. In truth, Britain is something of a hybrid. Neither contract alone nor solidarity alone adequately grasps its character. The ambiguity in its character intimates the different forms that political association may take. It may also intimate its eventual dissolution. The reconciliation in the idea of the constitutional people, which found expression in the language of the genteel tradition, assumed the following. On the one hand, the United Kingdom's contractual basis meant that no nation can be compelled to stay within the Union against its will. On the other hand, no nation within the United Kingdom (and this is where Ireland always caused difficulties) had any reason to leave because of the practical solidarity that flowed from a common Britishness. This is a view that, for all their policy differences, is shared by the narratives of the Conservative and Labour Parties.

Theorists who subscribed to the notion of a solidaristic British identity may have disagreed on exactly how to define it. Those theorists, socialist and liberal, who wanted to defend the redistribution of wealth may have disagreed on the extent to which it was necessary for British citizens to share a common public culture. Moreover, they may also have differed over the extent to which it was legitimate for the state to foster (or forge) a shared national identity. What they all agreed on was that the nations did well out of the Union and that that was a measure of its success. But such a utilitarian calculation of contractual self-interest ought not to be divorced from the ethical community which made it possible: Britishness itself. This was the point Canovan was making in defence of British nationhood. Acknowledging a contractual element to the United Kingdom was an admission of the principle of consent. Acceptance of that principle further acknowledged a residual right to self-determination for the nations of the Union. Stressing the element of solidarity was an attempt to make of Britain what Hegel had tried to make of marriage: a contract which transcended contract. This was indeed a supposed partnership for good in both senses of the word. For those generations weaned on the values of the genteel tradition, all of this was taken to be not only self-evident but somehow providential. It seemed solid enough within and secure enough without. And it was worth preserving.

What was Britain, then? The story of Britain was mainly what the genteel tradition had made of it. The fragments of its worldview can be expressed in a few simple lines: London at the centre, local patriotism, membership of a major power with global responsibilities and kinship connections throughout the empire or Commonwealth. The contemporary perspective, of course, is post-imperial and it is a perspective which is available only with the decay of that version of the genteel tradition we find in Barker. The perspectives on Britishness have changed significantly in the course of a generation. What was formerly seen as an inexorable and providential expansion of civilisation – and civilisation meant the inculcation of the genteel tradition – now appears morally questionable, politically wasteful and historically moribund – except when it comes to the international enforcement of human rights in places such as Kosovo. That changing perspective today has made relevant yet another question: Why is Britain?

3   Why Is Britain?

In his book *The Day Britain Died*, Andrew Marr suggested that the British problem was not so much: Is there an answer? Rather it appeared to be: Is there a question? There is, and the question is a truly subversive one. It is *the* question of the moment: Why is Britain? It is a subversive question because there is often no persuasive answer. There are some questions which no political order can address for that order's existence presupposes that they have been answered. Yet if historians and political philosophers have come to emphasise the 'imagined' or 'forged' nature of British identity, then the possibility opens up for a persuasive politics that claims: historically, it could all have been otherwise. Politically, it *should* now be otherwise. Historical imagination and political desire combine in a subversive project to unmake Britain.

Even posing the question implies that a popular imaginative space has opened up which is already, as Tom Nairn has claimed, 'after Britain'. It may intimate the possibility of dissolution and also be part of the process of that dissolution. In a famous episode of the TV series *The Prisoner*, Patrick McGoohan succeeded in destroying the computer which controlled his open prison by programming the question: Why? The question 'Why is Britain?' has been posed recently on a number of occasions. According to political disposition, it has been posed in a tone of despair, of apocalypse or of anticipation.

POSING THE QUESTION

The Conservative academic and peer Lord Beloff once noted the linkage between the general amnesia or bad conscience about the empire and the potential demise of the constitutional people of Britain (1974, pp. 428–9). If the history of the empire begins with Elizabeth I, asked Beloff, 'will Elizabeth II close not only the history of Empire but British history itself? After all we are being taught by Britain [sic] to think of ourselves in Britain not as Her Majesty's loyal subjects but as citizens of Europe' (1999, p. 15). Here, in a couple of lines, Beloff captures the vision of dreadful night which agitates one strain of contemporary Conservatism: a Britain without a memory, its constitution violated, its integrity dismembered and its future absorbed in a European superstate. Of course, dreadful night can appear to others as glad confident morning. From a different political perspective, David Marquand posed the question which he believed to be among the most explosive in the modern world. That question was: 'Of what are we citizens?' – the 'we' being the British. And that simple question provoked others. What 'does nationhood mean in this strange entity known as the United Kingdom of Great Britain and Northern Ireland? And if the answer to that question is confused or problematic, what can citizenship mean?' The looming difficulty, thought Marquand, was to give a generally acceptable answer to the question: 'what is the community to which British citizens might be expected to be loyal?' (1997, pp. 152–3). What caused Beloff deep anguish was what Marquand welcomed with enthusiasm. Devolution of power and acceptance of a European vocation were the destiny unfolding. For Marquand, the urgent political questions were about the how and when of this destiny, not about whether it was possible.

Reflecting on the character of the times, at least as it is interpreted by intellectuals of the New Left, Nairn argued that the gap between the form of the British state and the spirit of the age was astonishing. They were like two alternative universes, one in which time has stood still, the other in which life was energetically modern. The gap in Britain was experienced in the way in which Ethiopian intellectuals, returning home from studying abroad, encountered life there: '*How is all this still possible*? At the end of the twentieth century? With democratization of the globe in full spate, and Nelson Mandela running South Africa? *How dare it endure one day longer on earth*?' (2000b, p. 77). These questions may not be so urgent amongst the population as Nairn or Marquand assume. But Nairn is surely correct to argue that a feeling of absurdity is potentially as great a motor of political change as economic discontent. Appearing ridiculous is a danger to which every governing order is, or ought to be, acutely sensitive.

Is there anything new in this? Is it not the case, as Richard Rose pointed out (1982, p. 4), that too many books have been written explaining events which have not happened in the United Kingdom, and that prominent amongst the events that have not happened is the break up of Britain? There is something to Rose's argument. One should always be aware of the danger of exaggerating the significance of the present. And yet there is a particular urgency about the question of Britain today. The 'British disease' a generation ago tended to be understood in socio-economic terms. Intellectual energy was channelled into explaining the culture of British business, the ethos of labour or the decline of the industrial spirit. The assumption was that the proper diagnosis and the appropriate cure could be applied by an interventionist government. There was a concern for the conduct of governance but it was mainly a concern with efficient procedures of diagnosis and effective administration of the cure. Rose, from that perspective, could be genuinely critical of the tendency to extrapolate too much from the constitutional debates of the 1970s. He saw no reason to overplay the nationalist challenge to British identity (except in Northern Ireland). The business of government was functional, addressing material issues common to all British people. The academic bias is rather different today. The general acceptance of the limits which the global market imposes on domestic decision-making has moderated expectations about British economic policy and what the state can actually do. This recognition has encouraged a shift to concern about what the British state is. The influence of postmodernism in the academy has encouraged research into the question of political identity, especially when difference and diversity appear to loom larger than unity. Consequently, it is the meaning of Britain rather than the functioning of Britain which becomes a focus for research. This is not a self-generated academic enterprise. It matches a detectable change in political mood.

In 1959, the Conservative journalist Peregrine Worsthorne sensed that there would come a point when the magnificence and grandeur of the British class system would begin to look 'foolish and tacky' when related to a second-class power in decline (cited in Gamble 1974) – and not only the class system but so too everything associated with it: the monarchy, the House of Lords, the honours system, the British constitution itself. That point may have been reached a generation later. Thirty years after Worsthorne, Stephen Haseler was still arguing that the British system of governance encouraged a maudlin medieval nostalgia which sustained the snobbery of class and held the country back from modernisation. In this he was repeating much of what Nairn had argued in his critique of the monarchy, *The Enchanted Glass* (1988). He was also anticipating David Marquand's critique of the 'whig-imperialist' vision of the British constitution. Things had changed.

Marquand's criticism was more plausible than Haseler's. The vision of which he wrote was the majesty of the sovereign Crown-in-Parliament, the buckle which fastened together the old imperial state. The fate of that vision, claimed Marquand, was brutally plain. It may linger in parts of the British establishment, but its meaning has been exhausted: 'You can't be an imperialist if you have no empire.' Though the Crown retains some of its old magic, political changes since 1945 have destroyed the unique and mysterious multiple monarchy which Barker once celebrated. Along with it has gone the balanced statecraft which gave meaning to the traditional idea of the constitutional people (1993, pp. 217–18). If the political secret of the constitutional people in the *ancien régime* was, as Leo Amery once put it, 'government of the people, for the people, with but not by the people', then its day had passed. Moreover, the subtlety of the relationship between encompassing Union and nations, which subordinated the populism of the second to the institutions of the first, could no longer be sustained. Britain's decline, as its consequences had slowly filtered through the political generations, now made the question 'Why is Britain?' the dominant one for the present generation.

The reason was to be found in three related developments: the loss of empire, the rise of national sentiment and Britain's entry into the European Community. All three moves had challenged the popular identity and political institutions of the *ancien régime*. Shorn of empire, the British could not be such a people any longer. And here was the rub, thought Marquand, they could not be anyone else. Imperial Britain was not one of several possible Britains, 'Imperial Britain was Britain'. Thus the fatal and logical conclusion for what *was* Britain. 'Empire was not an optional extra for the British; it was their reason for being British as opposed to English, Scots or Welsh.' Deprived of empire and plunged into Europe, Britain had no meaning (1997, p. 200). What is left after the sun has set on the imperial state are the separate nations on the one hand and, on the other, the 'bloodless, historyless, affectless' administrative structure of the United Kingdom. This is what Nairn had called Ukania, a term which made comparison with the dissolution of the Habsburg monarchy. Marquand reversed the view advanced by Canovan and which Britishness benignly claimed to embody, namely that the British are a nation by way of a shared ownership of something external to them and not necessarily by the similarities within them (1996, p. 72). The renaissance of non-metropolitan ethnicities which animates national separatism proclaims that, on the contrary, it is the similarities *inside* us which are the real basis of political association. Sharing the British thing *outside* us has lost much of its meaning and must be rethought or discarded. It can no longer unite us into a nation – if it ever did.

Marquand is rightly concerned both that the old constitution is dissolving and with the shape of what will replace it. The opportunity now presents itself for a more radical form of democratic self-government than the old genteel tradition permitted (2000, pp. 274–6). The European Union provides the opportunity for the diffusion of territorial power. Some empirical justification for this can be found in the research conducted into British national sentiment. The conclusion was that British national sentiment may be destined for gradual decline as the older generations die and are replaced by younger, more internationalist, cohorts. In Scotland this internationalism coincided with support for independence (Heath et al. 1999, p. 173). The trends in both internationalist and nationalist dimensions would seem to go some way towards confirming Marquand's view that things cannot hold. Nevertheless, there is room for caution because earlier predictions based on theories of political generations have not been noted for their accuracy. To make some broader assessment, it is important to look a little more closely at the central claim – that without the empire to give Britishness political cohesion there is today 'a vacuum of language reflecting a vacuum of feeling' and that this seriously threatens the integrity of the state (Marquand 1995, p. 189).

THE EMPIRE

The meaning of empire for theorists such as Marquand is unproblematic. However, as Tomlinson (1982, pp. 70–1) has pointed out, historians of empire often disagree about the scope of the subject. The most difficult problem they actually face is deciding what they mean by empire. Other factors complicate the picture. Class had an important influence on how empire was understood, and how it was understood also depended on where one lived (Baucom 1999). One interpretation, which chimes somewhat with Marquand's view, can be found in a wide-ranging essay by A.G. Hopkins. It is impossible to do justice to all Hopkins' insights and in what follows a few relevant observations are merely extracted.

For Hopkins, one of the most striking features of modern British experience has been the separation of the history of the state from the history of empire. Hopkins judged that it was hard to find an influential interpretation of modern British history – as opposed to an ideological one – that was based on a close reading of imperial matters (1999, p. 208). There is no doubt that empire was indeed a British (as opposed to an English) enterprise and one that helped to produce a distinctive British identity. Images of empire had indeed entered the British soul and suffused popular and official identities on the Left as well as the Right (see Howe 1989). This official culture had now vanished, like tears in rain. For Hopkins, it was a truism that empires end partly because they have served their purpose. The engine of growth in world trade is no longer sustainable along the lines of the old imperial pattern: metropolitan finance and manufactured goods in return for colonial raw materials. The reorientation of global trade has meant, in its turn, a reorientation of British political interest towards Europe. And that reorientation has encouraged the pressure for a reorganisation of a now disunited kingdom. That is the (globalised) material basis for nationalism in Britain. In a brilliant summary, Hopkins seized upon that trend which more than any other has led to the question 'Why is Britain?' Imperial power had promoted a political culture that strengthened its own sense of national identity. Today, however, global forces have generated the opposite effect. Their tendency is to weaken established institutions and identities. The consequences have become visible in recent British politics. The attraction of Scottish nationalism, for example, is a response to the decay of the imperial state, an insurance against the penetrative consequences of new globalising forces (Hopkins 1999, p. 243).

However persuasive this idea of the imperial British state appears, and however systematically an historian such as Hopkins may provide evidence to substantiate its 'gentlemanly' basis, it is an idea which is not unchallenged or unchallengeable. In the 1994 Creighton Lecture, P.J. Marshall criticised the contemporary vogue of resorting to phrases like 'an imperial state' and directed his criticism particularly towards those in the constitutional reform movement Charter 88. British institutions, Marshall argued, were certainly prepared to add an imperial glamour to their domestic role. But accepting fundamental change as the price of an imperial role was another matter. What sounded loud and clear, and still does, was an objection to any surrender of British sovereignty. Directly contradicting some of the claims of the Ukania thesis, Marshall argued that the British state 'developed its own trajectory with very little regard to what was happening in the empire'. In his judgement, Britain's political leadership rarely allowed the supposed needs of empire to upset the requirements of domestic politics (1994, pp. 382–3). Barker's formulation of the operative principle of the British empire, 'indirect rule', is here elegantly restated. Indirect rule was about keeping the colonies and their problems at arm's length from British domestic politics.

It would be absurd to deny, of course, that the empire was a major component of the British sense of identity. Marshall does not deny it, but that still leaves much open to debate. It is the openness of the historical debate which is closed off by the fashionable Ukanian thesis. The diversity of empire meant that it could easily fit diverse, even opposed versions of Britain. Indeed, one could argue that the use of the term Ukania is a further example of the diversity of empire, in this case to promote the subversion of Britishness. Marshall's conclusion neatly suggests this: 'Whatever one's view may be about the institutions of the present British state, it is unlikely that empire has had much to do with shaping them.' In attributing what one dislikes to a convenient idea of the imperial past showed, in Marshall's opinion, the real and lingering influence in politics, of both Left and Right, of the empire itself (Marshall 1994, p. 393).

J.G. Darwin was of much the same opinion. In continental European countries, the retreat from empire had contributed to serious political upheaval and social convulsion. In Britain it had left few visible traces and never threatened the viability of British insti-tutions. What intrigued Darwin was the acquiescence of British public opinion in the face of dramatic imperial decline (1986, p. 29). He believed that it could be accounted for only by the attitude of the political elites. Even the bombastic imperialists, found mainly but not exclusively within the Conservative Party, thought that 'empire was meant to serve the party and not the other way round' (1986, p. 33). And those, such as Joseph Chamberlain or, later, Julian Amery, who looked to defence of the empire as a measure of Britain's will to rule, were always marginalised by party managers more interested in domestic affairs. It is precisely because of the reluctance to mobilise opinion on imperial issues that it has become difficult to gauge the force of popular sentiment. Public opinion appeared to receive the death of empire with equanimity and Darwin thought that the main reason for this was the priority given by political parties to domestic strategies.

The other reason for the ease of decolonisation was historical luck. Being on the winning side in two world wars provided favourable circumstances in which to adjust to new global realities. These victories, though, also helped to foster the illusion of geopolitical power and diverted attention from the fact of decline. This is something with which the Ukania thesis agrees. So too is there agreement that much of twentieth century British political history has to do with concealing the real reasons for the retreat from empire. That reason was the eclipse of British power (Barnett 1986). To the present generation, the Age of Empire now seems like a fantasy. To deny the former imperial character of the British state is ludicrous. To assume that there is a simple reading of the British imperial experience is equally ludicrous.

It does seem rather unlikely that Britain *only* had an imperial meaning and could survive *only* on the life-support system of empire if only because empire itself had no single meaning. Moreover, if one's identity is entirely defined in relation to what is external and different, then one has no identity at all. This is what the Ukania thesis does assert about Britain today. But that is surely a gross exaggeration. It fails to do justice to the solidarities and communities of interest which do, for the moment at least, depend on there being substance to the idea of Britain irrespective of imperialism. And even if it were true that the institutions are all that remain of Britain, it would still not be a clinching argument for its inevitable dissolution. That one sort of Britain is dead, the Britain of the Raj, cannot be doubted. That does not mean, necessarily, the death of Britain itself. The British state may have been lucky enough to sustain the illusion of imperial greatness long enough for the retreat from empire to be relatively painless. One of the costs, however, may now be popular cynicism about what Worsthorne called its tacky institutional residue. The cost of that residue is not only to be found in football hooliganism, but also perhaps in a loss of political vision. The importance of Marquand's work is to remind us of that. The linkage of imperial decay to the inevitable dissolution of the institutional identity of Britain, whether true or not, strikes a blow at another of the lingering self-congratulatory assumptions of the genteel tradition, the 'constitutional' element of the constitutional people.

3M SelfCheck™ System

Customer ID: 30014095

Title: Nationalism, devolution and the challenge
to the United Kingdom state / Arthur Aughey.
ID: 3554147400
Due: 04-03-13 10:00AM

Total items: 1
28/02/2013 21:46

Thank you for using the
3M SelfCheck™ System.

THE CONSTITUTION

The understanding of British history as the history of a free people underpinned generations of constitutional study. They were free, though, in a very particular and in a very British way. Indeed, *the English ideology*, as George Watson put it, echoing a long line of similar commentaries, 'is the idea of liberty expressed through parliamentary institutions' (1973, p. 1). The genius of this free people was thought to lie in its capacity to fashion institutions which reconciled order with personal liberty. The English character had forged a constitution of ordered liberty which was the inheritance of the British as a whole. That constitution had become the wonder of the world. As Sir John Seeley argued in 1883, England had discovered the secret of constitutional government 'and taught all the world how liberty might be adopted to the conditions of a nation-state' (cited in Watson 1973, p. 215). The significance of this constitutional celebration was that it became a substitute for an overt and official ideology of British nationalism. Constitutionalism demanded a practical ability to know how rather than a theoretical ability to know what. And that practical knowledge was vouchsafed to the rule of gentlemen.

A.V. Dicey's nineteenth-century work on the law and the constitution set a pattern, the authority of which became hard to shift. In Dicey's opinion it was the very absence of a populist, nationalist tradition in Britain which assured the preservation of freedom and representative government. The rule of law was celebrated as a reflection of the character of the constitutional people. The practical wisdom of slow, piecemeal constitutional change was taken to be second nature (Stapleton, 1993, p. 5). The lack of a sense of deep kinship was thought to be a boon, not a disadvantage. England's institutional mission had already achieved its objective in the construction of Britain's distinctive public culture, even though the majority of the Catholic Irish had refused to acknowledge it and had seceded by 1922. It was the philosopher Michael Oakeshott who best expressed that style of thought well into the contemporary era. Reputable political behaviour, Oakeshott once wrote, is not the product of nor is it dependent upon sound philosophy, never mind ideology. British constitutional tradition was a good substitute for both (Oakeshott 1948, p. 476). One might put that otherwise. There was no need for an ideology of British nationalism – there was the British constitution.

That is certainly not the mood today. The virtuous, gentlemanly assumptions of British constitutionalism have gone the way of received pronunciation at the BBC. The mood today makes the old style of constitutional argument appear quaintly Ruritanian. The self-satisfied notion that the traditional form of the constitutional people adequately reconciled the legal sovereignty of parliament to the political sovereignty of the electorate has come under severe attack. Though the traditional constitution still has its defenders they are increasingly on the defensive (see Norton 1989). In his survey of recent writing on the British constitution, Neville Johnson argued that much of that work has been strongly critical. The literature has also become more obviously 'committed' in the sense of advocating radical change. In his view, 'the "old constitution" has been under attack for some considerable time and it looks now as if it is being replaced by substantially different institutional relationships and procedural conditions' (Johnson 2000, p. 127).

One important reason for this pressure for change comes from membership of the European Union. As Prosser has persuasively argued, it has been contact with the different tradition embodied in the legal arrangements of the European Union which is 'leading to the rapid demolition of previously cherished constitutional fundamentals including parliamentary sovereignty itself' (1996, p. 486). Permeation of the British system by influences from the rights-based European system has had the effect of stimulating a more contentious debate about democratic politics and individual rights (Harlow 2000). But there is another, and larger, cultural reason. Part of the ruling self-confidence of the British tradition (at least in its more bombastic forms) was that its experience of ordered liberty was not only unique, it was exemplary. Others could not hope to match the symmetry of the British achievement, but at least they had a model which they might try to emulate. That sort of political Podsnappery is now treated with derision. In the European engagement, the British model of constitutional democracy appears less attractive. The hollowing out of confidence in the value of the British way contributes immeasurably to the question 'Why is Britain?' because it has encouraged a sort of inverted Podsnappery.

Dickens' Mr. Podsnap, as is well known, believed that the constitution was something to be proud of because it was bestowed by providence in order to make Britain the most favoured country in the world. As Johnson observed, in contrast to Mr. Podsnap, 'the majority of modern commentators on the constitution appear to assume as a matter of course that foreigners generally do it better than we do, especially if they are our partners in the European Union' (Johnson 2000, p. 127). That they do order these things better abroad is highly questionable. But whether they do or not, the important point is the general intellectual disaffection with the way things *are* done in Britain. That may be the real price of the gentle management of decline in world status. There is now a backlog of constitutional discontent to be dealt with. Such discontent was cleverly channelled into the public realm by Charter 88 and more directly by the Scottish Constitutional Convention. Nationalists have simply gone one logical step further. If the thing doesn't work properly any more why bother to fix it at all? The alternative – independence in Europe – is there for the taking.

What of that coping stone of constitutional identity, the monarchy (Vincenzi 1998)? It was in 1969 that the Duke of Edinburgh asserted: 'it is a complete misconception to imagine that the monarchy exists in the interests of the monarch. It doesn't. It exists in the interests of the people' (cited in Bogdanor 1996, p. 421). This remark was to be put to a severe test in 1997 with the death of Princess Diana. Momentarily, one had the impression that the survival of the monarchy itself was in doubt. Yet the demise of the British monarchy is something which has long been predicted. In 1871, Joseph Chamberlain wrote: 'The Republic must come, and at the rate at which we are moving, it will come in our generation' (in Cannon 1986, p. 143). That is the historical tradition of radical expectation which helps to explain why so much importance was attached to Diana by some on the Left.

Anthony Barnett, for example, in his manifesto for constitutional renewal, *This Time*, devoted a whole chapter to Diana, Princess of Wales, and her spectral presence hovered over the whole book (1997, Ch. 5). Barnett argued that the way in which the public had influenced Diana's funeral had transformed the traditional relationship of monarchy and people (1997, p. 2). The 'spirit of Diana' had made the Duke's words come true and compelled the Windsors to justify themselves in the interests of the people. It is perhaps understandable that what Nairn called the 'September Days' of 1997 should provoke the sort of interpretation advanced by Barnett. The opportunity presented itself of using the September Days permanently to shame and embarrass the Royal Family. That might be the very wedge republicans have always sought to prise apart the monarchy and people. Superficially, it also intimated a sort of 1789 of the democratic emotions, an assertion of loving people-power which, if channelled properly, could rock the deferential foundations of the *ancien régime*. It was understandable that these opportunities should be seized upon and rhetorically exploited. But it showed a lack of judgement not only about the times but also about the people.

The idea of a deferential people had been in academic disrepute at least since the early 1970s. That the people might not be deferential and yet still incline to support the monarchy has been a lacuna in radical thinking. Equally, that the fevered and frequently intolerant populism of the September Days revealed a new, emotionally demonstrative British people ignored other more specific and localised examples of that mood, such as the response of Liverpudlians to the Hillsborough tragedy in 1989. Even some on the Right lost their sense of proportion. Anthony O'Hear, in a headline-making intervention critical of what he saw as Diana worship, thought that the country had witnessed a defining moment in its history (1998, pp. 183–90). Hardly. What Diana bequeathed to the monarchy was rather different: it was a lesson in the cult of celebrity. When the Duke spoke of the monarchy existing in the interests of the people he had in mind the moral uplift and seriousness of the genteel tradition. What the term means today is the celebrity value of a glamorous niche market. If the royals choose to live by it (and in Prince William they have the perfect product) the chances of the monarchy's survival are reasonable. It may not be magnificent, but it is a life. If they do not, then its days may be numbered. For those seeking change, however, it may not be all that important. Neal Ascherson surely specified accurately the radical agenda when he wrote: 'If the cult of the archaic nation is demolished, the monarchy – no longer called upon to sanctify it – will reduce to the scale of a harmless focus of affection and newspaper scuttlebutt' (1986, p. 304). For the Conservatives that is a demoralising thought (Hitchens 1999). There is a demoralising perspective amongst Conservatives today which raises the question 'Why is Britain?' and this encourages, and is encouraged by, apparent nationalist self-confidence, especially in Scotland.

FATAL ANXIETY

The two sides of this particular coin are wish-fulfilment and fatal anxiety. Wish-fulfilment can be detected in Ascherson's (1999) comments on the funeral of Diana. He detected in the behaviour of the crowds the return of an older English nationalism. The mind may still be British, he thought, but the English heart was now learning to be a nation once again. Whether that is true or not and, even if it were true, whether Ascherson's interpretation is the correct one, is not the issue. Rather it is that the articulate repetition of this view has a political effect. What Ascherson, like Davies and Samuel, wishes is for Britishness to go the way of *Homo sovieticus*. There is evidence that the repetition of the wish has brought forward a pessimistic but also aggressively Conservative response, one that can be called fatal anxiety. For individuals, that is usually produced by a sense of despair, the anxiety of those who live scared to death because of a presentiment of the end. For Slavoj Žižek, this behaviour matches the Lacanian notion of 'symbolic castration', the moment when the possibility of castration takes precedence over its actuality, when its mere threat produces real effects in our thinking (1994, p. 69). The disorder in this case is the perceived disorder of Britain, its break-up. It is the English psychic economy which it affects.

Ironically, this view of the world may bring its own comforts. Certainty, even the fatal certainty of loss, orders the world and arranges its materials, providing a defensive barrier against complexity. Having abandoned hope it accepts fate with bravado. So it is not necessarily the case that a fatalistic disposition is entirely without political dividends for the contradictory drive of fatal anxiety lies in this. Fearing the coming break up of Britain, it may help to bring it about in order to end the uncertainty. In short, if Britain cannot stay the way it has been, then why *is* Britain anyway? If *they* – the Scots, the Welsh and the Irish – don't want it, why should *we* – the English?

Simon Heffer's *Nor Shall My Sword: The Reinvention of England* expresses the code of fatal anxiety perfectly. Opinion polls in Scotland seem to confirm the inevitability of separation. 'So, finally the English end up feeling that if the Scots want to be rid of England, then maybe it is not, after all, such a good idea for the English to cling on to the Scots' (1999, p. 10). It is not the English who want to break up Britain, but if that is what the Scots want, then good riddance to it. The tone of jingoism is clearly detectable. Nationalists in Scotland and some Conservatives in England may, wittingly or unwittingly, jointly exploit the idea that Britain is being abolished. That is exactly where wish-fulfilment and fatal anxiety intersect and support one another. For some an element of self-justification may also be involved. Thus, John Major feared that Scotland was already lost to the United Kingdom because all the warnings he had given from 1992 onwards were not heeded. As a result, within ten years or so Scotland will have moved towards divorce from England (2000, p. 10). This sort of thinking caused Donald Dewar great unease because he thought it carried with it the seeds of its own fulfilment: 'If it becomes received wisdom in England that the Scots have given up on the English, that will encourage the English to give up on the Scots' (1998, p. 18). That is a dangerous intellectual game for it plays straight into the hands of nationalism.

Unquestionably, British nationhood is in doubt. Its former sources of pride have been under assault for more than a generation. These – pride in the Commonwealth, pride in the country's distinctively virtuous constitution, pride in the country's institutional continuity compared with Europe's instability, pride in the status of being a world power – have become confused or confounded. But political identity is not about pride alone; it is also about interest. A stable identity makes interest one's pride and pride one's interest. What interest remains in sustaining Britain? One way of approaching a tentative answer to this question is once again suggested in a thoughtful article by Margaret Canovan.

PRAGMATISM AND REDEMPTION

The view proposed by writers such as Nairn and Ascherson, and repeated in the work of Marquand, is that political identity has now returned to the constituent nations from its three-century British sabbatical. All that remains is the tired dance of bloodless institutions which is 'Ukania'. This view articulates a modern populism, detached from the socialist cause and attached to the nationalist or regional-ist cause. As Canovan remarked, populism is not just a reaction against established structures of power, it is also an appeal to a recognised authority. That authority is the people, the democratic sovereign. It is certainly not that corrupted entity, the constitutional people, the so-called British *ancien régime*. Populism makes a case for the energetic, the fertile principles of political life – the nation – to free itself from moribund Britishness. In this regard, Canovan has argued that democracy has two faces, the 'redemptive' and the 'pragmatic'. All stable modern states require a creative balance of the two, but that is often hard to sustain. Populism and nationalism always thrive on the tension between the two (1999, p. 8).

Pragmatic democracy stresses rules and practices which moderate the competing claims of modern society. Democracy is understood as a form of government, the value of which lies in its effectiveness at adjusting the claims of competing groups. Democracy, therefore, 'means institutions: institutions not just to limit power, but also to constitute it and make it effective'. Redemptive democracy, on the other hand, is one of a family of radical visions which hold out the promise of secular transformation. Indeed, the contemporary appeal of populism, if one listens carefully, has historical echoes of the radical democracy proposed by the New Left in the 1960s (1999, p. 15). Transformation will take place when the people, the only source of legitimate authority, take charge of its own destiny. Ultimately, 'the romantic impulse to directness, spontaneity and the overcoming of alienation' is at the heart of the project (1999, p. 10). Applying Canovan's model to Britain, the Ukania thesis clearly assumes a profound distinction between redemptive democracy – nations and regions in the European Union – and pragmatic democracy – the contemporary British state; as she observes, pragmatism alone 'without the redemptive impulse is a recipe for corruption'. Not only that. It is also a recipe for the cult of formality and empty ritual. And that is what the Ukania thesis takes Britain to mean – formality, empty ritual, a hollow shell, making a lot of portentous noise but signifying no popular content. The anti-Ukanian appeal is made 'past the ossified institutions to the living people' (1999, p. 14).

If the Ukania thesis were true, of course, then nothing *could* be done for the British state. It would be unredeemable. There would be no point in talking about the intrinsic value and dignity of sovereign British statehood because that is something to which nationalists aspire for their own people. Nor would there be much point in using the contrary argument, that in the modern world the sovereign independence of small states is an illusion. If sovereignty as political independence is dismissed as mere legality, so what? Legal sovereignty and self-government are not trivial matters. They are the very qualifications required to play a role in world politics. And if this means an independent status for ambitious politicians within the European Union, then the attraction is obvious. The trappings of national dignity and independent statehood may be preferable to the collective British alternative. In short, it is a powerful incentive to put the question 'Why is Britain?' It does not mean that the Scots or the Welsh have to believe that they suffer discrimination at the hands of the English. It does not even have to mean that they feel hard done by in Britain (though both these claims are part of the small change of nationalist argument). The attraction of sovereign independence, as Alan James has noted, does not seem to be exclusively determined by such treatment (1999, p. 470). Pragmatically, Britain might not be altogether despised. Redemptively, for the nationalist, it has nothing to offer. What, though, are the elements of a positive response to the question 'Why is Britain?'

DUALITY

The Russian artist Wassily Kandinsky believed that in the course of the twentieth century we would see the triumph of 'and' over 'either/or'. For Kandinsky, this would represent a great achievement of civilisation. A defence of Britain must begin with the proposition that Britishness has for a long time represented the triumph of 'and', a relaxed duality of identity, over 'either/or', an assertive belonging. This has certainly been a dominant theme of the literature and exemplifies a modern, liberal updating of the genteel tradition. Bernard Crick identified duality as the soul of Britishness and has chided the English for not being sufficiently aware of it. Most Scots, he argued, 'think of themselves as Scottish and British, perhaps a dual sense of identity, perhaps a more functional differentiation'. On the other hand, most English people have a tendency to assume that to be British is simply to be English (1991, p. 97). Things in Scotland have changed somewhat. Joyce McMillan has reminded us that a third of Scots under the age of 35 do not feel British at all. As she argued, some would apply an iron rule of national identity politics to this and assume 'that where cultural cohesion and confidence begin to falter, political and institutional decay cannot be far behind' (1999, p. 30). For Scottish nationalists this *is* the argument. It is Britain which lacks cohesion and is in a state of political decay. The future belongs to Scotland. McMillan's article provides a note of caution for that sort of simple-minded triumphalism.

McMillan observed that the politics of national identity (our side of the contract) can become a dim-witted substitute for the politics of British solidarity. The reluctance to speak of socialism should not become an excuse for ignoring the commonality of experience throughout the United Kingdom. McMillan was clear about the disposition within nationalism to pose the 'either/or' question and to dismiss the possibility of 'and'. When she told a senior Scottish nationalist that she felt herself to be both Scottish and British, his reply was: 'You've got a problem, then, haven't you?' In her view, there is a tendency to regard complexity of identity as something to be suppressed (McMillan 1999, p. 33). It was experience of this pluralism in British identity which another Scot, Andrew Marr, thought to be the appropriate model with which Britain could interest its partners in Europe. It could no longer be the stuffiness of Rule Britannia (Marr 1998, pp. 25–7).

A variant of this vision is to be found in Jonathan Freedland's *Bringing Home the Revolution* (1998). Freedland asks the decisive questions: *When* was Britain? *What* is Britain? What is Britain *for*? The difficulty providing clear answers, he thought, is because Britain is bereft of a civic faith. That may be found – in this case, repatriated – by looking across the Atlantic to the United States. 'The founding principles of the US,' argued Freedland, 'were British ideas of liberty and democracy, which somehow slipped out of our hands and drifted across the Atlantic' (1998, p. 14). The difference is that in Britain power flows from the top down and in America it flows from the bottom up. America's energetic, populist citizenship is contrasted with the stuffy formalism of the current British way. It is a neat distinction, politically suggestive but not entirely true. Politics is never that neat. The main problem with it is the lack of subtlety in his consideration of populism. Freedland is honest enough to acknowledge that it can have what the British Left would consider illiberal effects such as legal enforcement of the death penalty. However, his confusion of republicanism and populism and his failure to acknowledge the different kinds of republicanism weaken his argument. As one authority has put it, the essential character of the American constitution is that 'while all its parts are *derived* from the people, none of them *is* the people' (Mansfield, Jr. 1983, p. 55). Put that way, the difference between Britain and the United States does not appear to be so dramatic. On the other hand, the passion of popular republicanism always needs to be cooled and American constitutionalism is designed to make deliberative reason paramount over the passions 'by the *public's* passion since this is not an aristocracy of the wise' (1983, p. 57). That is rather different from Britain, where the real aristocracy of the wise, colloquially known as 'the great and the good', has always thought itself to be *more* liberal than the people.

Freedland's project represents one intelligent response to the question of Britishness. It attempts to provide a British national project of democratic renewal which could become the basis of national pride. None the less, one is reminded of Gillray's famous cartoon of 1793 *'Fashion before Ease. A good Constitution sacrificed for a Fantastik Form'*, in which Tom Paine tries to pull the corset of American republican ideas (unsuccessfully) onto a rather ample and buxom Britannia (Mellini and Matthews 1987, p. 19). Freedland's message, rather like Tony Benn's a generation ago, is that Paine's time has come again. His 'nationalism of ideas' is faithful to that earnest tradition of democratic improvement which is to be found in Paine's (and Benn's) work.

Another variant is to be found in Britain's ethnic communities. In Crick's opinion, it was these new Britons who 'have a truer sense than many of the English that being a British citizen does not and need not imply a common culture' (1995a, p. 173). The 'pragmatic' value of Britishness is acknowledged, but so too is a 'redemptive' faith in the potential of its democratic renewal. Previously marginalised from the mainstream, these views are now at the centre of a positive renewal of Britishness. What one finds is an intelligence which thinks through the question of British identity with a passionate intensity. This is not to say that this intelligence is confined there and is without wider sympathy. That would ignore, as nationalists are keen that one should, majority support for the Union. It is only to say that this intensity allows a sharper focus on the merits of the important solidarity in Britishness, a solidarity which is more than economic.

One of the most acute theorists of modern national identity is the political philosopher Bhiku Parekh. His clarity of thought and subtlety of exposition have been a vital contribution to contemporary debate. In the pragmatic sense, argued Parekh, every national identity is paradoxical. A community needs some shared view of its collective identity, yet every such view has the potential 'to demean those outsiders who constitute its acknowledged or unacknowledged point of reference'. Pragmatism alone is not sufficient, for every national community needs to modify its identity according to a redemptive vision of what it ought to be. And rather like Bosanquet's quest to resolve the paradox of self-government, Parekh sets out the criteria which are necessary to resolve the paradox of national identity (2000, p. 7). It should be as inclusive as possible. It should be open to revision. It should acknowledge its history not for the purpose of nostalgia, but for the purpose of imagination. It should not inspire collective loyalty alone, but also critical reflection on that loyalty. It should not be confused exclusively with difference. The fact that a nation differs from others in certain respects need not mean that it has no features in common. It should encourage a solidarity which links different classes and cultures. It must have popular roots and not be imposed. Finally – and this is the key summary point of Parekh's formulation – national identity should be defined in political rather than ethnic or cultural terms (2000, pp. 7–8). For Parekh, then, British national identity must embrace the complexity of a society which contains a significant proportion of the population who do not feel obliged to cheer the English cricket team. The value of Britishness is that it may be more capable of embracing that complexity, given its traditional politico-institutional emphasis, than an identity that is self-consciously national. In other words, what the Ukania thesis ridicules, this vision of Britishness cherishes.

Equally, Harry Goulbourne's important work on ethnicity and nationalism acknowledges that Britain 'developed a civic culture which has contributed massively to notions such as the rule of law, parliamentary sovereignty, individual freedom, and certain common assumptions about individual freedom and group tolerance in a wider social collectivity'. It is from these basic materials of the British genteel tradition that a new, fairer, more inclusive society can be constructed (1991, p. 238). What Goulbourne deplored was the rise of the ethno-cultural paradigm, whether it be that of group or nation. That sort of ethnicity vacates the common space and, however well-intentioned, can retreat into exclusivity. The civic quality of Britishness should not take second place to the ethnic. In this regard, some of Ernest Barker's reflections on the relationship between individual liberty, pluralism, law and the constitution find a new relevance.

Others have articulated the problem – even the fear – of national separatism more directly. In a series of essays, Yasmin Alibhai-Brown has acted as a dissenting voice and has been frequently critical of the Panglossian view of nationalist resurgence. She has criticised some of the pronouncements by members of the Scottish National Party as smacking 'of the worst kind of French cultural and political arrogance which is built on the idea of absorption into a greater culture, not diversity and equality of respect' (1998, p. 47). In doing so, she has highlighted one of the traditional differences between the French and the British ideas of the people, which was explored in Chapter 2. The fear is that minorities would be locked out emotionally from the nationalisms of Wales, England and Scotland. Many black and Asian Britons, she claimed, were alarmed lest the more capacious British identity be discarded (2000a, p. 26; Marr 1999, pp. 156–7). What is needed is that tradition of historical fudge which informed the liberality of the genteel tradition – 'a Britishness which is a civic device to bind people together without recourse to ethnicity' (1998, p. 47; 2000b). Her work is important for she recognises more clearly than most what is at stake in asking the question 'Why is Britain?'

The old Britain has passed away. That is almost universally accepted. And why should it not? Only something that is outside history can be changeless. For Alibhai-Brown, a number of possibilities open up. One can say good riddance to Britain and then get on with the business of fashioning distinctive national and regional identities within the European Union. Or one can use the opportunity to redefine Britishness as a vigorous, modern identity (2000a, p. 28). Paradoxically, in demanding less of its citizens as a vigorous modern identity this ideal of Britishness may expect too much of politico-institutional allegiance. It remains an open question whether there is the political will or the civic energy to make out of modern Britain the attractive and inclusive national identity that Alibhai-Brown, Goulbourne, Parekh, McMillan, Marr and Freedland, in their diverse ways, would like to see. For the ancestral voices of resurgent Scottishness or reawakened Englishness, promising a comforting home in an uncertain world may be too strong to make it happen. Maybe it could never happen. Nairn, for instance, has argued that this mongrelisation, a self-conscious embracing of multicultural diversity, is not a solution. Put in that way he is correct. As Parekh himself has consistently argued, no identity can ever be constructed on difference alone. There must be some commonality.

It may be a sign of the times that many of those who make the most persuasive and unrepentant intellectual case for a positive Britishness and who seem to care most about it are not of British 'stock'. What they seek, as Simon Partridge (1999) puts it, is a British Union state which is a 'flexible citizens' home' and not the old folks' home of the Ukania myth. And in this endeavour, the voices from the margins have engaged directly with the mainstream, with the great hope of New Labour's constitutional project. It is this project itself which, inevitably, has become the target of the sort of nationalist attack one finds in Nairn's *After Britain* (2000a).

The British party system has traditionally served to integrate the British people into a common political identity. The ideological competition of the parties assumed a common ideology of national unity. The claim has recently been made, however, that the present question 'Why is Britain?' and the doubts about its unity have arisen mainly because of the decay of the ideologically integrative narratives of the Conservative and Labour Parties. Before 1979, as J.C.D. Clark has argued, the British electorate generally identified itself with one or other of these narratives: the working class supported Labourist socialism and the middle class Conservative constitutionalism (1990b, p. 41). This has changed. The great historical narratives of socialism and Conservatism have lost much of their appeal. Without them it becomes difficult to account for the British state. This coincides with, indeed has brought forth, renewed nationalist self-confidence. What was excluded from the traditional language of Britain's integrative narratives has reasserted its claim to right. Nationalism (within Europe) has become a respectable narrative once again. The apparent vulnerability of the British state, therefore, has as much to do with the problem of a convincing political narrative as it has to do with chronic economic problems. Sustaining such a narrative is certainly one of Blair's concerns. In that enterprise, argues one critic, the traditions of twentieth-century British party politics provide little sustenance upon which to draw (Barker 1996, p. 17). These traditions, the British narratives of Conservative and Labour, now require some examination.

Narratives

4   The Conservative Nation

George Dangerfield famously wrote of *The Strange Death of Liberal England* (1936). Sixty years later Patrick Cosgrave wrote of *The Strange Death of Socialist Britain* (1992). It was *Conservative* Britain which appeared to have survived in rude good health. The narrative of the twentieth century, as one text maintained, was the story of the Conservative nation (Gamble 1974). It was a narrative that claimed to reconcile the Englishness of Conservatism with the Britishness of public culture. Its apparent solidity had been the frustration of generations of radicals. Today, things look rather different. The fragility of the Conservative nation, rather than its solidity, can now be better understood. Its fracturing has provided an opportunity for New Labour to raise social-liberal Britain from its grave and give it new life. The endurance of the Conservative nation may have flattered the ideological strength of its narrative. The central historical idea – a secure relationship between Englishness and Britishness – was never fully settled in Conservative politics.

Stanley Baldwin provides an interesting example in the shifting rhetoric of the Conservative nation. When he addressed guests at the annual dinner of the Royal Society of St. George in 1924, he tried to define the meaning of Englishness. He did feel a certain freedom, in that particular company, from the requirements of what today would be called political correctness. The first thought in the Conservative leader's mind was 'a feeling of satisfaction and profound thankfulness that I may use the word "England" without some fellow at the back of the room shouting out "Britain"'. How very different it would be, he went on, if an Englishman were required to say, 'For in spite of all temptation to belong to other nations, he remains a Briton' (1926, p. 1). Englishness, for Baldwin, was sensuous and emotionally evocative. Britishness obviously was not. In the same collection of speeches there is also a record of Baldwin's address in 1925 to the St. Andrew's Day Festival of the Royal Scottish Corporation. To that audience he claimed that the English had always taken the Scots to their hearts as blood-brothers. He did not claim any reciprocal embrace. At the same time he felt sufficently at ease in that company and, one supposes, with the fellow-feeling of a common Britishness, to be capable of making a joke at the expense of the kilt – 'the garb of the robbers of the North' (1926, p. 239) – which would assuredly be beyond the bounds for any English Conservative leader today.

Together, Baldwin's comments are a curious mixture for anyone interested in Britishness. He articulates a profound sense of his own English identity. He expresses a strong sense of fellow-feeling for the Scots. He acknowledges an equally profound sense of Scottish national distinctiveness. He thinks that the expression 'Briton' is somehow an inadequate term which does not capture the meaning of Englishness or Scottishness, never mind Irishness or Welshness. He accepts that a Conservative leader should be careful not to assume that England is Britain or that Britain is England. Finally, he knows that when one does speak of Britain one is speaking politically. At the same time, Baldwin tells us that it *is* easy to confuse England with Britain and Britain with England; that it *is* easy to give little thought to national identity. (Why else would that tiresome fellow at the back of the room be complaining?) Baldwin was English, some might argue quintessentially English. The image he assiduously cultivated was of a very English leader of a very English party. His speeches involved a celebration of English distinctiveness within a diversified Union. By implication, the Scots, the Welsh and the Irish were equally distinctive. The 'Englishness' of Conservatism, though, was not understood to be at odds with the 'Britishness' of the state. Englishness was compatible with Britishness because the cultural and national institutions of the Scots were embraced by it, neither absorbed nor extinguished. Therefore, Baldwin's praise of England was not thought to be controversially nationalistic. Nor was it. It might irritate the Scots, but there was little evidence that their irritation implied resentment at 'the imposition of a dominant culture and institutions on a subject people' (Mitchell 1996, p. 31). The commonality was more vital than the irritation.

The relationship between commonality and irritation had changed somewhat by the end of the twentieth century. It was a sign of changed times for the Conservative Party and its leader when one compares the note struck by Baldwin's thoughts about England with the derision that greeted John Major's attempt to appropriate George Orwell's imagery of the old maids cycling to church on a misty morning. This *was* judged to be controversial because when 'he spoke of British values and traditions and linked them with references to warm beer and cricket matches on the village green, he was reflecting on life in southern England' (Jones 1999a, p. 144). This was not Major's intention. His British patriotism was genuine, and his speech was intended to convey the message that the European Union was not a threat to British identity (Paxman 1999, pp. 143–4). What had happened in the 70 years between Baldwin and Major was the attenuation of the embracing constitutionalism of political Englishness. The consensual image of Conservative England/Britain no longer resonated as it once did.

The older consensual image of the Conservative nation had not emerged fully formed. It had been worked at in the 1920s and 1930s by Conservative Central Office and by the BBC. Baldwin had seemed its perfect embodiment (Nicholas 1996, p. 140). While the press tended to be more hostile, the BBC maintained a deferential relationship to the Conservative and Conservative-dominated governments of the interwar years. As Nicholas argued, the self-conscious political function of the BBC was to unite, not to divide, and its image of unity was that projected by Baldwin. In short, it 'drew upon and embellished those shared conceptions of the nation and national identity that Baldwin had done so much to embody in words and manner' (1996, p. 141). By the time Major was premier the media no longer saw their task as one of fostering national consensus. Rather it was to interrogate, to challenge, to deconstruct. Irony, not received patriotism, was the dominant value. Major's personal qualities, though generally acknowledged, were treated as irrelevant to political reportage. A different age meant that the old conceptions could no longer suffice.

It would be wrong to give the impression that things used to be unproblematic. That is recent myth-making by those on the Left and and those within the Conservative Party who opposed Thatcher. The relationship between Englishness and Britishness or between nationhood and statehood in traditional Conservative politics has never been a particularly easy one. The truth of this has only recently come to qualify the assumptions of earlier work on Conservatism (Francis and Zweiniger-Bargielowska 1996, p. 6). The Conservative nation revealed neither complete self-assurance nor an uncomplicated identity. The party has always had intimations of disaster. Radical critics have tended to credit Conservatives with a self-confidence which was not there. How might one characterise the Conservative nation given the fluidity of both British identity and of 'England's interests'?

THE MAKING OF THE CONSERVATIVE NATION

In the late nineteenth century, the Conservative Party reinvented itself as the party of the empire, the party of the Union, and as the patriotic party. It has been one of the claims of Conservative politicians ever since that their party is a 'national party or it is nothing'. It is the true people's party because it expresses the interests of 'One Nation'. This Delphic term can be understood in two senses. First, it was taken to mean that the Conservatives had a definite view on the 'condition of England' question. In short, the Conservative Party was the party of class harmony and understood its task to unite the 'Two Nations', the rich and the poor. This was not to be done according to the alien nostrums of liberal radicalism or revolutionary socialism, but in accordance with the venerable procedures of the British constitution. Second, the idea of One Nation had a territorial complexion and stood for the Conservative commitment to the Union of England, Scotland, Wales and Ireland (later Northern Ireland). The nation was at the core of Conservative thinking and unifying the two themes was a belief in the ultimate identity of interest shared by all British people.

With that sort of pedigree one would imagine that the reflections of Conservatives on the question of British identity would be clear. One would imagine a public sensitivity about the use of the terms British and English (if only as far as Baldwin was prepared to take it). In fact, there is no historical consistency at all in the way in which the terms 'English' and 'British' have been used by party publicists. The historical irony would seem to be this. As it made greater efforts not to offend the Britishness of Baldwin's fellow at the back of the room, Conservatism was increasingly perceived by the electorate in Scotland and Wales to be the organised expression of Englishness. There is nothing novel about the Conservative Party's Englishness. By the end of the twentieth century, however, that Englishness was now working against the party in Scotland and Wales.

Lord Blake has stressed the familiar pattern of Conservative electoral support throughout most of its history. He reflected that from one aspect the Conservative Party was the party of English nationalism. However, he also identified Conservatism with the continuity of British constitutionalism (1985, pp. 361–2). If one accepts Blake's description of these matters, how does one explain the Conservative Party's electorally successful reconciliation of its English 'nationalism' and its traditional Britishness, given that, as

Blake admitted, the logic of its English-based support argued *against* opposition to Home Rule? Part of the answer lies in the complex amalgam of the 'Conservative nation'.

The Conservative nation has been a compound of two traditions of British Conservatism. The first is rooted in the pre-modern notion of the authority of the Crown. The nation is held to be founded on the patriotic allegiance of the people to the person of the monarch, an allegiance which embraces all subjects irrespective of their regional, cultural or national differences. Allegiance to the monarch transformed itself into allegiance to the constitutional people headed by the monarch. The Conservative nation, therefore, is the political community united in acceptance of the legitimacy of that traditional relationship. In the latter part of the nineteenth century this perspective adapted itself to liberal constitutionalism and began to parade its democratic credentials. As A.J.P. Taylor once jokingly observed, the consequence of this was a common wisdom that history was now best conducted on the principle that Whig plus Tory equals eternal truth (1977, p. 21). That was the sort of eternal truth with which Margaret Thatcher grew up.

The second tradition of Conservative thought is to be found in the late nineteenth-century concern to pacify the working class and head off the challenge of organised labour. It assumed a distinctive sort of popular unity in which 'popular' did not entail social equality. The Conservative Party itself was the country party, suspicious of such liberal metropolitan fashions. Snobbery too was an important element, the supreme law of life for those who thought it best to maintain the standards of social rank. One of the historic purposes of the party, one well understood by its aristocratic leadership, was to justify social rank to a democracy. And one of the reasons for joining the party was to feel at home in a world where the code of snobbery was second nature. These two traditions might be profitably termed the patriotic and the populist styles. They may be analysed separately though their practical significance for the success of Conservative politics was to come from their fusion in the late nineteenth century. The erratic career of Benjamin Disraeli appropriately traces this fortuitous construction.

Disraeli remains important in the history of Conservative politics as a purveyor of both its illusions and its potential. Disraeli's writing, especially in his Young England period of the 1830s and 1840s, developed the theme of 'the King at the centre, the people at the circumference', the idea that the people were better served by the Tory tradition of Church and Crown than by a self-serving oligarchy of the Whigs and Liberals. The faithful servants of the Crown – Tories like Disraeli – would be the true representatives of the people. As John Vincent interpreted it, Disraeli conjured up 'an anti-elitist or popular doctrine of national solidarity' (1990, p. 23). That was a populist trick which Conservative leaders have used ever since, especially against the Labour Party. The message was that the constitutional people – in this case government at the centre and people at the periphery, must not be seduced by radical misrule, which would upset the proper balance.

That populist style served its purpose by helping the Conservative Party adapt to the demands of democratic politics in the twentieth century. There may have been cynical flattery in the Conservative courting of the masses, but this was only the formalisation of what was a long-standing social reality. Those 'angels in marble', especially the English working-class Conservatives whom Disraeli is supposed to have perceived, did not object to a little jingoism and responded well to the image of traditional stability. The nineteenth-century Conservative Party was not, and never had been, a serious party of social reform. But it had been rhetorically well positioned to take advantage of the opportunities which came its way when the Liberal Party split over Home Rule for Ireland.

Few Victorian Conservatives would have believed it possible to make Conservatism popular, and the Tories were astonished that they could elicit a sympathetic response from a growing electorate (Pugh 1988, p. 273). What enabled that to happen was the appropriation of patriotism. Yet there was no automatic relationship between patriotism and Conservatism – the ideology of patriotism had to be cultivated; the identity of the Conservative Party with it was a matter of luck. There were difficulties too getting a proper balance between patriotism and populism. The task of the party's leadership was to ensure that an electorally successful equilibrium was achieved. What governed and regulated both these aspects and reconciled them was the old, though refurbished, idea of the balanced constitution. The emotion of belonging to the constitutional people was attached to integrative symbolism of the Crown-in-Parliament. Englishness, Britishness and the Conservative nation were presented as a seamless union. Electorally, this proved to be a very profitable image for most of the twentieth century.

It associated the proper governance of the territory of Britain with the institution of the Conservative Party and with the particular competence of its political leadership. It assumed that 'the interests of the British nation state are best served by contriving the perpetuity of a Tory administration whatever *apparent* sacrifices of principle or policy this may entail' (Clark 1999, p. xix). This Tory version of patriotism retained a very English cast despite its intense commitment to the integrity of the United Kingdom. The aristocratic assumption of that patriotism was clear. However condescending the perspective, it was based upon a recognisable tradition which took the notion of the balanced constitution seriously. In Lord Salisbury's words, the politics of the constitutional people, for all its local inconveniences, was to be preferred to the French model of the sovereign people. Efficiency, he thought, argued in favour of centralising power. But efficiency was not everything, and the drawbacks of the French approach were so serious that the freeborn English had to reconcile themselves locally to the inconvenience of being governed by squabbling juntas of shopkeepers and tenant farmers (Pinto-Duschinsky 1967, p. 114). That was the Tory version of Barker's genteel tradition.

The governing assumptions of the Conservative nation have been remarkably enduring. Talk of the twentieth century as the Conservative century is not entirely misplaced (Seldon and Ball 1994). Even in the 1980s, R.W. Johnson could still believe that something called 'Tory culture' ruled Britain, something that went beyond the Conservative Party, which was just its central core. This Tory culture, rather like Scottish or Welsh nationalism, was greater than party (1985, pp. 234–5). Perhaps it was *English* nationalism. Equally, Patrick Wright thought that the idea of the nation to which Conservatives appealed made the Labour Party version seem bureaucratic and uninspiring. The Conservative nation, he thought, had colonised the memory of the country (1985, p. 87). To Conservative activists such as Jim Bulpitt, on the other hand, there was nothing inevitable about this and much of it, especially Johnson's and Wright's description of it, was nonsense. Few Conservatives felt comfortable with modern Britain and did not recognise this 'Tory culture'. For Bulpitt, the party had been lucky. It was merely the 'Great Survivor' (1991, p. 7).

Ireland was the exception which seemed to prove the rule. The Irish policy of the Conservative nation in the early years of the twentieth century had threatened the very existence of the constitutional people. The First World War changed all that. Ironically, opposition to Home Rule had been the glue which had held the party together for some 20 years and helped to establish the Conservative Party as the 'national' party. By contrast, the patriotic demands of the war had served to marginalise much of the dangerously populist rhetoric about Ireland. Special provision for Ulster became the escape route. The Union of Great Britain and Ireland which Conservatives had defended *was* broken by the encounter of Irish republican separatism and Ulster Unionist loyalism. Northern Ireland was compelled to accept the sort of Home Rule which Conservatives up to 1914 had opposed for the whole of Ireland. But by that time most Conservative activists were bored by the Irish Question.

After the Second World War, the shock realisation that the party of Churchill was blamed for both unpatriotic appeasement and unpatriotic unemployment was an incentive to pull the fragments of the Conservative tradition into a new populist shape. Socialism, it was argued, believed that the 'gentleman in Whitehall knows best' and had centralising pretentions. It was the Conservatives who recognised the diverse character of the kingdom and wanted to defend it – so long as the integrity of the constitutional people was maintained. It was the Conservative Party which wanted to set the people free, albeit free within the accepted boundaries of the Welfare State. What was required, above all, was the proper sort of (Conservative) leadership to run the country. In 1950 Churchill was arguing that the nationalisations promoted by the Labour government were contrary to the spirit of the balance between Englishness and Britishness: 'If England became an absolute Socialist State, owning all the means of production, distribution and exchange, ruled only by politicians and their officials in the London offices, I personally cannot feel Scotland would be bound to accept such a dispensation' (cited in Marr 1992, p. 113) – Churchillian exaggeration, of course, and only for purposes of Opposition. Moreover, the Conservatives happened to be at that time the majority party in Scotland. Yet it helps to emphasise the extent to which acknowledgement of Scottish distinctiveness was part of the general currency of political argument, even if Home Rule for Scotland (or Wales or the English regions) was not. This was exploited in Scotland by Conservatives such as Walter Elliot, who argued that north of the border nationalisation meant denationalisation (Findlay 1996, pp. 120–1).

In its own pragmatic fashion the Conservative Party had on occasion reassessed how the state should operate. It had done so with a sceptical view of constitutional change and with a principled assumption of the intrinsic good of the British constitutional people.

It had been a Conservative government that created the Scottish Office in 1885 and upgraded the status of the Secretary for Scotland in 1926. It had been a Conservative-dominated government that transferred the functions of the Scottish Office from London to Edinburgh in 1939. Conservative governments had frequently modified the procedures for the conduct of Scottish business in a way they were reluctant to do for Wales. It was a Labour government that established the Welsh Office in 1964. Reform of administrative and institutional procedure, therefore, had not been a major problem in Conservative politics. What had been contentious was the argument that the cultural and national distinctiveness of Scotland and Wales required any serious modification of the exercise of Westminster sovereignty. By the late 1960s, even this seemed susceptible to change in the same pragmatic or opportunistic fashion.

In May 1968 Edward Heath announced an initiative to the Scottish Conservative Conference, which became known as the Perth Declaration. It was a pledge to 'give the people of Scotland genuine participation in the making of decisions that affect them – all within the historic unity of the United Kingdom' (Conservative Party 1977, p. 518). A Scottish Constitutional Committee was established under the chairmanship of Sir Alec Douglas-Home to make proposals to that effect. Its Report, *Scotland's Government*, published in March 1970, suggested the creation of a directly elected Assembly which would form, in effect, a third chamber of the United Kingdom parliament. The Heath government of 1970–74, however, became overwhelmed by other pressing matters. Devolution was not a priority even though it continued to have its strong Scottish advocates within the party.

Thatcher, who succeeded Heath in February 1975, had other ideas. She had little sympathy for devolution. In this she was in tune with the sentiments of her party. Most English Conservative MPs were opposed to the idea, as were their Welsh colleagues. Scottish Conservative MPs were divided on the issue. In the referendum campaign on Labour's Scotland and Wales Acts, the Conservative Party argued for a 'No' vote. This, it was made clear in Scotland, did not mean that the party would not consider a less threatening form of devolution in the future. There was some relief when the Acts failed to generate sufficient public support in the referendum vote of 1 March 1979. By this stage, the party supported 'devolution in theory while opposing it in practice' (Bogdanor 1980, p. 93). As far as

Thatcher was concerned, that meant not supporting it at all, a position confirmed when the party won office in May 1979.

CONSTITUTIONAL CONSEQUENCES OF MARGARET THATCHER

There has been something of a consensus amongst critics of the Conservative Party since 1979 that the traditional order of the United Kingdom has been damaged, perhaps irreparably, as Thatcherism ran its course. The damage did not start under Thatcher, but it is thought that her approach to government not only promoted tendencies towards disintegration, but seemed almost to turn them into a definitive style of politics. There was a nostalgic air to much of this criticism, a feeling that one was witnessing the passing of a more civil, albeit patrician, era of politics – the genteel tradition. In this new abrasive age, the theme of mixed and limited government had given way to one of ideological dogmatism. In particular, there developed the notion by the people 'on the circumference' that Conservative England no longer felt obliged to acknowledge the interests of non-Conservative Britain. Bernard Crick, for instance, argued that the old English governing class had been historically-minded and had a sense of the diversity of the country. The new Conservatives did not understand the United Kingdom and were Anglocentric in mentality and mid-Atlantic in culture (1990, p. 111). There is some truth in Crick's claim. Thatcher, as her autobiography makes clear, had no time at all for the patrician style in the Conservative Party and even less for the patricians themselves. It and they were seen to be just as much the cause of Britain's decline as socialism. The thrust of Crick's criticism was really that the particularity of Thatcherite populism (its Englishness) weakened the patriotic identity of the party (its Britishness).

Within the party, Sir Ian Gilmour (later Lord Gilmour) also found it difficult to accept the intellectual hubris of those like Thatcher who argued that the Tory Party had been wrong for 30 years (Gilmour 1977, p. 12). His judgement on the Thatcher era was similar to Crick's. For the Conservatives, government demands continual adaptation, patience and reflection. It is unsuited to ideologues like Mrs Thatcher (Garnett and Gilmour 1996, p. 80). That response may very well confirm Thatcher's view of the patrician class with all its subtle codes of gentlemanly exclusion.

Whatever the reasons for the Thatcherite ideological turn, it could not be put down to the electoral geography of Britain. Certainly, Conservative support was increasingly concentrated in the south and midlands of England, but then the historical bias of the Conservative vote always had been English. As Lord Blake pointed out, the distribution of Conservative strength in the last quarter of the twentieth century would come as little surprise to a Tory Rip Van Winkle who fell asleep in 1840 (1985, p. 361). Of course, by the 1980s and 1990s things were much worse in Wales and in Scotland. This was bound to cause political difficulties for the Thatcher administration whatever its policies. And perhaps, as she herself believed, there was little she could have done anyhow about the recrudescence of nationalist sentiment, particularly in Scotland. Nevertheless, it was the attitude towards the government of the United Kingdom which was important and not electoral geography or national sentiment alone. In this both Gilmour and Crick are correct. An indication of a change of attitude is to be found in Thatcher's appeal to the Conservative Philosophy Group: 'We must have an ideology. The other side has got an ideology they can test their policies against. We must have one as well' (cited in Gilmour 1992, p. 8). This *was* a rather different emphasis from the Oakeshottian belief that the constitution was an adequate substitute for a philosophy. The trouble with a philosophy is that there is an incentive to make things clearcut when one of the secrets of the Conservative nation had been to leave things vague and conventional. It is, of course, possible to overdo the ideological consistency, but it is impossible to ignore. There were two things which Thatcherite ideology wanted to make clear and which caused political trouble with the nations of the Union. They were the doctrine of individualism and the doctrine of parliamentary sovereignty.

Thatcher's individualism owed something to Enoch Powell and his quest to reaffirm British identity in the post-imperial era. But her conflation of individualism with British identity had a unique inflection. Liberal constitutionalism, with its history of rights and liberties, was to be expressed again in a modern economistic idiom. Parekh identified the significance of this restatement of ordered liberty as a defence of the free market and limited state. British liberty, for Thatcher, 'did not create disorder and conflict, and required only minimum intervention by the state' (1994b, p. 101). This idea of liberty was an achievement of the Conservative nation. In this achievement of civilisation all British people shared. Speaking in Scotland, Thatcher linked Conservatism, Scottishness, Britishness and traditional personal values: 'Scottish values are Tory values – and vice versa. The values of hard work, self-reliance, thrift, enterprise – the relishing of challenges, the seizing of opportunities' (1989, pp. 247–8).

The crucial point is that individualism was taken to be a universal cultural attribute and the natural birthright of every British citizen. It transcended all regional, local and national differences. It was the condition of both unity and singularity. Therefore, its claims overrode all qualifications and resistance. Its message for the nations and the regions of Britain was the same as the message to ethnic minorities on the famous race relations poster of the 1983 general election. Underneath a picture of a black man the message ran: 'Labour Says He's Black. Tories Say He's British.' In other words, there would be no special cases, only equality of citizenship and freedom of opportunity throughout the whole of the United Kingdom. And this view continues to resonate powerfully within the party. Conservatives have argued that the Left have assiduously attempted to redefine British citizens as members of minority groups and deny their truth as sovereign individuals (Gove 1999, p. 15). Sovereign individuals under a sovereign parliament were the ideal; or, as Andrew Gamble (1989) once put it, a free economy and a strong state. The logical consequence of the thought that British values were individualistic soon became clear. Resistance to a project driven by individualistic premises was anti-British. Defence of those institutions which opposed individualism or preserved the 'dependency culture' of collectivism was anti-British. The Scots and the Welsh who did not vote Conservative were not being true to themselves. It was thus legitimate to force them to be free. Thatcher's governments did not necessarily act on the basis of that legitimacy. For most of the time her Secretaries of State in Wales and Scotland, adjusting ideology to local circumstances, tended to deflect the rigours of the Thatcherite revolution (Jones 1999, p. 131). Nevertheless, it was an attitude which allowed nationalists to argue that the 'people on the periphery' should become the centre of their own government. In this case, national populism confronted the claims of central legitimacy. It was a feeling that went beyond the Scottish National Party in Scotland or Plaid Cymru in Wales.

This is captured in an address by Canon Kenyon Wright, chairman of the Scottish Constitutional Convention, on 30 March 1989. Referring to Thatcher, Wright asked how the outcome of the

Convention's deliberations would be received: 'What if that other single voice we all know so well responds by saying, "We say no, and we are the state"? Well, we say yes – and we are the people' (cited in Marr 1992, p. 206). As it happened, the government – by this time John Major's government – did say no. Yet the substance of the question had not disappeared. Its persistence revealed the tears in the fabric of the constitutional people, the potential dissolution of its genteel bonds, and with it the Scottish flavour to the Conservative nation.

For there was a genuine revolutionary quality to Thatcher's approach. Its character was elegantly captured in Hugh Berrington's ironic analogy that Thatcherism owed far more to France than to Britain. The tradition that came closest to Thatcherism, he thought, was Jacobinism (1998, p. 9). Both shared a tradition of radical individualism, and populism was a common powerful ingredient. This populism caused problems for the integrative British patriotism of the Conservative Party, not because Thatcher was not patriotic but because her populism was seen by many of the Scots and Welsh to be distinctively English. Berrington thought Thatcher's hostility to locally representative institutions a peculiarly Jacobin trait which informed her defence of the British state: 'She saw the nation-state as the ultimate form of political organisation. She rejected union above as devolution below' (1998, p. 11).

Much of the irony had to do with the fact that, historically and ideologically, Conservative constitutionalism had defined itself against French centralism. Thatcher's 'Jacobinism' had mixed fortunes. In her memoirs she was candid about one failure during her term of office: 'There was no Tartan Thatcherite revolution.' This was always a surprise to her, for 'Scotland in the eighteenth century was the home of the very same Scottish Enlightenment which produced Adam Smith, the greatest exponent of free enterprise economics till Hayek and Friedman' (1993, p. 618). Scotland (and Wales), unfortunately, had succumbed to the anti-individualist, non-British, dependency culture of socialism, a culture which had infected all levels of society from the churches to the media. This was a national illness which needed the curative medicine of sovereign individualism. The old order had gone: 'whereas in the past it might have been possible for the Conservatives to rely on a mixture of deference, traditionalism and paternalism to see them through, this was just no longer an option – and none the worse for that' (1993, p. 619). That was the true voice of Thatcherite radicalism, exhibiting a distaste for the old genteel identity. The majority of Scots understood it differently – not only as a struggle between socialism and capitalism, but also as a struggle between Scottish traditions and an imposed English policy. Despite the references to Adam Smith and the Scottish Enlightenment, historians have indeed interpreted Thatcher's ideology as a peculiarly English one (Clark 1990b).

Yet in her denial of this English cultural bias, Thatcher herself tended to give some credence to it. She argued that part of the difficulty in Scotland was that 'the Tories are seen as an English party' and herself 'as a quintessentially English figure'. While Thatcher was proud of the second point, she denied the first: 'The Tory Party is not, of course, an English party but a Unionist one.' England, because of its population, happened to be the prominent partner in the Union. If the Scots wanted special treatment they would have to persuade the rest of the United Kingdom, particularly the English, of its merits. 'It was understandable,' she conceded, 'that when I come out with these kind of hard truths many Scots should resent it', but that had nothing to do with her Englishness (1993, p. 624). The Scots (collectively) were never persuaded of the merits of Conservative individualism.

As long as Thatcher remained leader, the Conservative Party would reject devolution. Her policy was different and one compatible with sovereign individualism. In a speech to the Scottish conference in May 1988 she defined that policy as devolution to the people themselves: 'devolution of housing, devolution of education, devolution of share-ownership and devolution of State-run industries to individuals'. In an echo of Walter Elliot 40 years earlier, she argued that individualism, privatisation and a self-determination of sorts went hand in hand: 'Nationalization took companies out of Scottish hands and into Whitehall; privatization will hand them back to Scotland' (1989, p. 245). Unfortunately, the one major populist initiative undertaken for her people in Scotland, the poll tax, became the very symbol of English political imposition and a threat to the government's legitimacy. The impression remains that the Scottish question, and therefore the *British* question, was one Thatcher did not take to be central to her project.

Part of the reason for this lay in the weight given to the principle of parliamentary sovereignty. As Bulpitt argued persuasively, it was the intention of the Conservative government after 1979 to re-establish that 'central autonomy' which the leadership felt had been lost under social democracy in the 1960s and 1970s. But this was not a Conservative leadership with a traditional governing perspective. It was a Conservative leadership with a programme to implement and a prime minister who wanted to change everything. A governing ideology, originally designed to maintain continuity and modulate differences in the interest of stability, was now pressed into the service of a radical regeneration of Britain. All those dangers of 'elective dictatorship', which Lord Hailsham (1978) had outlined, appeared to her opponents just as dangerous under a rightwing government as under a leftwing government. It was well within the *power* of the government to do this; but it was questionable whether it was within the *spirit* of the traditional notion of constitutional balance. As far as the ideology was concerned the answer was simple.

In her robustly sympathetic treatment of the anatomy of Thatcherism, Shirley Robin Letwin reduced to clarity and precision the relationship between central and local government in Britain. Local government was never an ancient bastion of autonomy and liberty under the British constitution. It was all a myth (1992, pp. 159–60). Of course, there is a lot of truth in this. Nevertheless, part of the success of British constitutionalism has been precisely in the pretence, for in the pretence lay the wisdom of respect for local, regional and national pride and sensibility. That was one of the old 'tacit understandings' which, despite its mythological status, sufficed for a constitutionally-minded, One Nation Conservative such as Gilmour. It would not do for an ideologically-minded Conservative such as Thatcher. This is not the place to examine the failings or successes of that style of Conservative politics, but it is the place to consider Letwin's conclusion. For her, the battles with local authorities in the 1980s were not about centralisation but about undermining socialism. The Thatcher experiment, she thought, led to the logical conclusion of reducing 'local government to being in practice the agent of central government as it always has been in constitutional theory' (1992, p. 198). If one compares that sort of constitutional understanding with that of Lord Salisbury, one can appreciate the extent to which the Conservative nation had changed in the course of a century.

The principle of parliamentary sovereignty actually played a double role in Thatcher's Northern Ireland policy. It was used to impose on Ulster Unionists the Anglo-Irish Agreement of November 1985. It was also the principle which informed the character that the Agreement finally took. One of the key British officials, Sir David

Goodall, has argued that Thatcher entered the negotiations determined not to compromise the Union and was primarily interested in finding ways to improve the security situation. On the other hand, the main thrust of the Dublin position was towards joint authority over Northern Ireland for which the Irish government was prepared to trade Articles 2 and 3 of the Republic's constitution, which contained the 'territorial claim' to the six counties. Thatcher would not go that far. Thus emerged, according to Goodall, the central concept of the Agreement which was Irish acceptance of the Union, though without repeal of Articles 2 and 3, as a basis from which the Irish government 'could be given a systematic and institutionalised influence on British decision-making there without any diminution of British sovereignty' (1993, p. 130). Ulster Unionists did not accept this concept, nor any of its propositions. They felt betrayed by a Conservative leader whose patriotic and populist view of Britishness they thought to be in sympathy with their own. They saw the Agreement as an illegitimate use of parliamentary sovereignty against the spirit of the constitutional people. They were not alone.

AFTER THATCHER

Alistair Moffat thought that Thatcher herself had been the midwife of devolution for Scotland. The Scots began to distance themselves from England by trying to become very Scottish. This was one way of rejecting Thatcherite Conservatism (1999, p. 35). This had been predicted by academic research in the early 1980s. As Miller et al. had found, the Conservative Party was seen not just as anti-devolution but as anti-Scottish (1981, p. 213). The decline of Conservative support in Scotland was a long drawn-out affair and it would be too simple to correlate the rise of nationalistic sentiment with that decline. Michael Fry argued that things only turned disastrous when the party in Scotland imported its policy from England under Thatcher's leadership. He concluded that the strong roots of Scottish Unionism have been steadily destroyed because of its displacement by a bloodless and rootless English Conservatism (1999, pp. 467–9). However, Gerry Hassan's research on party activists in Scotland reached a different conclusion. He found that party members did identify with Thatcher's English nationalism (1994, p. 16). It was not the imported but the indigenous views that were dangerously out of touch. Both these judgements need a degree of qualification. A valuable corrective is to be found in Seawright and Curtice (1995). They believed that the emphasis on nationalism may unfortunately underestimate material issues. The short-term economic record of the Conservatives at election times has been more unfavourable than Labour's and this might count for part of the party's problems (1995, p. 339). Nevertheless, they agreed that the loss of an ability to appeal to the symbols of Scottish culture has been a crucial ingredient in the party's decline (1995, p. 335). The attempt to recover that appeal is now the task of contemporary Conservatism.

Under Major the Conservatives had returned explicitly to an old argument which had currency at the time of the Irish Home Rule debates a century earlier. The argument ran that there is no half-way house between unity and separation (Seldon 1997, pp. 261–3) – except, that is, for Northern Ireland. In Scotland, this proved to be reasonably successful if only to stem the decline of the Scottish Conservative vote in the general election of 1992. However, that had the unintended effect of appearing to put the Scottish and Welsh position within the Union on an all-or-nothing basis. They could have separation; but they could have no self-government short of that. Major's autobiography clarifies his point of view. He saw the United Kingdom without Scotland 'as a diminished power: less able to punch its weight at European Councils or in the world; without its place as one of the permanent members of the UN Security Council; perhaps excluded from the G7 Group of industrial nations' (1999, p. 415). And what was bad for Britain was even worse for Scotland. His irritation with what he saw as the insular world of Scottish politics was as marked as Thatcher's (1999, p. 419). Echoing Lord Blake, he thought this all the more galling for it was not the Conservatives who had gained from ties between England and Scotland; it was the Scots. Despite Major's more emollient style and greater sensitivity to the problems of a multinational Britain, and despite the energetic efforts of his Scottish Secretary of State, Michael Forsyth (1995–97), the Conservative vote in Scotland slumped to 17.3 per cent in the 1997 general election. The defeat meant the loss of Scottish Conservative representation at Westminster.

A similar Westminster annihilation was experienced in Wales. Ironically, it was Major's appointment of John Redwood as Secretary of State (1993–95) which brought for the first time Mrs Thatcher's English-style Jacobinism to the Principality. As Jones commented,

Redwood's impact on Wales should not be underestimated: 'For such hard-edged Thatcherite policies now to be applied, when Major's government appeared to be returning to more consensual policies, caused dismay and anger across Wales' (1999, p. 139). One important consequence was to convince many doubters in Welsh local government of the need for some form of devolution.

William Hague, who succeeded Major in 1997, inherited a difficult legacy. He had to adapt his party to the reality of New Labour's devolutionary settlement; at the same time, he had to try to make a case for a Conservative nation distinct from New Labour's supposedly 'rebranded' one. The task was to bring Conservative populism and British patriotism back together in a persuasive defence of the Conservative nation. In a keynote speech entitled 'Identity and the British Way', Hague repeated much that was familiar about the values of Britishness. Individualism remained one of them, but so too was loyalty to the institutions of civil society. One defining characteristic of British identity, Hague claimed, was that it continued to be a 'country of neighbourhoods' (Hague 1999). This is an interesting echo of what Ernest Barker called the spirit of English neighbourliness, a neighbourliness which protected Britain against the ravages of (European-style) nationalism. It also tracked closely Gordon Brown's adaptation of Amitai Etzione when he spoke of the need to create a 'community of neighbours' (Foote 1997, p. 343). And parliamentary sovereignty was to stay at the core of British identity. The British way, then, continues to be the way of ordered liberty under historic political institutions. It is because of the stability which those institutions have provided that the multiethnic and multinational character of Britain can flourish. In response to Lord Tebbit's view that nationality was more about culture than ethnicity, Hague argued that Britishness must be 'patriotism without bigotry', acknowledging that 'successive waves of immigrants have enriched our culture' (cited in Lynch 2000, p. 63). Some minority spokespersons have welcomed this approach, symbolised by Hague's visit to the Notting Hill carnival (Alibhai-Brown 2000b, p. 28). Others are less convinced (Parekh 2000, p. 11). Hague's claim that the identity of Britain is to be found in institutions rather than in ethnicity, however, seems close to Parekh's view that the distinctiveness of a society lies in its political way of life.

In Scotland, Hague accepted the popular will of the Scottish people. He also allowed his party there a greater degree of autonomy. Some senior members in Scotland have responded to devolution with equanimity. Malcolm Rifkind, long a supporter, has argued that Conservatives should not get too fatalistic because the history of British constitutionalism had been one of gradual evolution (1998, p. 87). The main task for Conservatives now was to prevent the Scottish National Party confusing patriotism with nationalism. Devolution, properly patrolled by a revived Conservative Party, could check and balance the state as well as encourage the popular legitimacy of the Union. The Conservatives could do that by becoming, as the novelist Alan Massie once recommended, the Gaullists of Scotland within the Union. This would be less extreme than the advice of the journalist John Lloyd, who thought that the future for the Scottish Conservatives was to make the case for an independent Scotland (Lloyd 1999, p. 31). In this regard, David McLetchie, the Scottish Conservative leader, has recently spoken of his party as 'Scotland's other national party', albeit within the Union. Local patriotism is the logic of the position taken by Rifkind, Massie and McLetchie. It might be sufficient to revive Conservative fortunes. In England, a federal system has been advocated by John Barnes, who believes that Enoch Powell's famous maxim that power devolved is power retained was unreal. The Conservative task is now to contain those forces of nationalism which New Labour has so carelessly unleashed (Barnes 1998). Federalism is about limiting the fissiparous tendencies of Britain, something which had concerned Lord Hailsham in *The Dilemma of Democracy* 20 years earlier.

The great difficulty for the Conservative nation is that New Labour has stolen most of its traditional clothes. Lynch is right that the old discourse of Conservative patriotism has lost much of its potency. Despite Blair's private worries, patriotism and populism are not always intimately identified with Conservatism. Lynch is also right that the patriotic argument now seems more effectively used by New Labour (2000, p. 66). The big question is: can it be used effectively at all? British patriotism has itself become problematic. But then the Conservatives have been here before. It would be foolish to deny the capacity of the party for reinvention. Yet the challenge of devolution should not be underestimated. If the Conservatives do win a general election, relations with non-Conservative Scottish and Welsh executives could test to the limit the Britishness of the party. In these circumstances, refurbishing a Conservative narrative of the nation may be very difficult. The demands of populism and patriotism may then coincide in an appeal, not to the people of Britain, but exclusively to the people of England. Unlike Baldwin, future Conservative leaders would no longer have to look out for the man at the back of the room. One possible development of such a diminished Conservatism could be an English nationalism which would ditch Scotland in order to save England (and Wales) from a European federal state. Hague's instinct has been to resist this drift, though he has to tread a very careful path between a genuine sense that New Labour's reforms have been unfair to England and an irritable Conservative English nationalism, made even more irritable by the party's exclusion from office. There is a real temptation to exploit that grievance by playing the 'English card', which some would see as the most effective way of challenging the legitimacy of a future New Labour government. The party has not yet fully succumbed to that temptation even though its idea of permitting only English MPs to vote on English matters at Westminster suggests the seductiveness of the temptation. Moreover, if the predictions made by Conservatives about the disintegrative consequences of New Labour's constitutional reforms come true, the English nationalist answer may become the obvious, if self-fulfilling, response.

5   The Labour Nation

The implication of an influential study of electoral behaviour in Britain by David Butler and Donald Stokes, first published in 1969, was that the future belonged to Labour (1974). In the 1970s Harold Wilson was confident that Labour would replace the Conservatives as the natural party of government, for as the numbers of deferential Tory voters declined, working people would enter into their inheritance. History was moving in Labour's favour. By the 1980s that historical self-confidence had gone. Eric Hobsbawm declared that the forward march of Labour had come to a halt (Jacques and Mulhern 1981). That crisis of Labour politics had a significant impact on the party's approach to constitutional matters. It may be gauged in a confession by one of its intellectuals.

In a contribution to a book marking the 300th anniversary of the Glorious Revolution, Bernard Crick described the new approach to constitutional affairs which he thought the Labour Party had to take. The transformation he recommended matched that in his own views. In 1964 he had published the influential *The Reform of Parliament*, in which he argued that there was no conflict between the sovereignty of parliament and personal liberty so long as a few minor adjustments were made to the procedures of the House of Commons. The key thing was that the rules of the parliamentary game should be strictly adhered to (1988, p. 57). Those rules meant that governments had the power to govern, but only within proper limits. Proper meant acting in accordance with the (best) sensibilities of the people. In assuming this definition, Crick wrote in the style of the genteel tradition, adapting it to socialist priorities. The Labour Party could use the powers of government to promote social change and could do so in the expectation that the Conservative Party, when in office, would consolidate or mitigate but not reverse such changes.

Twenty-four years later, Crick had changed his mind. He argued that hardly any intelligent member of the Labour Party did not now believe constitutional reform to be a major issue. One might have expected the source of this new belief to lie in the experience of a decade of Thatcherite government. But that was only the half of it. The other half was traditional Labour culture itself, a culture which tended to understand the constitution in instrumental terms. That was a big enough error. But it was compounded by a larger mistake, a belief that the big push towards socialism made the sovereignty of parliament a tool of emancipation. That was not just a leftwing dream, but common ground in Labour politics. For Crick it was the heart of the problem (1988, pp. 59–60). It was more important to change presuppositions about parliamentary sovereignty and cen-tralised power than to propose a model constitution like that of the United States. It was advice which radicals such as Jonathan Freedland have not heeded. Crick thought that devolution of power to the nations would not come about by reason but only by the con-sequences of Conservative failure. He was right – up to a point.

A decade after Crick, and with New Labour in office, Peter Hain made more or less the same distinction between old-style socialism and new-style Blairism. To the Left's historic disadvantage one tradition had come to dominate the constitutional thinking of the Labour Party in the twentieth century. This was the statist version of socialism, which had contributed to Labour's reputation for bureau-cracy and greyness. Centralism, argued Hain, was the real problem, for it had marginalised individual empowerment and local control. In the past socialists had exploited the possibilities of centralism in the quest for equality. This was no longer acceptable (1999, p. 25). New Labour now emphasised 'decentralisation, democracy and popular sovereignty' and refused to accept that 'collectivism means subjugating individual liberty'. It had committed itself to the dispersal of power because that was the only way to encourage (lib-ertarian) socialism to take root. The imperative for devolution is not nationalism, it is a new common citizenship. The reconciliation of liberty and equality could be found in the participatory democracy which the politics of devolved institutions should foster.

Evans had delineated the three interlocking features of Labour's traditional constitutional thinking which justified Old Labour logic: 'state collectivism forwarded through an electoral majority; a con-stitution which legitimizes executive dominance; and constitutional arrangements which are amenable to manipulation by the executive' (1999, p. 73). It was these assumptions which Crick challenged, Hain came to bury and from which the party, in principle at least, has decided to move on. In the 1990s, therefore, the Blair 'project' intimated a new Britain, a Britain which had learned, as Tony Wright once put it, a painful constitutional education in the Thatcher years. It suggested that Labour had awoken from the illusions of parliamentary socialism, British-style. The implied theoretical break with tradition is deep and profound. That the practice of New Labour has been less radical is not surprising. Democratic politics is not about theory or logic alone. It is not even about constitutional change alone. It is about the complex business of reassembling the fragments of party tradition in an imaginative manner in order to make the party electable and to sustain it in office. This is what New Labour believes to be its historic task, even if it means offending old sensitivities. Furthermore, the circumstances of government are not always conducive to consistency. For a party of the Left, the criticism will always be that it has not gone far enough.

In recreating the image of the Labour Party in the way in which Blair has attempted, there is a tendency to create myths about the old order. The stark distinction made by Hain is one example of that. It expresses a vision and defines a purpose. Whether Hain is giving an accurate or a fair assessment of the historical achievements of Labour politics is irrelevant. 'Victors construct appropriate mythical histories', wrote David Howell on New Labour, 'in which complexities and ambiguities are lost, and alternatives hidden' (1997, p. 1697). If the Conservative Party can lay claim to being part of the very fabric of Britishness, then the Labour Party can also make that claim. How could it be otherwise? That being so, how could Labour politics avoid the challenge of trying to make the best of being British? Equally, how could it avoid the self-deceptions and hubris of being British even when it was trying to make the best of it (Ward 1998)?

LABOUR AND THE NATION

Neal Ascherson provides a good example of what is at issue here. He criticised what he took to be Labour's unreflective effort to claim the heritage of Britain for itself and to compete with the Conservatives as the party of the nation. In Ascherson's opinion, this was both unhistorical and doomed to failure. The Tories would always win the game. In whose name, asked Ascherson, should the Labour Party speak? 'Not in the name of the nation, but not in the name of one class either. How about in the name of the people?' It was not a nation or a class which demanded Liberty, Equality and Fraternity. It was the living people (1986, p. 303). The Left had to develop this notion of the people 'free of British national mythology'. Only a rigorous doctrine of popular sovereignty rigorously carried through could free political life of this British mythology. That is an enticing project for radicals and Conservatives would argue that a vestige of its spirit is to be found in New Labour (Rose 1999, pp. 42–4). It is not Ascherson's call to reform which strikes one as problematic. It is the assumption that Britishness can be the preserve of Tories only; the assumption that radical politics and the idea of the nation are incompatible (a truism, it now seems, which no longer applies in Scotland); and the assumption that the constitutional peculiarities of Britain are mere obstacles to fulfilling doctrinal logic.

One is reminded of E.P. Thompson's criticism in the 1960s of Perry Anderson and Tom Nairn. Following Anderson and Nairn, Ascherson's view is that the peculiarity of the British state lies in its failure to imitate the French model. For Thompson such intellectual strategies, 'which thirst for a tidy platonism very soon become impatient with actual history'. It was the actual history of Britain which had shaped, continues to shape, but does not condemn the Labour tradition. 'But only the platonist supposes that politics is an arena in which the enlightened can pursue, in a single-minded way, only teleological ends, such as "the conquest of class power"' (1978, p. 47). That is closer to the meaning of 'unhistorical' than Ascherson's use of the term. Thompson's own work, like that of Christopher Hill, has sought to establish the lineage of an alternative, radical patriotism. Of course, there were and remain large problems in distinguishing this patriotism from its Conservative variant. Critics are right to argue that the practice of Labour politics has been often uncertain and frequently contradictory.

This is because the Labour Party, like the Conservative Party, contains within itself sedimented layers from its past. It has been as internally diverse as the people it has sought to govern. Geoffrey Foote (1997) has examined with archaeological precision the various strata and specimens which constitute the party's political inheritance. In particular, Foote notes that 'while liberal internationalism is strong in the Labour Party, the anti-British nationalism of many Marxists is unacceptable'. That is because the nation state is the arena in which social and economic struggle is carried on. Part of that social and economic struggle involved competing definitions of patriotism. This is the source of Harold Laski's (1939) famous critique of the cult of the 'gentleman' in British politics. For Laski, the snobbery which sustained the Conservative nation was nothing more than a collective inferiority complex on the part of working people, the result of 200 years of public indoctrination in the thesis that only the gentleman is fit to govern (1939, p. 28). Having been born to power, the ruling class never knew how to share it. After his own brief flirtation with pluralism, Laski's project became one in which the Conservative gentleman was replaced by the socialist planner and by a system of government which did not share power either. The ideology of the constitution found in his work, which influenced a generation of Labour politicians, has been brilliantly explored by Tony Wright.

Laski became converted to an instrumental view of the constitution 'whereby a people defined in terms of interest and ideology could directly pursue its purposes through a two-party system and the formidable resources of a strong, executive-dominated legislative system'. This, argued Wright, became the way in which constitutional issues were understood by the Left for most of the twentieth century. It was a view which endorsed a unified British system. Power would be transmitted via the Labour Party through parliament to be returned to the nation as social and economic enablement. Labour's programme required effective governmental machinery to translate it into legislation. 'The British constitution was, happily, such a constitution, a unitary state driven by a powerful executive rooted in an electoral system which produced majorities, a Parliament which registered what governments did and a judiciary which knew its place' (Wright 1990, p. 335). This was the Labour version of the constitutional people. Why would any radical wish to change it? It appeared direct and efficient. And if that were the case, what hope was there that less radical elements within the labour movement would be moved to change it either? Patriotism and self-interest coincided in support of the British constitution.

Wright argued that though the model was not wrong, it was inadequate and relied upon a too restrictive notion of democracy. If it was restrictive it was so because the ideology on which it was based, the ideology of a class interest, was conducive to such restrictiveness. For those on the Left of the party, all other issues were bourgeois distractions. For others in the party, parliamentary democracy was as important as social change itself. Evan Durbin, for example, may have had a restrictive view of democracy, but he also believed that there was a national and emotional unity that was deeper than purely class interest (Foote 1997, p. 191). In an age of extremes, this Labour version of the genteel tradition saw its task as educating the party in the responsibilities of governance in order to deliver the triumph of the Labour nation. Socialism and Labourism supposed uniform needs.

Both traditions saw fit to leave constitutional matters alone. In its constitutional thought, the Labour Party can be justly criticised for its lack of imagination. But it was not 'wrong'; nor was it 'unhistorical'. Its reformist strategy of amelioration meant improving the lot of the people and creating a nation based on solidarity and equity. For most of the twentieth century the choice was made to put uniformity of provision before (to use Hain's terms) 'decentralisation' and 'local control', because that was thought to be the best way to achieve 'individual empowerment' in a world of hierarchy and inequality. If times have changed, that historical imperative ought not to be forgotten. Hain, though, is right when he argues that it was not nationalism which informed Labour's idea of the nation; it was solidarity. For the Labour Left that meant solidarity of class; for the Labour Right it meant solidarity of citizenship. It was solidarity which was to be the basis of a decent society based on equal citizenship. The Attlee governments of 1945–51 did not create a social revolution, but they 'did establish a society with much less poverty, and a much greater degree of equality, than had previously existed in Britain' (Tomlinson 1998, p. 101). Labour politics for most of the rest of the twentieth century was dedicated to furthering Attlee's achievements.

THE SOCIAL DEMOCRATIC STATE

The Labour nation was to be sustained by the social democratic state. The state's capacity to promote national solidarity through welfare, redistributive taxation, full employment and social justice assumed an economy which, like the British constitution itself, was single and sovereign. Just as the purpose of international politics was to ensure the security of the state, so the purpose of domestic politics was to assure the security of public welfare. The sovereign powers of government would enable Labour to manage the economy according to nationally determined priorities in order to satisfy the needs of the national community. Nationalisation, in other words, was an idea greater than Herbert Morrison's organisational form with which it is usually associated. It summed up the political ideal of a generation. The security it sought was a consequence of the crises of the interwar years. There was to be security of employment; security of health care; security of housing; security that the prospects for one's children were brighter than for previous generations. The delivery of security demanded stability. Here the ancient virtue of British constitutionalism fitted neatly with Labour's social objectives and with the managerial instincts of Labour's intelligentsia. In Ernest Bevin's phrase, this island of coal surrounded by a sea of fish, this Britain, was a bountiful resource to be managed so that its wealth would be fairly distributed. Britain was to become, in the words of socialism's most articulate critic, an 'enterprise association' (Oakeshott 1975). The enterprise – socialism – and the association – collectivism – would give real egalitarian substance to the British nation.

The Labour government's legislative programme of 1945–51 aimed to democratise the capitalist system. The price, in terms of bureaucratic regulation, appeared to be worth it. Yet, social democracy encouraged citizens to delegate their power to experts and institutions. The result was often 'cold organisations embodying, at best, a technocratic noblesse oblige dispensing standardized benefits to clients' (Rose and Ross 1994, pp. 442–3). There is some truth to that sort of criticism. In mitigation the objective of personal empowerment was thought to be one which could be attained only through state provision. And in the 1940s and 1950s, the popular demand for what were thought to be reasonably stable and universal needs made the collectivism of Labour appear perfectly rational. And not only rational, it was also successful. It assumed the proportions of the inevitable and was thought to be permanent. This was an error. The network of relationships and expectations which constituted *that* Labour nation was unlikely to survive indefinitely. Anthony Giddens provides one clue to its unravelling. The postwar social democratic consensus, which had been ushered in by the Attlee government, was actually 'a tensionful combination' of two strands of socialism. On the one side was Keynesianism, which was concerned with the directive control of national economic life; on the other was ameliorism, which was concerned with the protection of the economically underprivileged. 'For some while global economic circumstances made this combination not only tolerable, but even propitious. When these circumstances altered the edifice started to decay' (1994, p. 74).

It is perhaps one of the major ironies of the Labour nation that its armoury of political instruments, designed to provide security and stability, was generally successful when the world economic order itself remained relatively secure and stable. The decay which Giddens notes began in the 1970s when the world economic order started to experience dangerous instability. The consequences were to be profound for the old social democratic faith upon which the Labour Party had staked so much. The transition was to a new stage of globalism in which the old social democratic policies no longer appeared to work (Rose and Ross 1994, p. 443). Even sympathetic commentators made decisive judgements on this era. Donald Sassoon, for example, argued that old-style social democracy and its sovereign administrative machinery was part of a world which has now disappeared. There can no longer be social democracy in one country (1994, p. 94). John Gray has been equally emphatic. The ability of world markets to constrain national policies is the new fact of economic life to which politics must adjust. Not only the policy of social democracy but also its constitutive morality 'have been rendered utopian by the ruling forces of the age'. It is for these reasons that traditional social democracy is redundant (Gray 1996, pp. 26–7). It is a narrative which no longer persuades.

Not only did the old theory of the social democratic state take a severe, perhaps fatal, battering in the storms of global economic restructuring in the 1970s and 1980s. The idea of the Labour nation also unavoidably came under pressure. Labour's traditional strategy of national solidarity had aimed to resolve disparities between the nations and the regions in Britain. It was in the 1970s and 1980s that the Labour nation underwent insistent questioning. Whether it was a national community at all and whether its solidarity could be sustained became issues for debate. Schwarzmantel, for example, believed that the integrative successes of British statehood and the solidarities fostered by the welfare policies of the postwar decades had rendered the claims of the nations unproblematic as long there was economic growth. When growth faltered and when Britain's diminished world standing could no longer be ignored, things changed. The emergence of Scottish and Welsh nationalism was a powerful challenge to the old Labour nation (1991, p. 107). The response to this challenge appeared as confused and divided as the Labour government's policy of 1974–79 appeared cynical.

OLD LABOUR AND DEVOLUTION

Historically, the question of devolution was one which the Labour Party had not so much avoided – for Home Rule was frequently endorsed by the party's Scottish Council – as evaded. Resolutions in favour of devolution tended to carry little weight and were largely ignored by the party leadership (Drucker 1977, p. 192). Devolution simply appeared irreconcilable with Labour's strategic ambitions. For some, sympathy for Home Rule represented the last vestiges of the Celtic liberal-radical tradition which lingered romantically on the fringes of modern British socialism. It was given a renewed lease of life when the leadership felt obliged to consider constitutional reform as a way of dealing with the threat of Scottish and Welsh nationalism. However, this also aroused a passionate defence of the Labour nation. And, as Drucker noted, the record was full of paradoxes. Scottish Labour seemed to be in favour of devolution as long as there was no nationalist threat. When that threat appeared, the Scottish Conference recoiled from the prospect (1977, p. 192). Welsh Labour was consistently hostile. By contrast, the Labour leadership had little interest in devolution so long as there was no nationalist threat. As soon as there was, it rediscovered that Britain was not a monolithic state after all and set about recognising its historic heterogeneity.

When one reflects on the debates of the 1970s there is the sense of an enormous amount of energy and intelligence being squandered to little effect because of the profound divisions within the party. There were genuine devolutionists, such as Michael Foot, and Scottish and Welsh MPs who thought that decentralisation would benefit their communities economically. But most Labour MPs believed that their own government's strategy was misconceived. It would not see off the nationalist threat but actually feed it. It is an argument yet to be disproved. Devolution was a distraction from the real business of advancing the interests of the Labour nation. Even when the legislation was secured, dissident backbenchers, who feared for the integrity of the state, had already achieved a fatal amendment: the 40 per cent rule. This stipulated that 40 per cent of those entitled to vote had to vote 'Yes' before the legislation could come into force. In Scotland while 51.6 per cent voted in favour, this represented only 32.8 per cent of those entitled to vote. In Wales devolution was rejected by a margin of nearly four to one (Balsom and McAllister 1979, p. 397).

The government's failure was probably well deserved. In one of the most perceptive surveys of this episode, L.J. Sharpe argued that the impetus to devolution had always been external to government. It reflected no measured or developed strategy. At no time could it be said that the majority of the Labour leadership acted with any enthusiasm for the principles of devolution. That half-heartedness was matched throughout the party, not only in England but also in Wales and Scotland: 'The task facing the Labour government was always seen as an essential prerequisite for possibly winning back electoral support in Scotland and Wales.' Sharpe was correct in his estimation that the Scotland and Wales Acts were seen as distractions. Labour politics desired to stick with a conception of Britain as differentiated by income and class and not by geography, except in Northern Ireland (1985, pp. 88–9). The party continued to see itself as a self-consciously unifying force.

After the electoral defeat of 1979, Labour's policy became even more incoherent. On the one hand, in opposition to Mrs Thatcher's economic radicalism, the party committed itself to an Alternative Economic Strategy which would have involved strengthening centralised control of the economy. On the other hand, in opposition to Conservative policy on local government, there emerged a socialist strategy which sought to use local authorities as sites of resistance to Thatcherism. As the Conservative Party strengthened its hold on southern English constituencies, Labour's position in Scotland and Wales became ever more dominant. This encouraged a reconsideration of the value of devolution, not as a way to defeat the nationalists but as a way to protect Scotland and Wales from the Conservatives (Mitchell 1998, p. 486). That a clear consensus on territorial policy eluded the party would be putting it kindly (Jones and Keating 1985, p. 201). In the 1980s, Labour was to learn a lot.

In this state of confusion, James Naughtie has pointed to a moment which had immense significance for Labour's territorial strategy. After the crushing general election defeat of 1983, the temptation was to argue for a separate Scottish mandate, bringing the party dangerously close to the position of the Scottish National Party. It was Gordon Brown, then Scottish chairman, who organised an alternative approach to persuade Labour MPs from England of the inevitability of devolution but which stopped short claiming a Scottish mandate (1989, pp. 162–3). This view has been challenged by Geekie and Levy (1989), who argued that the 1980s indeed witnessed a progressive 'tartanisation' of the Scottish Labour Party. They claimed that by 1989 the idea of the Scottish mandate had become common currency in the Labour Party. 'By emphasising the negative consequences of Westminster government for Scotland, while raising expectations about the power of a Scottish Assembly to arrest or reverse them', Labour spokesmen had effectively undermined the authority of the House of Commons and promoted the Scottish National Party's cause (1989, p. 402).

The devolution desired by Labour was not such a capitulation to nationalism as Geekie and Levy have suggested. What Scottish Labour proposed was a compromise between the claims of the sovereign (Scottish) people and the traditional claims of the constitutional (British) people. Gordon Brown, along with Donald Dewar and John Reid, was to become one of this compromises most articulate advocates. In the light of the experience of 1979, what Labour had come painfully to understand was that if devolution was to be successful, it needed the widest possible measure of public acceptance. It encouraged the cross-community consensus which Labour sought to secure in the Scottish Convention.

It is also interesting to note how, in this period, some academic critics were writing Labour's obituary in England. Gregory Elliott called on the Labour Party to abandon its illusions and pretensions that England could become part of the Labour nation. For Elliott, who had drunk too deep at the well of Tom Nairn, the 'strange death of Labour England' was all too obvious: the English were a hopeless case (1993, p. 199). However, the only credible measure of a Labour recovery, the only hope of reconstituting the Labour nation, was the degree to which it could fight the Conservatives in their own English heartlands (Johnston and Pattie 1989). This did appear a daunting but not an impossible task. Neil Kinnock, who had done so much to reform an unelectable party after 1983, was unable to deliver sufficient votes in England to secure victory in 1987 or 1992. However, he had begun to set Labour on the course of 'a new constitutionalism' and this was one of the more surprising aspects of the new model Labour Party he built, given his own fervent opposition to devolution in 1979 (Evans 1999, pp. 73–8). Blair's New Labour Party set out to disprove those who argued that England was lost forever to the Labour nation. New Labour's new Britain owed much to a general refurbishment of social democracy elsewhere in Europe (Jahn and Henn 2000, p. 42).

NEW LABOUR'S NATION

The Blair 'project' (the 'third way') is an attempt to reinstate a progressive British narrative. If Old Labour paid some deference to the claim 'we are all Marxists now', New Labour's refrain might well be that 'we are all Gladstonians again'. That is why the spirit of Ernest Barker finds expression in the very different language of New Labour. As a number of commentators have observed, its language owes more to social liberalism and its variant, ethical socialism, than it does to traditional labourism. John Gray has argued that the collapse of the grand narratives of socialism and Toryism has witnessed the unexpected rebirth of liberal Britain. Of course, those ideas do not entail a consistent view of the world. Gray detected an uneasy truce between the traditions of materialist market liberalism and of social liberalism. Upon the reconciliation of these two liberal traditions would depend the future shape of British politics. For Gray, it was the social liberal tradition which would be a more reliable source of policy inspiration for New Labour because it acknowledged the value of social cohesion and national solidarity. These homely truths would be vital to a New Labour government in hard times, especially if the market liberalism to which it has adapted faltered in an economic downturn (1998, pp. 28–9).

Indeed, in his lecture to the Fabian Society to mark the 50th anniversary of the election of the 1945 Labour government, Blair stated that to establish the new British consensus he sought it was as important to value the contribution of Lloyd George, Beveridge and Keynes as that of Attlee, Bevan or Crosland (1995, p. 4). Blair gave as much space in the section 'Eternal Values' to New Liberals such as L.T. Hobhouse and J.A. Hobson as he did to Labour Party stalwarts such as Sidney Webb. The message was clear: the working-class, trade union, socialist character of the Old Labour nation was dysfunctional. The New Labour project must connect to what Britain is now. The commitment to the disadvantaged in society, as Chris Smith put it, must 'march hand in hand with the aspirations of the great majority of ordinary people' (1996, p. 14). That great majority now thought of itself as middle class. The objective was to do what the Liberal Party had done historically – tap the progressive instincts of those middling sort of people and channel them into a reforming style of politics.

The disputed components of this New Labour ideology were highlighted in an interesting exchange between Michael Freeden, and Steve Buckler and David Dolowitz. Freeden examined with forensic precision how New Labour had located itself between the ideologies of liberalism, conservatism and socialism. However, it was not equidistant from them and tended towards an older form of liberalism (1999, p. 48). This could be gauged by its concept of equality, now redefined as equality of opportunity, fairness and a modest redistributionism. Its main claim to radicalism, thought Freeden, was the focus on modernisation. Even here the grammar of devolution appeared to be countered by the practice of centralism (1999, pp. 50–1). It was a point made by others (Marquand 2000, p. 270). The New Labour nation, then, had become 'that patriotic group of groups and focus of a new national identity which is replacing the failed collectivist projects of the past' (Freeden 1999, p. 49). That view was challenged by Buckler and Dolowitz, who thought that New Labour's position was best understood as social-liberal. It embraced liberal individualism, but retained a commitment to redistributive social justice. Indeed, New Labour had made a shift from 'equality of outcome to procedural fairness as the principle of redistribution' (2000, p. 102). Yet it retained a clear sense of national community, which would not be out of place in the work of Ernest Barker. Where Freeden could see only incoherence and political opportunism, Buckler and Dolowitz could see a distinct social-liberal direction which dovetailed well with Labour's constitutional reforms.

Ideological consistency or not, there would appear to be some common ground here. Just as the Labour Party adopted a socialist constitution in 1918 so has New Labour readjusted itself to another tradition. If the pitch of Old Labour was somewhere between working-class radicalism and working-class conservatism, the pitch of New Labour is now somewhere between middle class radicalism and middle-class conservatism. And the project is to 'include' the working class and the underclass somewhere on that territory in a manner which corresponds to social-liberal notions of justice and fairness. This is not a return to Crosland and Gaitskell, who remained firmly within the Old Labour nation (Plant 1999, p. 34). It is, rather, an attempt to pick up the historical threads of a progressive alliance which fragmented in the early years of the twentieth century into the competing organisations of Labour and Liberal Parties. It is that repositioning which has drawn the anger of socialist commentary (Alavi 1997; Kennedy 1998). For David Howell, Blair's project was not so much New Labour as pre-Old Labour, a Labour Party reinventing a progressive style of politics which owed little to the party's later self-conscious proletarianism. It was, then, not so much the spirit of 1945 as the spirit of 1906. Howell did acknowledge Blair's progressivism on the constitution, but again with caveats: 'The party leader's modernising enthusiasm embraced constitutional reform but without over-enthusiasm' (1997, p. 1703). That is just about right.

The willingness on the part of New Labour to reconnect with the liberal-progressive tradition also involved a desire to fashion a new association with the Liberal Democrats (Mandelson and Liddle 1996, pp. 205–7). The vision is of a progressive twenty-first century as a successor to the Conservative twentieth century. This elusive dream of realigning the centre has haunted the Blair project (Joyce 1999). It motivated Philip Gould, one of the creators of New Labour's success in 1997. For Gould, the great misfortune of the last century was that Labour had broken with Liberalism and split the radical forces of British politics. It took Gould a long time to see how the two could mesh again. He found the answer in the ideology of Blairism (1998, p. 27). To achieve a lasting alliance one of two things would need to happen: either the Liberal Democrats and Labour would become one party or New Labour modernisation would accelerate, 'broadening the party's appeal so that the Liberals are driven to the margins and New Labour alone becomes the broad progressive church of British politics' (1998, p. 398). The better course, thought Gould, was unity. Neither of these things might happen, though both are logical in the theory of 'the project'. The lukewarm response of New Labour to the 1998 Jenkins Commission Report on proportional representation, potentially a vital contribution not only to this realignment but to stability in Britain, illustrates the practical problems involved.

Gould was also clear about another key New Labour objective. It was that the 'One Nation' strategy of a modernised party could not be achieved without the middle-class vote. The middle classes were now the great majority of the electorate. They would constitute a vital part of the coalition necessary for Labour to win power. This did not go down well with socialist critics. New Labour, some might say, shows all the contradictions and the heartlessness of a socialism without the workers (Rose and Ross 1994, pp. 449–52). Others have claimed that New Labour is a label designed to extinguish all memory of anti-capitalism (Žižek, 2000, p. 37). But the need to become middle-income friendly was the message of Gould's focus groups. In the soundbite of the times: 'Winning the century means winning middle-class support' (Gould 1998, p. 396). It meant drawing those voters into trusting the Labour Party rather than the Conservative Party to look after their interests. It would be the centre which would hold New Labour in power. Building this coalition meant building support in the south of England.

In 1992, Giles Radice pointed to the critical need for Labour to re-establish its presence in southern England. Part of the problem was that for many of the middle classes Labour represented a past from which they have escaped (1992, p. 7). Changing the 'cloth cap' image of Labour politics had been an aspiration of revisionists since the late 1950s. But in the 1950s and 1960s the collectivist faith of the party had not been questioned. If the party was to have any hope of recruiting the south of England to the New Labour nation, argued Radice, it 'must show that it stands for the freedom of the individual' (1992, p. 15). Research conducted showed that there was no future for a trade union-dominated party: Labour 'must be the party of the individual citizen, which not only bases its own decisions on one member, one vote but speaks up for the individual against all vested interests' (1992, p. 24). In short, here was the model for Blair's reforms of the party organisation, his revision of the party message and his use of a new political vocabulary. For Blair, government is about the good having power and he believes that the New Labour middle class – as distinct from the old, nasty Conservative middle class – is a force for good (Simon 1999a, pp. 11–12). Here is the authentic view of postmodern social-liberalism, and it delivered success in 1997. The danger for New Labour, of course, is that it may be seen in Scotland and Wales to be soft-focus Conservatism and therefore English. In its traditional English constituencies it could be seen as Conservatism full stop.

It is difficult to know whether a New Britain has brought forth New Labour or whether New Labour needs a New Britain in order to feel at ease with itself. Advocates of a New Britain based on the devolution of power have argued that New Labour had to enter into new arrangements with a commitment to a pluralist style of politics. In a revealing juxtaposition of the sources of New Labour inspiration, the purpose of devolution should be to emulate Asquith's Liberals and Attlee's Labour (Tindale 1996, pp. 10–12). However, the question remains: To what extent is the New Labour nation founded on an enthusiasm for a pluralist style of politics? Or to what extent is policy driven by a calculation of the minimum the government can get away with? The experience, as one might expect, is mixed. For some, New Labour's caution on the economic front is matched by recklessness on the constitutional front (Ryan 1997, p. 16). For others, much more was expected. These people, whom Stephen

Tindale called disappointed ex-Marxists, tend to see constitutional reform as a panacea (1996, p. 2). That has certainly been the source of much of the criticism of Labour's sincerity about constitutional reform (Barnett 1999, pp. 25–7). Some of that criticism is well deserved, some of it is not.

David Sanders, for example, argued that constitutional change would fail to produce the new style of politics that reform was supposed to encourage. A comprehensive constitutional settlement, he thought, should be pigeonholed, because it would be too much of a diversion for Labour's first term (1996, p. 291). Sanders may have been correct, and it is well known that Blair has little time for Charter 88. Critics might also find confirmation of their worries in Blair's reported aside at the party conference in 1998 to the effect that 'constitutional reform was Year 1 business: the party had been there, done that, and could now get on with the bread and butter issues of more direct interest to its supporters' (Hazell et al. 2000, p. 260). Elections to the new Scottish parliament and assembly in Wales had not gone according to plan. In London, citizen empowerment was the cause of Labour's mayoral electoral failure. A cooling of interest in reform was understandable. However, the main charge which has been levelled at New Labour's reforms is incoherence, the fact that little thought seems to have been given to the way in which the institutions of the New Labour nation are to interact. Hence the judgement of 'control freakery', that having set up institutions of devolved authority, Blair has tried to diminish their independence through centralised party manipulation (Marquand 2000, p. 269).

In a brilliant attempt to make sense of the constitutional paradoxes of New Labour, Peter Mair began with that apparent contradiction. New Labour has been marked by a substantial commitment to institutional pluralism and an unprecedented shift towards consensus democracy. This has involved a partial dismantling of the Westminster model of government upon which Old Labour relied. This runs contrary not only to traditional British notions of politics but also to the British style of adversarial democracy. Mair believed that Blair's purpose is not to put the party at the centre of a web of control, but rather to evade partisanship altogether: 'this would certainly prove compatible with New Labour's drive to reform the traditional majoritarian constitution' (2000, p. 26). This is New Labour and New Britain joined together as the New Labour nation. There is an eerie echo of Conservatism here. It is Disraeli's view of the ideal constitutional arrangement: the monarch at the centre and the people at the circumference. Certainly, New Labour's vision is not that of the nineteenth-century Conservative nation. The voice of the people is important, but it does not establish the political agenda. The role of the people is pervasive but not immediate. They 'serve as the ultimate check on their governors, endorsing or rejecting policies and programmes designed by the inner circles of relatively autonomous political institutions' (Mair 2000, p. 33). This is government by the good, the administrative dream of social-liberal Idealism. Mair may have imposed a too consistent ideological frame on the Blair project (Barnett 2000); none the less, the tendencies to which he points have been unmistakable.

REBRANDING BRITAIN

Establishing an identity for the New Labour nation meant confronting three challenges. The first was the Thatcherite Conservative nation, with its appeal to a different sort of middle-class individualism. The second was the view, found in Norman Davies' *The Isles*, that Britain's time is up. The third was the trend perceptively captured by Joyce McMillan. She wrote that whilst Scottish and Irish nationalism had become fashionable, Britishness appeared to be dead in the water as a style item (1999, p. 32). McMillan put her finger here on the real motivation behind New Labour's concern to 'rebrand' British identity. Rebranding Britain is a serious venture in the context not only of the international competition for capital investment in which the task is to promote an image of modernity attractive to inward investors. It is also a serious venture in the context of deflecting the challenge of nationalist separatism. It is a style issue, but not only a style issue. Rebranding Britain is New Labour's attempt to provide the answer to the question: Why is Britain?

The seminal text here is Mark Leonard's *BritainTM: Renewing our Identity* (1997). Following Linda Colley, Leonard argued that 200 years ago Britain invented an identity 'that proved enormously successful'. That job had to be done again. It was going to 'be a slow burn, not a quick fix'. The important thing was to make a start now to prevent the country becoming, with an unconscious reference to the Italian Futurists, 'a museum'. The renewal of British identity would not tolerate the exclusive nationalism of the past. On the other hand, renewal did not involve doing away with all tradition and heritage. It 'means regalvanising excitement around Britain's core values – as a democratic and free society in an interconnected world – and finding a better way of linking pride in the past with confidence in the future' (1997, p. 72). Leonard was trying to substitute a softer and inclusive British narrative to replace the harsh and combative one of Thatcher; an optimistic narrative to counter the fatalistic one of Davies; and an attractive, Britpop one to check the cultural nationalism described by McMillan. Remarkably, the focus remained profoundly metropolitan. Northern Ireland was never mentioned; Scotland and Wales rarely. Leonard thought that 'Britishness has never been an equal arrangement' and, ironically, his pamphlet seemed to confirm it.

For all the limitations of the enterprise, especially the ridicule with which 'Cool Britannia' was greeted – a ridicule which said much about the good sense of the country – it acknowledged openly that image is important in modern politics. The criticism directed at it was a curious mix of rightwing outrage and leftwing hostility. Rebranding was taken as a sinister plot to destroy the 'British way' (as Hague had redefined the Conservative nation). Like spin-doctoring and focus groups, those other characteristics of New Labour, rebranding was too easily dismissed by the Left for its postmodern flim-flam. At times the superficiality of *BritainTM* encouraged that conclusion. However, the suspicion is that if someone as politically astute as Tom Nairn (2000a) has devoted his considerable satirical gifts to dismissing the idea of rebranding that could be because it does pose a threat to the break-up of Britain. Of course, it may not be possible for New Labour to write a narrative that can satisfy middle England, a pluralised country and the new devolved governments. Even a democracy more literate about the nation than Davies' assessment of it may not save Britain. A British government is obliged to make the effort none the less.

BRITISH MATTERS

Vernon Bogdanor thought that if New Labour's programme of con-stitutional reform was to work, it would require 'a *greater* sense loyalty to the whole, to the United Kingdom, than is necessary in a unitary state' (1999a, p. 193). One could argue, as a consequence of its programme of constitutional reform, that New Labour has become the party articulating that greater sense of loyalty, claiming to be the only credible and effective party for the Union, socially and culturally. The fate of New Labour is bound up with a renewed Britishness. If the prime minister's statements often have a whiff of boosterism about them, some of his colleagues have been more consistently reflective in building up the case for Britishness.

Gordon Brown, for instance, in a series of articles, interviews and speeches, has set out the values of the New Labour nation. He has tried to put some real political flesh on the bones of *BritainTM* and to answer the questions about Britain raised in the first part of this book. For Brown, the old Conservative nation was 'ill-suited to deal either with new nationalities, that is people who have come into this country, as well as the old nationalities'. That is why the constitutional reforms are so vital: 'The cause of the growth of nationalism was the unreformed state.' He saw Britain as the first country in the world that could properly describe itself as a multicultural, multi-ethnic and multinational state. Was America not the model? Unlike Britain, argued Brown, America does not have to address the 'Why is?' (nationalist) question. Brown's vision was of a Britishness where diversity was a source of renewed political strength, a Britishness capable of drawing upon its own imaginative political resources (cited in Richards 1999, pp. 18–19).

It is a chance and not a certainty. In his *Spectator*/Allied Dunbar Lecture of 1997, Brown backed up his colleagues Donald Dewar and John Reid by arguing that Britishness mattered as much as ever. It was not an ethnic identity, not some 'mystery of the blood or a pattern on a flag'. When we talk of Britishness, argued Brown, we 'are talking about the qualities of a people, of the collective experience they have shared over time'. In an interesting reversal of the assumptions of the Conservative nation, Brown proposed that the lesson of devolution is that because national identity resides with the people, reform of institutions does not threaten British national identity. Brown's distinctive 'British way' was pro-European, but the British state would remain the focus of collective identity (1997, pp. 15–16). New Labour's task was to promote 'a new civic patriotism built on local democracy and strong communities' in a Britain, 'where people accept the personal and social obligations of citizenship as well as the benefits that flow from it' (2000, p. 23). The old rhetoric of class solidarity has disappeared, replaced by the social-liberal solidarity of citizenship.

This, then, is the outline of the bold New Labour nation where, as Hain has argued, faith is placed in decentralisation; where devolution is not about nationalism but about forging a new common citizenship in the shared space of the United Kingdom; and where libertarian principles do not conflict with collective purposes. The echoes of Ernest Barker are clear, but it is uncertain whether New Labour can quite fully believe in that vision even as it begins to take shape in British politics. It is that New Labour nation which must face the particular challenge of Scottish nationalism which, as one commentator suggested, 'bears most resemblance to the *fugu* – a Japanese fish which, unless properly cooked, causes instant death' (Pollard 1999, p. 163). The fate of New Labour and the fate of Britain are bound up, safely or poisonously, with the proper 'cooking' of Scottish nationalism. The political choice of Scotland affects not only the fate of New Labour's reforms, but also the whole future of Britain and Britishness.

6 National Peoples

The British narratives of the Conservative and Labour nations had one thing in common with Marxism and liberalism: they assumed that Scottish and Welsh nationalisms were romantic distractions from the real business of modern government. Those British narratives now share some of the problems of Marxism and liberalism in responding to the contemporary nationalist challenge. Ernest Gellner (1995) thought that Marxism and liberalism had been wrong-footed by history. Because their respective, universal logics were so impeccable, they thought that nationalism had no right to exist. This is because nationalism feeds off cultural differences and cultural differences are being eroded by modern social developments. Both these propositions, thought Gellner, were true. Was it not sound, logical reasoning to suppose that nationalism was on its way into the dustbin of history, if it was not there already? For much of the twentieth century, Britishness supposed that too. Unfortunately, history has not been so logical. 'The facts', observed Gellner, 'are quite different.' The question which Marxist and liberal narratives had to ask is: 'Where the devil did we go wrong?' (1995, p. 2). What British narratives need to ask is: 'How can the fact of nationalism be accommodated without destroying the constitutional people?'

History seems to have played a trick. What was once peripheral shall now be central. In the British case there was a particular historical irony. For those who had been confined to the incidental 'Celtic fringe' such questions involved a degree of conceptual revenge. The venerable edifice of British constitutionalism was Ozymandian after all. The fertile principles of political life now seemed to be flourishing once again in Scotland, Wales and Ireland. And this flourishing appeared to make the old British state all the more decrepit. But what is the character of this neo-nationalism? To what extent, if any, does it differ from the nationalism of the past? Providing an answer to these questions has become one of the central objectives of social theorists.

It is to Tom Nairn's credit that, in the company of Marxists and liberals, he recognised these problems before they became academically fashionable or politically urgent. Much of his work on British politics has been dedicated to providing a local answer to Gellner's general question. Like Gellner, Nairn has recently explored that question by way of a paradox: the more interdependent countries become socio-economically the more is independence likely (1997, p. 149). In other words, there is a double edge to changes in the modern world. Nationalism has actually become more important as globalisation gathers pace. Theoretical blindness to it is more politically disabling than ever. Nairn is never one to pull his polemical punches. There is no doubt that he has struck traditional Marxists on the chin or perhaps hit them when they are down. The principal target is the work of Eric Hobsbawm. It is an engagement which goes back as far as the publication of Nairn's *The Break-Up of Britain* in 1977. *The Break-Up of Britain* contained some brilliant insights which helped students of British politics to see the subject afresh even if that did not necessarily encourage them to accept Nairn's narrative or his conclusions. As Bertrand Russell once said of Hegel, deficient logic can have stimulating consequences.

Two questions ran through *The Break-Up of Britain*. First, why has the British state system lasted so long? Second, why has its imminent collapse taken the form of territorial disintegration rather than socialist revolution? In short, why has nationalism eclipsed the class struggle? (1977, p. 14). Getting nationalism wrong had always been Marxism's greatest failure. Nairn's book was an attempt to get it right. As such, his arguments shifted between Marxism and nationalism and these shifts gave the book its own Janus-faced quality. Nationalism appeared as a result of the uneven development of capitalism, a sort of economic epiphenomenon. It also appeared as an idea of the state which had deep popular roots. These two understandings sat uneasily together. Since many of Nairn's contentious conclusions have subsequently become absorbed into the collective consciousness of contemporary debate (and not only on the nationalist side) they now appear self-evident. However, that does not remove their contentious quality. Nairn was passing a judgement on the British state which he believed the world had accepted long ago: its days are numbered. Nothing could possibly revive the British *ancien régime*. The programme for the next generation of nationalists was to be 'outward-looking' which meant a politics which sought to re-attach Scotland and Wales to like-minded states in the European Community (1977, pp. 194–5). National self-interest and practical need, Nairn believed, would coincide in that project. European integration must weaken the old assimilative British state machine.

Radicals should not grieve over this. Secession from the United Kingdom by Scotland, Wales and possibly an independent Ulster would encourage a corresponding popular democratic revolution in England. This nationalist narrative was the point of departure for Hobsbawm's criticism. Although the intellectual engagement was conducted in the Marxist idiom, the points which are clarified and the developments which are intimated have gone beyond the confines of a simple debate within Marxism. They have become central to today's debate about Britishness and nationalism.

HOBSBAWM

In his original response to *The Break-Up of Britain*, Hobsbawm stated the classic Marxist (and liberal) case for historic nation-states. Whilst a strong case could be made for 'a certain type' of nation-state in the nineteenth century this had little to do with contemporary nationalism, 'except in so far as this also means a convenient form of emotional cement or civic religion to weld together the citizens of such states'. These 'historic' nation-states, like Britain, were the main building blocks of modern capitalism. However, the progressive interest in them was not nationalist at all. It concerned the capacity of these states to promote 'historic', that is socialist, transformation. The situation of neo-nationalism was totally different. What characterised nationalism today was the break-up of existing states. Whereas in the nineteenth century, nation-states were of world-historic significance, this was no longer the case. Neo-nationalism is 'no longer a major vector of historical development' (1990, p. 163).

The second of Hobsbawm's observations was that there had been a transformation of 'the concept of state viability'. Size used to be essential, but now it appeared irrelevant to neo-nationalism (1977, p. 6). Hobsbawm thought this was an illusion. This celebration of *Kleinstaaterei* would not lead to independent and sovereign states. It would make them dependent on the protection of whoever happened to dominate the international order. It would also threaten personal freedom and equality. Hobsbawm believed that liberty and cultural pluralism were better safeguarded in large states which know themselves to be 'plurinational and pluricultural than in small ones pursuing the ideal of ethnic-linguistic and cultural homogeneity' (1993, pp. 184–5). If the choice was framed in that way, of course, Hobsbawm's conclusion was self-evident. In the local context, here was a clear preference for the self-consciously plurina-tional and pluricultural British narrative over the claims of nationalist separatism. One is tempted to suggest that it has a peculiar force for someone of Hobsbawm's background.

It was expressed succinctly in an address he gave to the American Anthropological Association in 1991. Hobsbawm told his audience that he usually spent his holidays in a cottage in Wales. It would not cross his neighbours' minds that his living there made him Welsh. The 'concept of ethnicity is available to them, as it would not be available to my neighbours if I bought a cottage in Suffolk, unless they were antisemitic' (1992, p. 4). Ethnic self-consciousness become national exclusiveness is much to be deplored when the alternative is the capacious identity of British citizenship and, by implication, British tolerance. The large state was identified with openness, liberalism and democratic tolerance. The small state he identified with ethnic intolerance and possible exclusion. The break-up of the United Kingdom was a prospect to which the Left might have to resign itself. Yet he thought the prospect called not for enthusiasm but for foreboding. That is why he actually read Nairn's nationalism not as the basis for an optimistic politics but as a last retreat. In 1977, Hobsbawm considered that anybody can be a realist when prospects look good and he assumed that Nairn's nationalism was a conse-quence of things looking bad. It is a measure of Nairn's subsequent shift from Marxist qualification to nationalist certainty, and also a measure of the changing times, that he could now be classified as a 'realist' who believes that his prospects look even better.

A further aspect of Hobsbawm's criticism was nationalism's complicity, knowingly or unknowingly, in the demands of what he called the 'neo-colonial transnational economy', what today would be called globalisation. The optimum strategy for that form of capitalism was to maximise the number of states and to minimise their strength and power. This was 'sovereignty as dependence'. Few separatist movements hoped to go it alone but wanted to exchange one form of economic dependence for another (1991, p. 16). The idealism of contemporary *Kleinstaaterei*, like that of 1919, was no more realistic about the economic facts of life and no more realistic about the realities of power. Abandoning arrangements based on (large) nation-state solidarity, they must survive in a harsh new world of (neo-liberal) inter-state contract and carry most of the attendant risks.

The great betrayal had been the betrayal of universalism. The culprit was identity politics, or what Hobsbawm understood as the politicisation of ethnicity (1992, p. 5). Hobsbawm asked what identity politics had to do with the Left. His answer was that the Left could never base itself on identity politics because it had a wider agenda. The reason is that the project of the Left is universalist. Nationalism is not (1996, p. 43). However, Hobsbawm's universalism in this article, which was a direct appeal to the leadership of New Labour, had transformed itself into *British* universalism. It was a call for the British Left to seize the opportunity to speak for Britain, to speak for the constitutional people as a whole, to reappropriate from the Conservatives the language of patriotism. No good, he was certain, would come from the fashion of identity politics (defined as small-nation politics). But then Hobsbawm was certain that it would not last. The fact that historians and theorists were beginning to make progress on the study of nationalism intimated that the phenomenon was already past its peak. He saw the owl of Minerva circling round nations and nationalism (1993, p. 192).

HOBSBAWM'S CRITICS

The owl of Minerva proved to be an ambiguous intellectual ally. As Hobsbawm's critics were quick to point out, there appeared to be a contradiction in devoting so much effort to challenging neo-nationalism if one really did believe that its narrative was unconvincing (Smith 1995, pp. 8–28). He was also thought to have made a simplistic assumption that neo-nationalism meant always and everywhere ethnic exclusivity. Moreover, it was claimed that Hobsbawm's critique did not engage with the realities of the post-communist world or do real justice to their democratic potential.

For A.D. Smith, Hobsbawm supposed that a nation needed to have an economic threshold before it could become 'historic', before it could become a proper state. That, thought Smith, was a nineteenth-century view which was deaf to both the new nationalism and the new capitalism. The absence of economic viability in the sense in which classical Marxism or liberalism understood it was no longer a serious factor restraining the claims of small nations like Scotland or Wales. In the eyes of small nation nationalists at least, political independence is economically positive (1995, p. 26). Modern nationalism has simply revitalised long-standing national claims which contemporary global forces, far from crushing, are spreading and recycling. Those who talk easily of post-nationalism, Smith suggested, should remember the tale of Samson, 'whose strength ebbed when his hair was shorn, only to return with greater force when it grew again' (1992, p. 452). That analogy, some might think, ignores the fact that Samson, eyeless in Gaza, pulled the temple down around him in an act of self-destruction, the very concern which Hobsbawm has expressed. The moral which Smith takes is that we should show more understanding than the Philistines. None the less, there is a danger in this neat reversal of Hobsbawm's criticisms, that of asserting another form of historical determinism. This is a view which holds that large nation-states such as Britain are redundant and that global economies of scale naturally favour the intimate cultures of small nations. We should be wary of inscribing a new philistinism which propounds the inevitable demise of Britain.

In Michael Keating's opinion what has inspired neo-nationalism in Western Europe in general and in Britain in particular is not so much post-nationalism as post-nation-statism. This implied 'addressing a world in which sovereignty has ceased to be absolute and power is dispersed' (1996, p. 53). What is new about neo-nationalism, Keating believed, is the break with the idea that self-determination means cultural self-absorption and autarky. Neo-nationalisms are committed to free trade and the central question of their politics is how to become part of a free trading world on their own terms. It is this new form of self-determination which threatens traditional states such as Britain. There is an ambiguity which Keating acknowledged between re-energising national democracy on the one hand and making claims which rival the large nation-state on the other. This might be expressed as the distinction between, for instance, varieties of Scottish nationalism which fall short of a demand for independence and the project of the Scottish National Party; and between varieties of Welsh national identity and the project of Plaid Cymru. The former, though in a very different relationship to Westminster and the world than that envisaged by Dicey and Rait, is compatible with the survival of the British state. The latter is not. The nature of the political debate in Scotland and Wales and to a lesser extent, England, now revolves around which of these views will take precedence. Correspondingly, the soundness of British government strategy will be measured by its sensitivity to the distinction between them.

In response to Hobsbawm's assertion that neo-nationalism equals everywhere ethnic nationalism and cultural intolerance, critics have tended once again to emphasise the reverse. In Western Europe, in particular Scotland, the argument is that neo-nationalism espouses a civic style of nationalism. Neo-nationalism, therefore, does not entail rejecting pluralism and cultural diversity. Because the motivation is political – to improve democratic participation and to secure greater executive accountability – rather than cultural – to preserve a traditional way of life – there is no need to impose a single worldview or to demand conformity. 'If,' according to McCrone, 'a single and homogeneous national identity is a key feature of classical nationalism then plural and shifting identities characterise neo-nationalism' (1998, p. 138). The trend of neo-nationalism is to be postmodernist in its cultural emphasis, valuing diversity, rather than modernist, committed to unity. Unfortunately for the clarity of that distinction, it is far from obvious that there can be a strict demarcation between civic and ethnic varieties of nationalism. Rogers Brubaker has argued against the Manichean view that there are two kinds of nationalism: the good civic kind and the bad ethnic kind. It is for him one of those 'pernicious postulates' which bedevil a proper understanding of contemporary politics. A state-framed nationalism, of which Britain is an example, may be imbued with a strong cultural content even if that content is not necessarily ethnicised. A counter-state nationalism need not be conceived of in exclusively ethno-cultural terms. Indeed, argued Brubaker, such nationalisms may provide 'a particularly rich setting for the cultivation, display and exercise of participatory and thereby in some sense "civic" virtue' (1998, pp. 298–301). However, the truth is always ambivalent. If a state-framed nationalism is rarely exclusively civic, then it is unlikely that a counter-state nationalism will be either. Nationalism in contemporary Britain proclaims its impeccable civic credentials. The SNP and Plaid Cymru are very insistent on this point. In practice, as Hobsbawm observed in Wales, the recourse to ethnicity is always available and probably unavoidable. Which is not to conclude necessarily, as Hobsbawm does, that the consequence will always and everywhere be bad politics.

All these criticisms of Hobsbawm found their place in Nairn's *Faces of Nationalism: Janus Revisited* (1997), which is revealing because it represents a chart of the changing balance of the debate. When Nairn revisited the nationalist Janus he no longer found it looking two ways. It was now looking only one way: towards a civic liberation. Its impact was universally positive. Radicals should welcome a nationalist (as opposed to a socialist) future as the most tolerable and democratic one available. In *After Britain* he outlined a prospect of four nations and a funeral, charting a 'transition from the management of decline into the management of disintegration, leading eventually to a suitable testament and funeral arrangements' (2000a, p. 58). Nairn was concerned to hasten the end of Britishness as a 'short-lived pseudo-transcendence whose day is over' (2000a p. 154). If Nairn's Marxism has now gone, the habit has remained. This is a philosophy of historical inevitability in another guise. That is the reason for the distinctive tone of *After Britain*, for if the truth vouchsafed to the nationalist narrative is the end of Britain, then everything done to prevent it is futile. *After Britain* assumes the futility of New Labour's constitutional reforms and it may be that history will prove Nairn right. In the meantime, however powerful the rhetoric and however justified his remarks about the pomposity of New Labour, the case is not proven. Nairn as always is sensitive to tectonic shifts and the shift in nationalist self-confidence is accurately displayed in his arguments. How might this current self-confidence be explained?

QUESTIONS OF DEGREE

A.G. Hopkins concluded that imperialism had promoted a form of cosmopolitanism which strengthened a sense of state identity. Britain was an example of that process. Today the cosmopolitan process has had a destabilising effect on such state-framed identities. The 'global forces that impinge on the world today have challenged and often weakened national institutions and identities'. What Hopkins called regional and ethnic allegiances have been encouraged because they supply protective insurance against global influences (1999, pp. 242–3). This is a suggestive insight, though the idea that neo-nationalism is entirely defensive would not be accurate. This was partly true of Scottish and Welsh reaction to Conservative government in the 1980s. To confine it to defensiveness alone would do an injustice to the overt optimism which also characterises Scottish and Welsh nationalism today. Indeed, it would misrepresent the character of contemporary nationalism which sees itself in the vanguard of political culture rather than fighting a rearguard action for a traditional way of life. Nevertheless, Hopkins has intimated a changing set of priorities based on a re-evaluation of historical circumstances. It is that question of priorities which demands attention. Why has it happened?

Slavoj Žižek has suggested a Hegelian answer to this question. He argued that Hegel was the first to elaborate the paradox of modernity, the paradox of 'individualization through secondary identification'. Historically, this involved a shift in fundamental allegiance from the particular and intimate local community to the universal and abstract national community. In this shift, argued Žižek, a transubstantiation of primary identity takes place. These primary identifications 'start to function as the form of appearance of the universal secondary identification – say, precisely by being a good member of my family, I thereby contribute to the proper functioning of my Nation-State'. This secondary, nation-state identity will be 'abstract' and possibly precarious 'insofar as it is directly opposed to the particular forms of primary identification'. It becomes 'concrete' and therefore secure when 'it reintegrates primary identifications, transforming them into modes of appearance of the secondary identification' (1997, p. 41). The politics of modernity, then, can be tracked by the successes and failures of such a process. Britain (Ireland excepted) was traditionally seen as one of the success stories and its international standing had much to do with its sustaining a multinational constitutional polity. The problems such polities have today, Žižek proposed, are to be found in 'the unexpected *reversal* of the passage from primary to secondary identification described by Hegel' (1997, p. 42, italics in original). What does this mean?

It means that the modern state is increasingly experienced as a distant, external and sometimes alien experience which gives some weight to Nairn's Ukania thesis. What we are experiencing is the postmodern 'ethnicization of the national' in contrast to the modern 'nationalization of the ethnic'. This is a reaction to 'the universal dimension of the world market'. But it takes place on that market's own terrain. In an ironic twist of the Hegelian dialectic, what is taking place is not a return to the authentic form of immediate community but rather the appearance of its exact opposite: '*this very reassertion of "primordial" identification signals that the loss of organic-substantial unity is fully consummated*' (1997 p. 42, italics in original). Žižek supplies a sophisticated theoretical substantiation of the historical charges made by Hobsbawm. The precarious unity of the traditional state, hard won and enlightened, is threatened by the global market and its relationship to the 'ethnic Thing'. The destruction of a state such as the United Kingdom will signal not national liberation but 'the final emancipation of the logic of the market' (1997 p. 43). And the logic of that global market favours 'tribalism' and tribal identities, at least in so far as they represent a suitable consumption niche in the global economy. This is a universalism of sorts, the particular which has a global marketing potential. Whether one accepts Žižek's conclusions, what is striking is how familiar his explication would be to both Lord Acton and Ernest Barker.

In *National Character*, Barker noted how Acton had assumed that nationality existed in two degrees. In the first, nationality is a 'social fact'. It exists at the level of culture but has no political expression. In the second, it is a political as well as a social fact. For Barker, the Scottish and Welsh peoples were nations of the first degree and he thought they were content to be so because they participated in a larger democratic nation of the second degree, Britain (1927, pp. 16–17). However, Barker accepted that Scotland had some of the attributes of a state and if these were less visible in Wales, they could not be said to be absent there either. He also accepted that it might be difficult for a nation such as the Scots to remain satisfied with being a nation of the first degree if they were to become disenchanted with their experience of nationality in the second degree (precisely what is said to have happened under Thatcher). If the Scots desired independent statehood, they would have their way. One might argue today that the process Žižek identified and the possibility Barker acknowledged have remarkable similarities. One reading, for which there is some good empirical evidence, suggests that a shift in primary identity is taking place in Britain (McCrone 1998, pp. 138–40). As a consequence there has been a disturbing of national 'degree' within Britain. Nationalists in Scotland and Wales hope and expect that the first degree of identity will come to displace completely the second (British) degree and that the respective national peoples will slough off the constraints of the British constitutional people. This has coincided with what some have considered a transformation of the relationship of culture, class and nationality (Heath and Taylor 1999, pp. 149–68). Of course, one has to be very careful about making easy generalisations. Indeed, the electoral evidence for such changes is mixed. Politics remains British. What one can do is retail common observations about trends in popular attitudes and with them, the visible emergence of a more self-confident nationalism in Wales and Scotland.

That this nationalism has all the attributes of a post-industrial phenomenon is more persuasive now than it was a decade ago (Studlar and McAllister 1988). *Pace* Hobsbawm, the sociology of nationalism may no longer be confined, just as a nation's competitiveness is no longer confined, by a lack of iron and coal. 'These days,' according to Charlie Leadbeater, 'a country's competitiveness is held back by its inability to make the most of its knowledge, skills, creativity and entrepreneurship.' Culture, in its broadest sense, has become the key to success (1999, pp. iv–vi). This is the 'thin air' in which the new cultural class in the media, academia, arts, advertising, design and image consultancies now lives and breathes. Those who have criticised Leadbeater's 'thin air' as superficial metropolitanism have missed the point of its political attraction. Nationalists aspire to a metropolitanism of their own, and know well that the image of youthfulness and vitality in a media age is crucial to the success of their project. That is why the New Labour project is the subject of such nationalist scorn. It treads on that dream. New Labour's distinctive project is to be the arch-metropolitan of (devolved) British metropolitanism, a second degree which remains culturally cooler than the first. That is where the major subterranean fracture in contemporary British politics is to be found and the impact of this new 'cultural turn' on the fate of nationalism has been significant.

WALES

Nairn once identified Plaid Cymru's problem to be that of achieving a viable reconciliation of its cultural ideal with the urban, industrial experience of most Welsh people. The heart of Welsh nationalism was 'culturist', a movement of language preservation and cultural defence. The extent to which it adapted to emerging opportunities, Nairn thought, could make its experience central. Nationalism has always tried to connect a distinctive cultural vision with the need for social and economic development. That struggle was exaggerated in Wales by the traditional division between culture and modernism (1977, p. 212). Welsh nationalists have made better headway in this struggle recently (Evans and Trystan 1999, p. 113). There is intimated a pattern which, if it may fall far short of independent statehood, could be appropriate to a new politics of national autonomy. This was something which Marr thought to be characteristic of the new

Wales (2000, p. 79). Contemporary Welsh nationalism appears to have improved its appeal by playing down the old oppositions which always afflicted it. Balsom et al. summarised these oppositions as the conflict between realists and romantics, the former acknowledging the political limitations of cultural Welshness and the pragmatic advantages of Britishness, the latter 'seeing no virtue in a system which so fundamentally compromises the integrity of Wales' (1984, p. 180). Their conclusion was that Welsh identity was pervasive, but unfortunately for Welsh nationalists it fell short of political nationalism. The great middle, almost three-quarters of the population, were not Welsh-speaking or Welsh-identifying Cymrics and had little sympathy for 'culturist' politics. To pitch the nationalist message in terms of cultural purism was to court irrelevance. This was the problem identified by most researchers and appeared to be insoluble, even when the party tried to proclaim for itself a socialist or a green vocation (McAllister 1998, p. 517).

Welsh nationalism lacked, in other words, a persuasive idea of the people. Even worse, nationalist rhetoric was in danger of appearing to allocate Welsh people different social worth according to their linguistic background. The impression that this was Plaid Cymru's idea of Welshness became a cultural block to self-government. Nationalism got the worst of both worlds. A politics of cultural survival was not only defensive, it also appeared to be threatening. The broad-based suspicion of even limited self-government shown in the 1979 devolution referendum confirmed the weakness of *political* Welshness. However, the recognition of the possibilities of a strategy which stressed 'both/and' rather than 'either/or' might insert Plaid Cymru more intelligently into those currents of Welsh national sentiment which are 'ubiquitous but elusive'. One reason for this opportunity seems to be that the language issue has lost some of its power to divide. This has provided a possible avenue of escape from nationalism's historic ghetto, a point noted by K.O. Morgan.

Morgan attributed the more relaxed attitude to the success of all-Welsh schools and Sianel Pedwar, the Welsh TV channel, something detected by John Osmond much earlier (Morgan 1999, p. 26; Osmond 1988, p. 149). These factors raised cultural awareness and helped to create a more favourable climate for a politics of national identity. The potential for a third way in politics was therefore not confined to New Labour (Osmond 1995, p. 47). In the 1990s, the traditional oppositions of either Welsh or English language, either Welsh or British nation, either socialist, decentralised community

Wales or capitalist market, cosmopolitan Wales no longer seemed so clear-cut. This may have diminished the intensity of the old identity but it created the possibility to exploit a politics which, as Anthony Giddens suggested, was now beyond Left and Right. If this were the case, then why should not that new politics be more Welsh?

An intimation of this development may be found in the reflections of Emyr Williams in 1989. Williams thought that Wales was moving towards a pattern of identities broadly similar to that which had existed in the late nineteenth century. But there were two important differences. New state structures for Scotland and Wales would be required and the nations within Britain would have access to an emerging European identity. Significantly, Williams argued that in Wales, 'we are thus moving away from a context of conflict between British and Welsh nationalism, to a situation in which Welsh identity can be both an ethnic identity and a state identity within the evolving parameters of the United Kingdom and the Western European State' (1989, p. 58). This devolved and embracing state identity would be vital to nationalism's future. It would help to focus the diffused sense of Welshness in a manner which might strengthen national identity. The political flux suggested by Williams has also been traced in the literature of Wales. Tony Bianchi observed that the defeat of the miners' strike of 1984–85 was an historic moment when Labour's grand narrative of Welsh identity began to collapse. On the other hand, the temptation for Welsh novelists to retail a narrative of 'fixed and limiting oppositions between inside and outside, closed and open, parochial Welsh speaking and rootless English speaking' was also becoming redundant (1995, p. 45). The result was a new Wales of productive paradoxes.

These old 'either/or' distinctions had no longer the same emotional pull. The pessimistic reading of Welsh fiction suggested the decay of traditional Welsh identity, Labourist and nationalist. The optimistic reading suggested a 'moving beyond a deadening regret for lost certainties' and the embrace of 'a hybridity that abrogates all centres' (1995, p. 72). Perhaps a realistic reading would suggest a proper regret for the passing of a Welsh way of life, though a regret more than compensated by the fertile opportunities to redefine that way of life, especially for those who have felt burdened by some of the communal demands of traditional Welshness (Trosset 1993, pp. 6–7). And at least one commentator claimed to have detected that redefinition already taking place in Welsh popular culture. Rock groups such as Manic Street Preachers and Super Furry

Animals appeared to have fostered a unique pop hybrid, which itself goes beyond the old oppositions of Welsh society. This kind of Welsh cultural identity, at ease with global trends and weaving the Welsh language in and out of rock argot, has exploited an imaginative space to develop an identity beyond the dominance of London (Savage 1996, p. 38). Here might be found the modern spirit of a national people refashioned, like the second coming of Tom Jones, in a more accessible form. Of course, as Bianchi observed, there can be a lot of Welshness everywhere but this does not necessarily entail a political sense of nationhood, at least in the way it has been traditionally understood by Plaid Cymru.

There is no necessary connection between the sort of trends which some observers have detected and support for independence, never mind a vote for Plaid Cymru. Indeed, the very narrow margin in favour of devolution in the 1997 referendum is sufficient to qualify any large claims about a resurgent Welsh nationalism. And in his sparkling polemic, Tim Williams bravely challenged metropolitan complacency about the benign nature of Welsh nationalism and gave voice to those in Wales who remain unconvinced of the promise of devolution (1997, pp. 48–57).

The new Assembly, on the one hand, has the potential to resolve many of Plaid Cymru's ideological difficulties, succinctly captured by D.E. Owens. Written at the peak of Thatcherite hubris, Owens defined the division within nationalism not as romantic versus realist, but as regionalist versus nationalist. For the regionalist, Welshness may be defined as everything west of Offa's Dyke, but for the nationalist this civic definition is not enough. The idea of the nation cannot be rooted in place alone, something with which, from his holiday cottage, Hobsbawm would agree. Owens' painful question was 'who needs traditional, cultural Welshness?' If one thinks only geographically, if one sees Wales only as Britain, Western Region, then the answer must be very few. Even the leadership of Plaid Cymru seemed to speak for a denatured sort of Wales, 'where the green and the white have been entirely expunged from the flag' (1985, pp. 159–62). The red of socialism flown by nationalists, thought Owens, represented a greater abstraction than the love which dared not speak its name – the national people. But the other side of Owens' question, which he did not ask, is: who needs traditional, cultural Welshness if its purity requires you to live in a museum? The answer again must be very few. On the other hand, the assembly puts Plaid Cymru to a real test as a responsible political party, which it may struggle to pass (McAllister 2000a, pp. 221–2).

The trend under Dafydd Wigley's leadership after 1991 was to emphasise once again the national at the expense of both regionalism and socialism. Plaid Cymru tried to do this by identifying more sharply the opportunities of self-government within Europe. In this case, trends in popular culture were leading the way. The political focus of the new Assembly in Cardiff permits Plaid Cymru, if it can and, more to the point, if it is willing, to transcend the (British) regional and (Welsh) national division. Although the powers devolved to this Assembly fall far short of Plaid Cymru's demands, it does give some coherence to a distinctively Welsh political culture dealing with exclusively Welsh matters. This is a culture which the indeterminate nature of Welsh *national* politics had previously failed to achieve but can now deliver (Williams 1982, p. 193). Measures of national pride as distinct from nationalism are high (Curtice 1999, p. 128). And if the popular mood remains as buoyant as some commentators claim or hope for, then Plaid Cymru can aspire, in the words of Gwyn Williams, to 'as much self-government as is humanly possible' and to reattach the green and the white to New Labour's red (cited in Cohen 2000, p. 10).

SCOTLAND

Despite very clear differences in the relative strength of their nationalist parties, the difficulties of defining accurately the political force of nationalism in Scotland are similar to those in Wales. As David McCrone observed, nationalism could not be captured by a reading of the electoral fortunes of the SNP alone. Like Wales, a strong sense of nationality was ubiquitous but equally elusive, and also like Wales it was not necessarily politicised. For McCrone, 'nationalism can and does take non-political forms – in the culture, language and literature of the society' (1984, pp. 129–30). In this he would agree with Bernard Crick, who has consistently argued that many nationalists are not separatists. It is the London-based media which assume that all manifestations of nationalism are separatist (1992, pp. 387–90). According to Nairn, if Welsh nationalism was culturist, then Scottish nationalism tended to be philistine (1977, p. 197). The SNP would prosper only if it integrated politics and culture more deliberately and effectively than had been done in the past. And in a similar vein

Jack Brand pointed to the prevailing contrast between the roles played by the cultural elites in Wales and those in Scotland. In the former those elites have been central to the nationalist movement. In Scotland, nationalists had shown little interest in culture (Brand 1993, pp. 45–6). In his influential *Understanding Scotland: The Sociology of a Stateless Nation*, McCrone returned to this issue. He now pointed to a cultural renaissance in Scotland which had begun in the 1970s and which, in the 1980s, had helped to confirm the country's distinctive identity. Scotland now stood at the centre of sociological studies for it provided a model for post-national civic society (1992, p. 33). What evidence was there for this?

Joyce McMillan thought that things changed in the 1970s as assumptions about Scottish culture began to crumble. It was no longer seen as a nostalgic remnant but as energetically present 'in the world of sex, drugs and rock'n'roll'. She, like many others, experienced a 'sense of escape from a cultural hegemony that devalues, stunts or marginalizes a vital part of one's own identity'. What she really appeared to be saying is that she, like many others, changed their view of themselves as Scots. That is where her feeling of liberation and exhilaration seems to have developed (McMillan 1996, p. 76). Scots were doing it for themselves, as they had always done, only this time it was validated in a different manner. This, according to one historian, was a 'Quiet Revolution' in Scottish cultural life, which boosted the campaign for Home Rule (Devine 1999, p. 609; see also Harvie 2000, p. 328). Alistair Moffat thought that cultural identity was localising even though economic structures were globalising. By that he meant that popular culture, in this case Scottish, no longer required London's validation for access to global networks. That did not mean that whatever validation such cultural product had was merely parochial. Far from it. Particularly in the form of popular music, they have had a global impact. These developments had promoted a self-nourishing sense of public worth 'not dependent on boundaries of any sort'. However, Moffat continued to see this contemporary Scottish, especially youth, culture in tension with a global economy where 'marketing strategies drive out particularity in favour of homogeneity' (2000, p. 35). This is questionable. The local, now directly accessed to the global, is shaped by it, but also, if it is inventive enough, secures its own influential niche. There is no necessary cultural conflict, which is not to say that the marketing and distribution of that culture will always be locally controlled. Relationships of power may not be so fluid. This global–local experience has been the subject of much academic discussion (Featherstone et al. 1995). The evidence of this research is mixed and the judgements are reserved. Yet there is a common expectation amongst commentators that the symbolism of national cultures, if not necessarily their substance, will wax to the extent that globalisation proceeds apace.

Perhaps the new importance of national symbolism in all its forms reflects a popular mood more than the sort of project normally associated with traditional nationalism. Nationalist politics in Scotland, perhaps because it did not have any heavy culturist baggage, has become reasonably nimble in adapting to this new self-confidence. The embrace by nationalism of an attractive popular culture rather than a single-minded attempt to make traditional culture popular may now be its strength and its appeal to youth in Scotland. This is what Pat Kane has called 'Cosmo-Scotia'. For Kane, Scots did not seem to be concerned with national tradition or with the old notions of cultural colonisation. He referred to surveys which showed that young Scots are eclectic in their tastes and see no supreme worth in being selectively pro-Scottish. 'Perhaps the confidence to play fast and loose with Scottish culture,' thought Kane, 'comes from an even deeper shift yet.' It is that mental shift of degree between Britishness and Scottishness which must turn the country eventually towards independence (1999, p. 28). Do these trends necessarily dispose the electorate towards the project of the SNP? Things are more ambiguous.

The famous comment by the former SNP MP Jim Sillars illustrates the ambiguity. Sillars believed Scotland's greatest problem to be 'the ninety-minute patriots whose nationalist outpourings are expressed only at major sporting events' (cited in Jarvie and Walker 1994, p. 1). This is an old nationalist complaint. The assumption is that there must be conformity between patriotism in the first degree and nationalism in the second degree. Popular sentiment, however, is rarely that simple or straightforward. In football things are far from straightforward either and ninety-minute patriotism may be a thin veneer over a differentiated popular identity (Bradley 1997, p. 26). Nationalists often expect the intense emotional expression involved in sport to find its replication in political commitment. Why would they not? That is what drives them. But usually they expect too much of politics and demand too much of individuals. The exasperation revealed by Sillars is the exasperation of dissipated purpose, a falling by the wayside in the pursuit of national destiny. Scottish society is richer and more diverse than Sillars' imagination and its options are more varied (Paterson 1993, pp. 1–4). Independence is one of those options. But its intrinsic worth is not self-evident even in a society such as Scotland's which has a mature sense of its nationality.

National consciousness does not easily translate into support for separatism. Even the SNP no longer uses the word. Maybe it is a measure of the new mood that it no longer has to. Therefore, it might be suggested that one, perhaps the major, division in Scotland's national narrative is between an impatient nationalism which demands independence as soon as possible (free 'by 1993'; free 'within the first four years of the Scottish parliament') and a nationalism which would accept independence so long as it is without tears. That is a slightly different distinction from the one made by Richard Rose – intended and unintended independence – but would have the same effect (Rose 1975). This latter and largest constituency may never be persuaded that the break-up of the Union can be without tears for Scots or for the rest of Britain. It may be satisfied with its place as part of a refashioned constitutional people. The recent history of the SNP has been its tendency to let enthusiasm outrun the country's essential moderation. It has confused, as much as the London media, broad Scottish national sentiment with a desire for separatism. It remains, however, an act of nationalist historical faith that this wider constituency can be won over to the cause of the national people (Kellas 1990, p. 434).

What would be the character of that sovereign Scottish people? Critics have suggested one thing: anti-Englishness. Andrew Neil saw lurking behind the cultural renaissance lauded by the *bien pensants* a nasty sort of anti-Englishness pandered to by the tabloid press (1998, p. 11). The *Braveheart* phenomenon was taken as a cultural sign of the times and, more worryingly, a portent of political things to come (Martin 1998, p. 20). Anti-English feeling does exist in Scotland, although it would be incorrect to argue that SNP voting is built entirely on hostility to the English. The conclusion of Brand's research was that the enemy of Scottish nationalists was not the English people but those 'British institutions which can be portrayed as part of the English Establishment' (Brand 1987, p. 347). In practice, of course, it may be rather difficult to make the distinction between the English, whatever their accent, and the 'English Establishment'. What is true is that Scottish nationalism, like its Welsh counterpart, lacks what the veteran Irish republican Brian Keenan once called 'the Fenian thing', that implacable hostility to all things

English and/or British. Compared with events in Northern Ireland, the course of Scottish nationalism is defined by its remarkable restraint. Not even at the extreme edges does Scottish or Welsh nationalism approximate to the pathologies of Irish republicanism. McMillan's definition – Scotland's 'quiet nationalism' – is apt, particularly when she compared the way its constitutionalism was disparaged by a Conservative government willing to negotiate with Sinn Féin after London's Canary Wharf was bombed (1996, p. 82).

The real question which haunts nationalism is the ethnic/civic one. Scottish nationalism has been at pains to stress that it is exclusively civic in character and its history of cultural 'philistinism' gives it a better claim to this designation than traditional Welsh nationalism. However, it is difficult to conceive of a nationalism without ethnic influence and, as always, it is a question of balance. From a liberal point of view, both the Scottish and Welsh versions are generally benign and without serious racial connotations (Paterson and Wyn Jones 1999, pp. 186–7). The anti-Englishness detected by Neil cannot be attributed to the SNP alone. Scotland's national narrative does not depend on anti-Englishness for its meaning even if it cannot avoid it entirely.

By the end of the 1980s, then, there had emerged an academic consensus which held that while the old Scottish nationalism was essentially the province of the SNP, the new nationalism was much wider and deeper than before. Its characteristics also appeared to be more eclectic. In the 1980s the SNP, like Plaid Cymru, had tried to be self-consciously socialist. By the 1990s, again like Welsh nationalism, it could reassert a politics beyond traditional designations. Nationalists could now argue that far from having to accommodate themselves to British socialism, socialism was accommodating itself to the Scottish nation. And if nationalists could sufficiently muddle the distinction they could make serious advances into the dominant Labour vote. In Alex Salmond's words, the SNP's policy was 'social democracy with a Scottish face', and at least one journalist found it hard to escape the sensation when watching encounters between Labour and the SNP that here were two social democratic parties slugging it out (Milne 1999, p. 24).

Some confirmation of this view may be found in an academic study which concluded that the major problem for the SNP was Scottish identity itself. The Scottishness to which it appealed was felt as strongly by Labour voters. If nationalists were to emphasise Scottishness above material prosperity, they would suffer at the polls. If

Labour failed to proclaim its efforts to fight for Scotland, it would be a sitting duck: 'Both appeal to the same voters with remarkably similar policies, using the same sorts of imagery' (Brand et al. 1994, p. 629). Seen from a different perspective that similarity might not be such a problem for nationalism after all. That there is a switch vote from Labour (and from the Conservatives) to the SNP in Scottish elections has been shown and the task is to maximise it (Hassan 1998, p. 26). But things are not all one-sided. The desire of the Scottish people to see the Scottish parliament work, and Scottish nationalism's expressed willingness to help fulfil that desire, could equally establish a trend away from the impatient politics of independence towards a policy of independence without tears. That might indeed be the new dynamic. In that case, New Labour's (old) idea of 'independence within the United Kingdom' might deflect the nationalist challenge into functional devolution. Accommodating short-term political necessity to the long-term goal of independence will be the future task of the leadership of the SNP.

So the picture of an inevitable tide moving towards an independent Scotland needs to be qualified. There is as much cause for scepticism as there is for self-confidence. William L. Miller, for example, reconsidered surveys which seem to show that Scottishness is replacing Britishness in the degree of identity. He thought there was something unreal or forced in the choice pollsters put to people. Citizens do have difficulty making a clear choice between feeling Scottish and feeling British, and forcing them to choose for the sake of an opinion poll appeared to create an unreal result. To say that someone feels more Scottish than British 'is not to say *how much* more Scottish than British they feel'. Indeed, argued Miller, it was common throughout Britain for territorial identification to be multiple (1998, pp. 191–3). He was even sceptical of the significance of the new cultural card. Though Scottish culture is visibly different from England's, 'the visible differences are either superficial or irrelevant to politics' (1998, p. 188). Certainly, that political similarity, as Kane would argue, might conceal subterranean shifts in attitude of seismic proportions.

These are matters, of course, which cannot be decided by interpretations of polls. They will be decided by the Scottish – or English, Welsh or Irish – people, which is precisely what Ernest Barker taught us at the beginning of the twentieth century (1919, p. 142). Britishness, in a constitutional democracy, could not be imposed; it could only be acknowledged. What does the evidence of recent constitutional changes reveal about the state of contemporary Britain?

Futures

7   Modes of Self-Determination

The question of Britain's future may be called the Candido question. In Leonardo Sciascia's novel *Candido* the eponymous hero, a naive but well-meaning young man, finds himself estranged from his native Sicily through intrigue. A former member of the Communist Party, expelled for asking simple but awkward questions, he corresponds from exile with his old mentor Don Antonio, an unfrocked priest. Don Antonio has remained faithful to the ideals of the Communist Party. Each letter from Don Antonio contains the statement of a single axiomatic truth. Candido tries to combine these truths but finds that they do not hold together. He writes to Don Antonio that such conflicting truths cannot be reconciled. Don Antonio replies that they must. These multiple truths constitute the drama of progressive politics. It was a bit like the problem of free will and predestination for Christians: 'two truths that must co-exist'. Candido is not convinced. He recognises a potentially fatal flaw in the optimistic worldview. What if, he asks, together these two truths amounted to one big lie? That question identifies an intellectual divide in British politics today. It is not a new question. It is the question which tormented Gladstone's first Irish Home Rule Bill.

The Candido question still looms large. It was neatly posed by the title of Vernon Bogdanor's article 'Devolution: Decentralisation or Disintegration?' (1999a, pp. 185–94). The answer is ambiguous. Committed devolutionists must take Don Antonio's line: devolution will decentralise power *and* disintegrate an excessively integrated system of government. Disintegration does not involve dissolution. What it involves is denationalisation in the sense in which W.L. Miller understood it – 'the opposite of uniformity and homogeneity' (1983, p. 103). That 'opposite' is complex, but can be taken to mean an act of self-determination which does not entail independent statehood.

'It is generally accepted,' argued Archie Brown, 'that nations living in their historic homelands have a right to self-rule if a majority of their citizens want it' (1998, p. 216). Brown's careful use of the term 'self-rule' suggests an act of self-determination which falls short of the dissolution of the British constitutional people. The subtle politics of the issue was expressed with equal subtlety in Neil McCormick's formulation: 'the members of a nation are as such in principle entitled to effective organs of political self-government within the world order of sovereign or post-sovereign states; but these need not provide for self-government in the form of a sovereign state' (1996, p. 566). This formulation is particularly apt for the British case where it has been difficult to envisage a coherent constitutional settlement. This was even admitted by those seeking the most rational of constitutional settlements (IPPR 1991, p. 23).

It was a mistake to look for a simple, one-dimensional answer to the question of national self-determination in Britain for what mattered was an intelligent grasp of what the constituent nations wanted. Once that was known, the system should adapt accordingly (Kellas 1995, p. 36). Accommodating those wishes was urgent in Britain because it was alone amongst the large and culturally diverse states in the European Union in not providing its citizens with devolved institutions (Kellas 1991, p. 100). In the jargon of constitutional reformers, these perspectives translate into the expression 'asymmetrical devolution', meaning that different degrees of self-rule are appropriate for Northern Ireland, Scotland, Wales and England. As a slogan, Brown thought, it certainly lacked the resonance of 'Bread and Justice' in revolutionary Petrograd, 'but it is the price of union – and a price well worth paying' (1998, p. 222). Does 'asymmetrical devolution' adequately address the Candido question? Some doubt it.

Those sceptical of New Labour's constitutional changes think that it has, like Don Antonio's literary model Dr. Pangloss, made naive optimism the basis of British government. They interpret it as a set of incompatibilities which cannot be contained. The central incompatibility is this. How can devolution satisfy simultaneously the nationalist ambition to bring about the end of the United Kingdom and the equal and opposite ambition of New Labour to strengthen the United Kingdom? John Lloyd shared the scepticism which the question raises. The centre of the strategy, he believed, cannot hold and must collapse in Scotland and perhaps ultimately in Wales, to the advantage of nationalism (1998, pp. 10–11). He thought this an absolute certainty in Northern Ireland.

NORTHERN IRELAND

In Northern Ireland terms the Candido question is this. How can the Belfast Agreement of 1998 satisfy the Nationalist ambition to bring about the end of partition in Ireland and the Unionist ambition to strengthen the Union of Great Britain and Northern Ireland? The sceptical view assumes that constitutional politics is ultimately a zero-sum game. Sion Simon thought that the Irish problem does not lend itself to 'a loserless ending' (Simon 1999b, p. 30). By contrast, New Labour's third way constitutionalism is defined by the promise that there can be a 'loserless ending' not only in Northern Ireland but in the whole of the United Kingdom. Nowhere is this more hopefully stated, publicly at least, than in the case of the Belfast Agreement of 1998.

In Northern Ireland, the either/or (predestination versus free will) style of political thinking has always been disruptive of practical compromise. The reason for this has been the lack of belief in the possibility of compromise. It has a long pedigree in Irish politics. Stephen Gwynn thought the problem lay in 'generations of political passion without political responsibility' (1924, p. 197). This, he argued, did not produce creative political thought. After partition, it translated into the cold logic of a distinctive dogmatism of denial: no first step *because* it is a step towards Irish unity (the Unionist position); no first step *unless* it is a step towards Irish unity (the Nationalist position). That remains the view of those who understand the many truths of the Belfast Agreement to constitute one 'big lie'. The complex arrangements of the Agreement are simply designed to conceal the steps which have (or have not) been taken. This view is held by a substantial section, possibly a majority, of the Unionist electorate. It is also held by an unreconstructed element within Irish republicanism.

Supporters of the Belfast Agreement, on the other hand, argue that politics need not be strictly 'logical' in that either/or way. What present conditions intimate is the modification of the mutual frustration of those old dogmas of denial. The basis of the Agreement assumes that politicians and their respective electorates recognise the value of moving from self-defeating certainty towards what might be called creative flexibility. The subtitle of *Candido* is: *A Dream Dreamed in Sicily*. The Agreement is a dream dreamed in Belfast. It supposes acknowledgement of a common interest amongst those of whatever class and whatever religion who have a stake in peace, security and stability. The conflicting truths of Irish politics *can* be contained. Instead of divisive contention connection is envisaged between Unionist *and* Nationalist in Northern Ireland.

This connection potentially locks in an island-wide constituency in favour of stability. Everyone can be a winner.

Irish Nationalism and Ulster Unionism fostered a political code which froze relations for most of the twentieth century. We might, with some historical licence, call this the Craigavon/de Valera doctrine. In 1933, the Prime Minister of Northern Ireland, Lord Craigavon, famously remarked that he was glad to preside over a Protestant parliament and a Protestant state. His remark was made in response to the claim by de Valera, that the Ireland of the 26 counties was a Catholic state. Craigavon accepted that the government of Southern Ireland should be carried on along lines which were appropriate to its Catholic majority. Surely it was right, then, that the government of Northern Ireland be conducted according to the wishes of its Protestant majority (Hennessey 1997, pp. 61–7). For Unionists like Craigavon and in practice for most southern Irish Nationalists, the settlement of the 1920s had divided Ireland into two zones of majoritarian democracy. The Southern parliament embodied Catholic majoritarianism, exclusively defined as Irish, and the Northern parliament embodied Protestant majoritarianism, exclusively defined as British. That was the either/or of strategic separation.

Since the outbreak of the most recent Troubles in 1969 the view that communal antagonism is irremovable has been more than a countervailing force to models of political reconciliation. Compromise has been interpreted by political leaders and their communities to constitute a threat to their own positions and interests without satisfying the ambitions of the other side. Much of what has happened in the political life of Northern Ireland may be calculated by that practical rule of thumb. The longevity of direct rule from London after 1972 was a measure of it. The Anglo-Irish Agreement of 1985 was also a sign that London despaired of an internal accommodation. Indeed, until the moment the Belfast Agreement was signed most people believed it could not happen. What was the basis of this popular scepticism?

On the one hand, it has been a traditional republican assumption, held to some degree by a large vector of constitutional nationalism, that it is impossible for Unionists to concede equality. To do so would mean the collapse of the whole fabric of Northern Ireland which was designed to ensure Protestant supremacy. Agreement about a new dispensation with Unionists would be, by definition, impossible. That was the lesson read into the failure of power-sharing in 1974. Unionist 'supremacism' represented the obstacle to progress and should be dealt with accordingly. And 'accordingly' meant that the British government should confront the Unionist 'veto'. In sum, it should 'persuade' Unionists of the necessity of Irish unity. Unionists needed to be forced to be free. On the other hand, a traditional Unionist assumption has been that Nationalists can never accept the democratic legitimacy of Northern Ireland. They never acknowledged the justice of partition nor the right of Unionists to exercise their own form of self-determination. For Unionists, the obstacle to reason has been Nationalist expectation that somehow the 'wrong' of partition should be rectified. This expectation is the root of the problem and should be confronted directly by military or political means. What Nationalists could 'expect' was usually defined to minimise the possibility of nationalists achieving anything they believed to be of value.

It is with good reason, then, that scepticism was deeply ingrained in public opinion. There seemed no good answer to the Candido question. What Unionism and Nationalism traditionally sought was what they also believed the other side to be incapable of giving. The purpose of politics appeared to be not agreement but the allocation of blame, historical and political. Here was the difficult transition to make in Northern Ireland: from a politics in which winning the ideological argument was everything to a politics in which the sharing of risks attending a move away from old certainties was vital. The former is the politics of either/or; the latter is the politics of both/and. The objective is to shift the bias of politics from distinctive grievances to a common predicament. It seemed to be a benign yet futile objective. By the 1990s, however, the conditions existed which put its attainment within the realm of practical politics. The dream dreamed in Belfast is one where the two truths, Unionism and Nationalism, *can* coexist. But they can do so only by going beyond the exclusions of the old code.

A shape was faintly visible. For instance, the notion of 'post-nationalism' was emerging to define the Irish Republic's new political character as a member of the European Union. Post-nationalism had also become the ideological leitmotif of John Hume's constitutional strategy. In the Irish case, the purported objective was to 'unite people' rather than to 'unite territory'. This formulation was sufficiently vague yet sufficiently traditional to be at one and the same time grounded in Nationalist rhetoric (another way of making the same old claim) and yet appreciative of Unionist sensitivities (it was not so directly threatening). It was the basis of the approach by Hume's Social Democratic and Labour Party (SDLP) in its talks with Gerry Adams' Sinn Féin in 1988. The claim that the Irish people as a whole had the right to self-determination, the Nationalist assertion which denied partition, was restated, but Hume's qualification was that the Irish people were divided over the exercise of that right (Bew et al. 1995, pp. 219–20). The objective should not be to blast Unionists into compliance with the Nationalist view or to make the British government force them. It should be to construct a consensual alternative.

The spirit of this thinking, adjusted by John Major's consultation with the Ulster Unionist Party, found its expression in the Downing Street Declaration of December 1993. It set out the view of the British and Irish governments about any future settlement. The Declaration conceded the principle of *popular sovereignty* to the Irish 'people'. It also conceded the principle of *constitutional sovereignty* to the people of Northern Ireland. This balance was designed to accommodate two opposing truths: the Unionist idea of the constitutional people and the Nationalist idea of the sovereign people. The Unionist truth of the constitutional people fixes Northern Ireland's statehood as part of the United Kingdom. The Nationalist truth of the sovereign people transcends Northern Ireland's current statehood in an all-island framework. In the Declaration, the British government confirmed the status of the constitutional people. But it also restated that it would legislate for any agreement between the Irish people as a whole. The Irish government remained equivocal on this matter. The historic character of the Irish state has been defined not only by the gap between, but also by the claim to remove the gap between, the ideal of popular sovereignty and the reality of its own constitutional sovereignty. However, the Irish government accepted that the British concession of the metaphysics of self-determination for the Irish people meant Dublin conceding the formal legitimacy of Northern Ireland's position within the United Kingdom on the basis of consent. The wording of the Declaration was that 'it is for the people of the island of Ireland alone, by agreement between the two parts respectively, to exercise their right of self-determination on the basis of consent, freely and concurrently given, North and South'. This obtuse formulation suggested that it was possible to conceive of self-determination no longer as part of the divisive 'either/or' of Irish politics but as part of the 'and', Nationalist *and* Unionist, North *and* South, British *and* Irish.

Something of the character of 'post-Unionism' never established itself (and the jury is still out on post-Nationalism). However, in the 1990s talk of a 'New Unionism' became voguish, especially in the ranks of the Ulster Unionist Party (UUP). A number of distinctions were made, designed to establish the political space within which an historic compromise with Irish Nationalism could be made. A distinction was made between acknowledging an Irishness of place, which could be shared by both Protestants and Catholics, and a politicised Irishness determined to destroy the entity of Northern Ireland. A further distinction was made between self-government, a general movement throughout Western European democracies to devolve power, and political exclusion from the United Kingdom which would substitute an Irish for a British context of decision-making. Finally, a distinction was made between practical cross-border cooperation between the two parts of the island and cooperation driven ideologically by a nationalist agenda.

Furthermore, three key propositions were invoked. The first was that the principle of consent should govern the political arrangements within Northern Ireland and those between North and South. The second was that nationalists must abandon the idea of the British government being a persuader for Irish unity. The third was that in order to secure the proper atmosphere for relationships on the island the Irish government should remove the territorial claim in Articles 2 and 3 of its constitution. Most of these points had been raised during the Brooke/Mayhew Talks of 1991–92 (Seldon 1997, pp. 412–15). Of course, 'New Unionism' and 'post-Nationalism' were mere possibilities. From the public's point of view, there was little evidence of their political presence. The question, as Candido might have put it, was simple. Was it ever possible to absorb Sinn Féin/IRA and the Protestant paramilitaries into any stable political order?

The 'peace process' of the 1990s was actually an acknowledgement by republicans that their long war of attrition against Unionists and the British state had been a failure. In the 1970s the use of force outside the democratic process had been a dead-end. In the 1980s the use of force alongside democratic politics, the ballot box and Armalite strategy, had not delivered. The course of political debate in the 1990s was about convincing republicans that the alternative was not the threat of force as a tactic inside democratic politics. Rather, it required an unequivocal commitment to peaceful methods (Mitchell 1999). Upon that commitment Unionists have been insistent. It remains uncertain whether republicans will fulfil their obligations to 'put arms beyond use' (as the decommissioning of illegal weapons is now described), though they have good reasons to do so. To build on its vote Sinn Féin needs to move away from the ideology of violence. Securing the Belfast Agreement of 1998 and sustaining it are thus rational objectives. Sinn Féin has argued that its strategy in the 1990s was to achieve a transitional mechanism to Irish unity (Coogan 1995). If it really believes the Agreement to be that mechanism, then its institutions need to be sustained. Protestant paramilitaries, who always saw themselves engaged in 'secondary' or 'reactive' violence, have gone along step by step with the politicisation of republicanism. Their representatives claim that they articulate a more progressive form of Unionism than that of the UUP; certainly, they are contemptuous of Ian Paisley's Democratic Unionist Party (DUP). However, their politics too is reactive; they will do nothing in advance of Sinn Féin or the IRA (Rowan 1995, pp. 123–9).

On 22 May 1998, the Agreement was approved in a referendum in Northern Ireland and the Republic of Ireland. The vote in favour in Northern Ireland was 71.1 per cent and in the Republic of Ireland it was 94.4 per cent. However, the result of the elections to the Assembly, held on 25 June 1998, showed how finely poised support within Unionism actually was. Against the 28 pro-Agreement UUP were ranged 28 anti-Agreement Unionists (20 DUP, five UK Unionists and three United Unionists). The two members of the pro-Agreement Progressive Unionist Party, a party linked to the paramilitary Ulster Volunteer Force, held the balance. On the Nationalist side the SDLP had 24 seats and Sinn Féin 18. The remaining seats were filled by six members of the Alliance Party and two members of the Women's Coalition. David Trimble, leader of the UUP, was elected First Minister and Seamus Mallon of the SDLP, Deputy First Minister.

The Agreement involves a delicately balanced set of compromises designed to achieve political stability, communal reconciliation and an end to violence. Included are institutional matters, constitutional matters, equality matters and security matters. It provides for a Northern Ireland Assembly of 108 members elected by proportional representation. Measures passed by the Assembly require cross-community support. An inclusive Northern Ireland Executive is composed of ministers allocated according party strengths in the Assembly. On 15 February 1999, the Assembly approved ten executive departments covering all devolved matters, in addition to the Office of the First and Deputy First Ministers. The allocation of these departments resulted in the UUP and the SDLP getting three each, Sinn Féin and the DUP two each. The Executive meets without the DUP ministers being present because they refuse to sit with Sinn Féin. These departments are monitored by ten Statutory Committees which have the power to consult, advise, hold inquiries, initiate and approve legislation and make recommendations. They are the primary site of ministerial accountability in the Assembly.

There is also a North/South Ministerial Council in which ministers from Northern Ireland and the Irish government meet to discuss matters of mutual interest, and to develop, where appropriate, co-operation on an all-island or cross-border basis. All decisions in the Council must be consensual. Areas identified include aspects of tourism, health, education, agriculture, transport and the environment. The Council is accountable to the Irish parliament and to the Northern Ireland Assembly. Also under the supervision of the North/South Ministerial Council are six North/South Implementation Bodies, such as The Food and Safety Promotion Board and The Trade and Business Development Body. A British–Irish Council, involving the British and Irish governments, the new devolved administrations in Scotland, Wales and Northern Ireland, and the administrations of the Isle of Man, Jersey and Guernsey has the purpose of consulting widely on matters of mutual interest. A British–Irish Intergovernmental Conference replaces that set up under the Anglo-Irish Agreement of 1985. Ministers of the Northern Ireland Executive have the right to attend the Conference. On constitutional matters, both the British and Irish governments affirm that there can be no change in the position of Northern Ireland as a part of the United Kingdom without the consent of its citizens. The two governments gave effect to the consent principle in legislation. One consequence has been amendment to Articles 2 and 3 of the Irish constitution. The Agreement is also designed to foster a new civic order in Northern Ireland based on parity of esteem for different traditions. The hope is that all sections of the community will feel that they have a stake in the future of Northern Ireland.

On security matters, provision was made for the accelerated release of prisoners convicted of terrorist offences. The proviso is that the relevant paramilitary organisations remain on ceasefire. A Commission on Policing was established under Chris Patten, which reported in September 1999. The main recommendations were a new Policing Board, including political representatives and independents, with powers of oversight, and increased recruitment of Catholic police officers to achieve a 50/50 balance with Protestants. Patten also advised changing the name and the symbols of the force to achieve 'neutrality'. These proposals provoked strong opposition within all sections of Unionism, especially the changes to the name of the force and its symbols. This, for them, smacked of disbanding the Royal Ulster Constabulary. For anti-Agreement Unionists, police reform has become the measure of British betrayal.

The Agreement also committed the parties to use their best efforts to achieve the total decommissioning of all illegal weapons by 22 May 2000. The failure by the IRA to move on this issue delayed the establishment of the Executive until November 1999 and it was only then on the UUP's understanding that the IRA would soon begin to disarm. When this had not happened by February 2000, the Secretary of State for Northern Ireland, Peter Mandelson, was forced to suspend the powers of the Executive. Republican rhetoric – that decommissioning required the surrender of an 'undefeated army' – was always unpersuasive. The requirement has been neither surrender to the British army nor to a Unionist regime. The requirement has been surrender to the principles of the Belfast Agreement, principles endorsed overwhelmingly by the people of the island including Sinn Féin voters. The Executive was restored in May 2000 when the IRA agreed to independent inspection of some of its arms dumps and expressed its willingness to put its weapons beyond use. As a consequence of IRA prevarication on the arms issue, Unionist support for the Agreement has been ebbing. David Trimble secured only a marginal victory – 53 per cent to 47 per cent – when he recommended to his party that it should return to government. And there is the danger of his party fragmenting under the sectarian pressures of Northern Ireland politics. All this raises Candido's simple question: can the Agreement ever work?

Nationalism retains the aspiration to Irish unity. Ulster Unionism in all its forms remains committed to the Union. Pro-Agreement Unionists claim that the institutions are practical and sensible and that no one in the Unionist community need fear them. The Agreement has created a new situation in which old antagonistic strategies can be overcome. It cannot be a vehicle for unification except in so far as Unionists consent to this. The vision is one of practical cooperation to end what Trimble called the 'cold war' on the island. For the First Minister it is the British dimension which counts. The changes required in Northern Ireland demand much of traditional Unionism. But it is worth it. For Nationalists the expectation is that North/South cooperation will establish linkages the growing quantity of which will ultimately transform the quality of relationships on the island. In these circumstances Irish unity will become not only necessary but also desirable, even for Unionists. It is the Irish dimension that counts.

It is those distinctive British and Irish inflections which give succour to the Agreement's opponents who cannot accept its two truths. The big lie presents itself all too clearly. A substantial number of Unionists can see things changing only to their disadvantage. They are not persuaded that the things they value will stay the same. The instinct is to cling to the old certainties. Equally, there are those republicans who can see things only staying the same. The changes driven by the Agreement are insufficient to outweigh their sense of historic disappointment. The instinct is to keep the old faith in the primacy of violence. In both cases, the Agreement is another manoeuvre either to break the Union or to deny the Republic. There are no loserless endings. Something – or someone – will have to give.

The anti-Agreement case dislikes complexity. It argues that the procedures for the operation of the Assembly actually reveal the problem. If there were sufficient consensus between Unionists and Nationalists about the government of Northern Ireland, then its Byzantine procedures (*either* majorities of both Unionists and Nationalists present and voting, *or* 60 per cent of all members including at least 40 per cent of Unionists and 40 per cent of Nationalists) would be unnecessary. If there were not such a consensus, then arrangements of this sort will not work anyway. The political game will become one of shifting the blame. This is what experience of Irish history obliges them to believe. But then experience is not always a foolproof guide. Consider once again Candido's position.

Reflecting in Turin on his exile from Sicily, Candido thought that the north and south of Italy were bound up there. They sought to avoid each other. But they also sought to strike out at each other. They were like two scorpions in a bottle. For Italy one could substitute Northern Ireland and for Turin, Belfast. Belfast has been the site of communal forces which sought both to avoid each other (partition and sectarian separation) and to strike out at each other (ideological hostility and sectarian violence). In his correspondence with Don Antonio, Candido agonised about this political conflict. Don Antonio's original response has echoes of the IRA. It was time to smash the bottle. He thought twice about this revolutionism. Acknowledging Candido's criticism that all politics assumed some sort of bottle to give form to public life, he now argued that progress meant shaping one 'without scorpions'. Perhaps that is where Northern Ireland is today, engaged in the attempt to shape a new arrangement without the scorpions of political violence.

Supporters of the Agreement claim to glimpse, however faintly, a solution to Gwynn's old problem. It is that mutual responsibility might soon become the passion of Irish politics, North and South. The hope is that a new logic may be emerging and with it a new political code and that this hope is far from Panglossian. All of this remains dreamlike. The sectarian electoral dynamics of Northern Ireland politics continue to speak against it. Yet there is cause for some tentative historical optimism. Writing of the partition settlement in 1923, J.C. Beckett observed that everyone expected it to disintegrate soon: 'Though the settlement left a legacy of bitterness, issuing occasionally in local and sporadic disturbances, it inaugurated for Ireland a longer period of general tranquillity than she had known since the first half of the eighteenth century' (1966, p. 461). For very different reasons that might be the historian's judgement of the current situation.

SCOTLAND

Writing in the 1960s of Northern Ireland's experience of devolution under the old Stormont regime, R.J. Lawrence argued that Northern Ireland was not a good guide to devolution's potential operation elsewhere in the United Kingdom. Northern Ireland had evaded rather than refuted the Candido question: whether Union and Home Rule are two incompatible truths. George Boyce also thought that Northern Ireland was a poor guide. He believed that its experience showed that devolution worked only when it didn't work (1975, p. 290). Home Rule and Union were compatible, in other words, when there was no desire to push the limits of autonomy. In Boyce's view the opposite effect would work itself out in Scotland and Wales. The status of Northern Ireland as a violently divided place apart meant that there has been little subsequent enthusiasm to learn lessons. However, a version of the Candido question cannot be avoided in Scotland either. This is the insight which informed Geekie and Levy's (1989) charge of the 'tartanisation' of the Labour Party in the 1980s. They questioned the ability of politics to reconcile the Scottish equivalent of free will and predestination – Scottish popular sovereignty and British parliamentary sovereignty. Theirs was and remains a good question. And the brightest and best in Scotland have tried to give an honest answer.

Lindsay Paterson identified three key aspects of the Scottish case. First, Scotland's position in the United Kingdom has always involved negotiation and compromise. The Conservative fear that self-government would mean dissolution and the nationalist belief that real self-government is impossible within the United Kingdom are both misplaced. It is possible to renegotiate the British contract without destroying British solidarity. Second, the pressure for a Scottish parliament is only the most recent phase of this negotiation. However, there are a number of new factors which give it a peculiar intensity. These include the divergent voting patterns in Scotland and England and the growing importance of the European Union. Third, there emerged in the 1980s a popular consensus about the justice of the demand for self-government (1998, pp. 54–5). The logic of Paterson's argument can be seen in the way in which the question of political legitimacy played a unique part in the Scottish campaign against the poll tax. Refusal of payment was justified not merely on the grounds of social justice common to the whole of Britain (solidarity). It was also justified on the basis that it was an imposition against the will (contract) of the Scottish people (Barker 1992, pp. 531–3). That critical edge informed the demand for self-government and took shape in a distinctively Scottish fashion.

A Claim of Right for Scotland was the title of the report of the Constitutional Steering Committee presented to the Campaign for a Scottish Assembly in July 1988 (Mitchell 1999, p. 635). *A Claim of Right* drew on the historical resonance of its predecessor of 1689 which had accused James VII of 'inverting all the ends of Government'. This identification of the role of the community in rational decision-making assumed a political association based on the principle of consent and possessing the right to dissolve ties 'with a government destructive of the ends of government in general was a remarkable development' (Smart 1980, p. 193). The spirit of 1689 wove in and out of the CSA's recommendations. 'The existing machinery of Scottish government,' it argued, 'is an attempt either to create an illusion or to achieve the impossible' (Edwards 1989, p. 17). Whatever it was, it was not responsive to the voice of the Scottish people. Moreover, under the prevailing dispensation 'the Scots are a minority which cannot ever feel secure under a constitution which, in effect, renders the Treaty of Union a contradiction in terms' (1989, p. 19). *The Claim* concluded with a stark message that Scotland faced a crisis of identity, even of survival. 'It is now being governed without consent and subject to the declared intention of having imposed upon it a radical change of outlook and behaviour pattern which it shows no sign of wanting' (1989, p. 51).

It was Dennis Canavan who, in his commentary on the text, raised the Candido question. Is the first loyalty of Scottish MPs to the British state or to the people of Scotland? (1989, p. 78). There is here a slight hint of Don Antonio's desire to 'smash the bottle'. And Canavan's challenge to the New Labour machine in the 1999 Scottish parliamentary elections may suggest one minor crack on its surface. The task for non-separatists, however, was to prevent this smashing by reshaping the bottle to keep the scorpions of separatism on the outside. It was imperative to sustain the Scottish tradition which, in its rational deliberativeness and estimable moderation had avoided Sinn Féinism, and to find a way 'of taking back control without turning our backs on our neighbours' (Scottish Constitutional Convention 1995, p. 6).

The Claim proposed the establishment of a cross-party Scottish Constitutional Convention which would draw on the resources of civil society. The inaugural meeting of that Convention was held on 30 March 1989. It committed itself to agree a scheme for a Scottish parliament, to mobilise Scottish opinion behind it and to 'assert the right of the Scottish people to secure the implementation of that scheme' (Scottish Constitutional Convention 1995, p. 10). The SNP withdrew from a Convention which would not recommend independence and the Conservatives refused to join a Convention they believed already shared an independence mindset. Indeed, one critic of the Convention's presumption argued that if government in Scotland is the sole prerogative of the sovereign people there, then it followed that the constitutional people of the Westminster parliament had no say in the matter (Levy 1992, p. 226). That was a logical consideration (two truths cannot coexist) but not a political consideration (well, in this case they must). Crucially, the Labour Party saw the Convention as the appropriate vehicle, both to absorb Scottish discontent with Westminster politics and to develop proposals for devolution which would have a wide fund of support. Between 1989 and 1996 the Convention's slow process of consensus-building had the effect of helping to align popular opinion with the aims of civil society (Paterson and Wynn Jones 1999, pp. 180–1).

There was much that was predictable in the Convention's final proposals given the limits set by the acceptance of the British state. However, there was also much that was imaginative. The problem of the 'one-party state' was to be addressed by the use of the additional member system of proportional representation. If this system made it unlikely that Labour could secure an overall majority, it would also have an equal effect on the prospects of the SNP. Some have suggested that this was the purpose of PR (Taylor et al. 1999, p. xxxi). It also proposed that there should be equal representation of men and women. Both these objectives were set out in an electoral agreement signed by Labour and the Liberal Democrats. To ensure a degree of independence in financial matters, the Convention wanted the parliament to have the power to vary the basic rate of income tax by 3p in the pound. In a rhetorical endpiece, the future Scottish parliament was recommended as 'something better than the secretive, centralised, self-serving superstate that the UK has become'. Its report heralded 'the dawn of new hope' for everyone in the United Kingdom (1995, p. 31). The 'superstate UK' was not to be smashed, but its potential released to become something better. The Convention's report set the framework for New Labour's reform proposals. The one major departure from it was Tony Blair's decision in June 1996 to hold a referendum on both devolution and the tax-raising power (Leicester 1999a, p. 256). If devolution was, as Blair's predecessor John Smith believed, the 'settled will' of the Scottish people, then the New Labour leadership wanted to make sure. Though it angered leading members of the Convention, Blair's instinct was right. The referendum was a way of acknowledging that a devolved parliament within the United Kingdom was a legitimate act self-determination by the Scottish people. As the Labour manifesto of 1997 put it: 'popular endorsement will strengthen the legitimacy of our proposals and speed their passage through Parliament'.

In office, New Labour moved swiftly on its manifesto promises. The government's proposals on devolution were published in July and the Scottish referendum was held on 11 September 1997. The result was 74.3 per cent to 25.7 per cent in favour of a parliament and 63.5 per cent to 36.5 per cent in favour of the tax-raising power. All Scottish regions endorsed the parliament. Only two, Dunfries and Galloway and Orkney, voted against the tax-raising power (Surridge and McCrone 1999). This soundly-based support for the new parliament may be contrasted with the equivocal result of 1979

(Bogdanor 1999b, p. 190). Following the recommendations of most sympathetic advisers, the government avoided the mistake of the 1978 Act, which had tried to specify in detail the powers to be devolved *from* Westminster. This time it designated the powers reserved *to* Westminster – macro-economic policy, social security, foreign affairs, defence and constitutional matters. All other matters are devolved to the parliament in Edinburgh. Finance for the services within the competence of the parliament will be allocated by the Treasury in London. This Scottish bloc, based on the Barnett formula devised for the devolution arrangements of 1978, provided a budget of £14.5 billion.

The Scotland Act also addressed the question of Scottish over-representation at Westminster. The next Parliamentary Boundary Commission review will reduce the number of Scottish MPs from 72 to 57. This will also have an effect on the size of the Scottish parliament itself. Changes in Westminster boundaries will mean that by the end of its second term in 2007 the parliament will shrink from 129 Members of the Scottish Parliament (MSPs) to just over 100 (Hazell and Sinclair 1999, p. 163). What effect that will have on Scottish political culture remains to be seen. While the scope of powers devolved is wide, sovereignty remains at Westminster: clause 27 of the Scotland Act leaves no doubt about this (O'Neill 2000, p. 82). Whether this remains a theoretical formality also remains to be seen.

The first election to the Scottish parliament took place on 6 May 1999. The historic nature of the occasion did not encourage an historic turnout. At 59 per cent it was 13 points down on the British general election of 1997. This, thought W.L. Miller, 'was hardly a ringing endorsement for devolution itself' (1999, p. 307). In his view it confirmed the 'second order' nature of the election and the 'second order' character of the new parliament. However, this 'degree' could change in the future. The alternative member system gave the elector two votes: one for the 73 constituency MSPs elected on the basis of first-past-the-post and one for a regional party list. In each of these eight regions seven additional members, or top-ups, were to be chosen, making a total of 56. Labour won 56 seats (53 constituency and three list), the SNP won 35 (seven constituency and 35 list), the Conservatives 18 (all list) and the Liberal Democrats 17 (12 constituency and five list). There were also three independents. Labour did fulfil its pledge on gender balance (28 women). The SNP also achieved it (16 women). Overall, the proportion of women returned was 37 per cent. The result, as expected, denied Labour an overall majority. Equally, devolution would not be tested in an atmosphere dominated by nationalism. The failure of the nationalist challenge was, for Miller, the most significant outcome for Britain as a whole (1999, p. 322). On the Candido question – was it possible to satisfy national sentiment within the British state? – Labour seemed to have won the first round of the argument. The fundamentalist wing of the SNP attributed this to the ambiguity of the nationalist position, which was committed to independence while also promising to make devolution work. Yet it is difficult to see how it could have been otherwise. Any response to the Candido question is bound to be ambiguous. The ambiguity of the SNP does not seem to be purely a tactical matter. It seems to be inherent in Scottish politics.

However, Labour's ideological victory this time was just as ambiguous. As Miller noted, there had been a strange pattern of electoral swings. This had the effect of transforming Scotland 'from a country of safe seats into a country of marginals'. Elections to the second parliament could be less predictable than the first (1999, p. 321). Indeed, the political editor of *Scotland on Sunday* thought that the new parliament now gave the SNP a regular shot at victory. The electoral barrier put the odds against it, but odder things have happened. 'In essence,' he reflected, 'to keep Scotland in the Union for the next 40 years Labour, or another non-nationalist party, will have to win ten Scottish elections in a row. To call that a tall order is something of an understatement' (Martin 1998, p. 20). The SNP, therefore, waits to convert disaffected Scottish Labour voters, providing them with an alternative not available in England (Denver 1998, p. 215). That outcome, the sort evangelically predicted by nationalists, assumes that devolution is, as the former Welsh Secretary of State Ron Davies put it, 'a process not an event'. And it is a process which benefits only nationalists. That is itself a tall story, the story of historical inevitability.

Donald Dewar became Scotland's First Minister on 17 May and the official opening of the parliament in Edinburgh took place on 1 July 1999. Dewar negotiated a coalition government with the Liberal Democrats whose leader, Jim Wallace, became Deputy First Minister. Dewar had already alluded to the psychological importance of self-rule: 'The idea that Scotland as a whole is parochial, that devolution is driven by parochialism, simply does not wash' (1998, p. 18). This devolution-makes-you-stupid argument never did bear relation to any political theory, though it did have much to do with metropolitan prejudice. The value of the parliament was the possibility to disprove it in practice. It would also mean an end to what Peter Jones called 'alibi politics'. Formerly, the Scots could keep their hands clean and their consciences pure because everything they did not like could be blamed on the English. After devolution this would not wash (Jones 1998, p. 270). Nevertheless, the SNP appeared determined to stick to the good old cry, only this time the blame attached to middle England in the form of New Labour Party headquarters at Millbank. The object was to portray Labour in Scotland as the puppets of London, perpetuating English dominance by other means. And since a vote for the Liberal Democrats was, according to former SNP leader Alex Salmond, a *de facto* vote for Labour, they too were party to a conspiracy against Scottish nationhood (Ingle 2000, pp. 278–9). Yet as Jack Brand once noted, the SNP has never been able to mobilise the Scots for a sustained period on the basis of nationality alone (1987, pp. 347–8). It was difficult, then, to see that approach being credibly maintained for the life of a parliament.

Of course, there was to be more to Scotland's new politics. Expectations were high that there would be a qualitatively different and not just organisationally distinct approach. This was not new either. It was once thought that the 1978 Scotland Act would provide scope for a more publicly accountable and democratic style of government (Bonney 1978, pp. 198–9). In a similar vein, the final report of the Scottish Constitutional Convention claimed that a Scottish parliament would usher in a new style of politics radically different from Westminster: 'more participative, more creative, less needlessly confrontational' (1995, p. 9). Others thought that it would provide Scotland with the chance to pioneer a novel politics of pluralism (McCormick and Alexander 1996, p. 161). This is what Dewar implied when he argued that he had never been a supporter of the 'devolution difference', simply doing things differently just because of Scottishness. The importance of devolution was that it would bring 'added value'. Bringing added value was a rationalisation of the governing partnership with the Liberal Democrats, an example of breaking new ground in Scotland. The job of Dewar's government was not to impose but 'to connect, persuade, cajole, encourage, preach and lead'. This gave the First Minister even more reason for annoyance at the behaviour of the SNP. Like the Conservatives, argued Dewar, the SNP remained wedded to the old politics. 'For them, open government is simply an opportunity to wound.' And he homed in on what he thought was the SNP's weakness: its conflict with the settled will of the Scottish people. What the SNP was trying to hide was 'its determination to rip up the devolution settlement and divorce Scotland from Britain' (1999, p. 58). But what is really new?

As in Northern Ireland, powerful subject committees scrutinise departments, monitor the work of the Executive and have the right to initiate legislation (Brown 2000). However, evidence of added value is more elusive. The initial popular impression was rather different from the hopes invested in new politics. There were complaints about the 'pay and holidays' character of the early weeks of the parliament, a criticism also made by the Northern Ireland media of its own Assembly. Shrugging off such impressions, Graham Leicester adopted the modern management mantra that one could not expect a new politics until the system had moved to 'the edge of chaos'. For Leicester, initial signs of confusion were taken as encouraging. They suggested that things were moving apace against resistant forces and old habits (1999b, pp. 32–4). Unfortunately, the initial problem was deeper than that (Mitchell 2000).

The inflated expectations placed in the new politics may have contributed to a facile sort of anti-politics found in the remarks of Canon Kenyon Wright, former chairman of the Constitutional Convention, after his defeat in the 1999 election. Voters, he claimed, were already 'bored, cynical, and disillusioned'. They wanted a new kind of democracy, but 'the way the parties have behaved has shown that they are not getting it' (cited in Miller 1999, p. 301). On the contrary. The value of the Convention was that it gave deliberative shape to the generally accepted, but ill-defined popular view that devolution was necessary. It had the charm of potentiality. That sort of politics is often incompatible with parliamentarianism. Glorious possibility has now become humdrum legislative responsibility. That is where the real stamina for politics is to be found. As Douglas Alexander judiciously put it, the parliament will ultimately be judged not by what it is (*Scotland's* parliament) but by what it does. In truth, it will probably be judged on both counts for it does not lend itself to a simple either/or judgement. However, he did suggest a neat answer to Scotland's Candido question. For Scottish devolution to become a settled arrangement it 'requires its adherents at Westminster to continue to argue unashamedly for the virtues of Holyrood, while devolutionists at Holyrood advance unashamedly the case for Westminster' (1999, p. 36). For New Labour, this would contain the two truths of the new Scotland-in-Britain. The SNP expects that it cannot be done and that the old British bottle will finally break because of its own contradictions.

WALES

The Royal Commission on the Constitution which reported in 1973 found that many of its witnesses thought Wales should continue to have a strong voice at Westminster. Equally, it found a deep anxiety that national identity was eroding because of policies which paid insufficient regard to Wales (1973, p. 336). The political problem was more complex than the way in which the Commission presented it. These two views – the administrative and the cultural – were antagonistic rather than complementary. The generous spirit of Glanmor Williams identified the Welsh Candido question: How can Welsh-speakers and non-Welsh speakers understand each other's aspirations and remove each other's fears? He also tried to provide a context in which their two truths could find some form of reconciliation. Following the fault line of the Royal Commission, Williams detected on the one side 'those who conjure up a gigantic state conspiracy hell-bent on committing the murder of the language', on the other, those 'who detect what they believe to be a clique of extremist fanatics determined to impose themselves and their language on an unwilling majority'. What was required of each side was a positive act of sympathy with the concerns of the other. Williams believed that Welsh identity was more encompassing than the divisions over language. There was a strong case 'for emphasizing what the Welsh have in common rather than the differences between them. They are,' thought Williams, 'too small a people to indulge in the masochistic luxury of self-inflicted wounds' (1979, pp. 32–3). That large vision was held by others. Another celebrated historian, David Williams, believed that no one now could doubt the ability of the Welsh people to govern themselves within the United Kingdom and 'to build a society at least as culturally rich and resilient as that which it has inherited from the past' (1977, p. 304).

The result of the 1979 referendum suggested otherwise. All eight counties in Wales voted no and by substantial margins (Balsom and McAllister 1979, p. 401). The two truths of Welsh society seemed uncontainable on the narrow ground of a National Assembly. The vision of Glanmor Williams appeared to the electorate as one big lie. And perhaps there was an even more serious political problem: that the Welsh lacked confidence in each other. It has been suggested that the reason why many people did not want an Assembly was because they were afraid that the Welsh could not make a success of it (Holtham and Barrett 1996, pp. 75–6). It was argued in Chapter 6 that in the two decades since the first referendum on a Welsh Assembly there has been a change in Welsh political self-confidence and that Glanmor Williams' vision now appears far from being an illusion. The identity of Wales or Welshness varies in its meaning and remains politically contentious. Yet a more embracing identity is something that a number of commentators thought to be developing in the 1980s and 1990s (see Snicker 1998, p. 140).

Jonathan Bradbury identified three novel political pressures which encouraged a re-estimation of the value of Welsh devolution. First, devolution offered itself as one way of realising New Labour's concern for autonomy and responsibility within communities. It also served to distinguish Blair's strategy from the centralised approach of Thatcherism. Second, devolution was now more in tune with Welsh Labour sentiment. A decade of Conservative governance had reduced hostility to a National Assembly. Because it lacked a popular mandate in Wales, the Conservative style appeared more pro-consular than democratic. In these circumstances the Labour Party, perhaps even despite itself, had become a vehicle of local patriotism. This development alone had the effect of softening the rigid political boundary between 'socialism' and 'nationality' though it did not fully erase it. Third, the Thatcherite programme of privatisation shifted the focus of Welsh politics from a concern to maintain an economy heavily reliant on nationalised industries towards a need to attract inward investment. The imperative was to market Wales properly as an attractive nation/region within the European Union (Bradbury 1998, pp. 130–3). The debate about a Welsh Assembly moved partly from the sphere of emotional contention on to more neutral or rational territory. It now seemed a viable method of adjusting Wales to the challenges and the changing patterns of a globalised economy (Osmond 1988, p. 150). One might argue that in this case too Thatcher was the midwife of devolution.

The Conservative government, however, was determined to resist pressure to bring that particular baby into the world. John Redwood, then Secretary of State for Wales, played on the concern that an

Assembly would give too large a say to South Wales. He also tried to arouse the metropolitan rivalry of Swansea and Cardiff over the siting of the Assembly buildings. However, the constitutional card remained the traditional one. There was no half-way house between union and separation. These two truths cannot be contained by a Welsh Assembly. It was all a big lie. Devolutionists, argued Redwood, were sitting on an uncomfortable fence, with one part 'crying, "On to independence", and another shouting, "Preserve the unity of the Kingdom"' (1995). For Dafydd Wigley of Plaid Cymru, on the other hand, there were three constitutional options. The first was continued direct rule from London favoured by the Conservatives and influential figures in the Welsh Labour Party; the second was a devolved Assembly with executive powers favoured by the leadership of New Labour. The third option, supported by Plaid Cymru, was not devolution at all but 'full self-government'. The sovereignty of the Welsh people would be acknowledged as of right. That right would not be exercised to attain independent statehood immediately, a formulation which allowed Plaid Cymru, like the SNP, to eschew the separatist label. Wigley, like the Labour Shadow Secretary Ron Davies – albeit with different intent – envisaged self-government as a process, not an event. Self-government could go only as far and as fast as the people of Wales would allow, but its logical direction would be towards independence in Europe (1995). This was an intelligent agenda for nationalists, the subtleties of which were to fascinate the national media during the referendum campaign of 1997 (Jones 1999b, p. 325). Given the history of the debate within Wales, Laura McAllister's judgement of Plaid Cymru appeared apt. Self-government appeared the utopian solution to every difficult question (1998, p. 502).

Both Redwood's and Wigley's interventions were in response to the Labour Party's 1995 proposals set out in *Shaping the Vision*. These were designed to address the democratic deficit in Wales by establishing an Assembly without legislative or taxation powers but one which would take control of the responsibilities and budget of the Welsh Office. For Ron Davies these proposals would give the people of Wales the opportunity to reflect their distinctive aspirations. It would also secure the union with Britain. Labour would not provide a stalking horse for those who wanted to break the British connection (1995a). For all its banality, that was as comprehensive a statement of Welsh Labour intent as it was possible to give, acknowledging the need to reflect what was distinctive about Wales but with barriers put against separatism. Davies believed that the Welsh Assembly should represent the broadest possible consensus. That was the only way to ensure that it would retain popular support in Wales and have the authority to secure its priorities with Westminster (1995b).

A fine objective, but here was the problem. Commentators were sceptical of generating sufficient consensus for an Assembly. Blair's determination to hold a referendum on Labour's proposals before legislation led many to believe that this had destroyed the hope of devolution. The vote might not be as decisively against as in 1979. None the less, it was still expected that the Yes camp would lose, even if the result in Scotland was positive (Bradbury 1998, p. 135). The reason for this was that the broadest possible consensus genuinely desired by Davies had not been cultivated outside the Welsh Labour Party (or even within it). Wales stood in stark contrast to Scotland and even to Northern Ireland. Whilst the former had its Convention and the latter had its multi-party talks, the proposals for devolution in Wales were almost entirely generated from within the Labour Party itself (Wyn Jones and Lewis 1999, p. 41). The introduction of the referendum changed the character of the debate. Until then the task had been to construct a consensus *within* Labour's ranks in Wales to prevent the fatal divisions of 1979. Subsequently, the task became one of convincing the Welsh public *outside* Labour's ranks amongst whom devolution was not the main issue.

The idea that in Wales the government could count on anything like the 'settled will' of the people was laughable. The process of devolution, if it were to be successful, would need to operate in reverse order to the experience in Scotland. As it turned out, Davies secured victory by the barest of margins. The result of the referendum in September 1997 was 'the most grudging of mandates' for the new assembly (Wyn Jones and Trystan 1999, p. 65). Even that is being generous. On a low turnout of 51.3 per cent the Assembly was approved by just 50.3 per cent of the electorate. A mere 6,721 votes separated the two sides. The referendum exposed once again the fault line in Welsh politics. 'Welsh' Wales backed devolution; 'British' Wales was opposed or equivocal. Apathy decided the issue. The Assembly, only marginally acceptable to those who had bothered to vote, would have difficulty legitimising the claim that it could confidently speak for the Welsh people. Rather, the task of the Assembly would be to create its own legitimacy. That means developing a voice for the Welsh people, fostering a clear sense of

national political identity and encouraging a healthy civic contribution to a new Welsh political system. There seems to be no good
reason why this cannot be done. Intelligent proposals have already
been made (Osmond 1998). As Paterson and Wyn Jones put it: 'while
Welsh civil society was not the precursor of devolution, it may yet
be among its progeny' (1999, p. 183).

The Assembly of 60 members was elected by the same additional
member system that operates in Scotland. Forty Assembly Members
(AM), or Aelod y Cynulliad (AS), are elected from Westminster constituencies and 20 are elected from regional party lists. This PR
system had been reluctantly accepted by the Welsh Labour Party. It
was concerned, reasonably enough, to retain its political dominance
in Wales. The New Labour leadership, on the other hand, was
concerned to make the new Assembly as broadly representative as
possible. Blair's view prevailed. The small size of the Assembly was
another product of Welsh Labour's ambivalence about having one at
all. However, it is not just a product of Labour ambivalence but also
of popular ambivalence. John Major's famous rule of thumb – if the
answer to your question is more politicians, then you are asking the
wrong question – made sense to more than Conservatives in Wales.
The size of the Assembly also suggested a concern to avoid criticisms
of over-government from Cardiff (McAllister 1999, p. 641).

The election campaign revealed Plaid Cymru adopting a similar
tactic to the SNP. It accused New Labour, as it once accused the Conservatives, of operating a rebranded sort of Thatcherite centralism –
'Millbank McCarthyism' – and of being dominated by the interests
of middle England. It had the perfect opportunity to exploit this
tactic after Ron Davies' unfortunate resignation from office in 1998
and his replacement as candidate for First Minister by Alun Michael.
Michael's experience was perhaps even more unfortunate than that
of Davies. He was perceived as an imposition by New Labour 'control
freaks' in London in order to prevent the 'off-message' Rhodri
Morgan from leading the new administration in Wales. The divisions
within the party and the suspicions raised within Wales had nothing
to do with Michael's abilities, which are considerable. He simply
suffered from the placeman syndrome. This provided Dafydd Wigley
with a good cry to 'woo Labour's heartland', formerly a nationalist
desert. It was an affair which brought good results. On a low turnout
of 46 per cent, the nationalists made inroads into Labour's South
Wales bastions, even winning the constituencies of Islwyn, Rhondda
and Llanelli. Plaid Cymru won 17 seats (nine constituency, eight list)

on 29.5 per cent of the vote. Labour remained the largest party with 28 seats (27 constituency, one list) on 36.5 per cent of the vote. The Conservatives secured nine seats (one constituency, eight list) on 16.2 per cent and the Liberal Democrats six seats (three constituency, three list) on 13 per cent of the vote. The 'Welsh factor' appeared to have been the source of Plaid Cymru's unexpected successes (Jones 1999b, pp. 329–30). This transcended its usual meaning, a concern with culture and language (either/or), and embraced a broader political concern with local Welsh affairs (both/and).

Some Labour politicians chose to interpret the election as an example of what happens when the leadership insults the intelligence of its own natural supporters. This it appeared to do in manoeuvring against Rhodri Morgan. 'The historic dominance of Labour in Wales,' argued Jones, 'was replaced, perhaps permanently, by a multi-party system' (1999b, p. 332). Plaid Cymru emerged as the second party in the Wales administered by Cardiff. It is still unlikely, but not impossible, that it can become a serious challenger in the Wales governed by Westminster. Following the election, Labour chose to form a minority administration rather than follow the Scottish example of coalition. Michael became Wales's First Secretary only to resign in February 2000 in advance of a mischievous vote of no confidence tabled by the three opposition parties. It was a poor reward for Michael and an inauspicious start for 'new politics' in Wales. Morgan, whom Blair had done so much to obstruct, succeeded him.

On 17 October 2000, Morgan agreed to a 'partnership' with the Liberal Democrats to secure stability and continuity in the administration. Though this brings Wales into line with Scotland the approach was very different. Whereas in Scotland Labour's coalition with the Liberal Democrats emerged from years of cooperation in the Scottish Convention, in Wales it emerged as an intra-Assembly deal. Whether it secures the stability (and advantage for Labour) which Morgan has sought remains to be seen.

The Assembly has taken over the Welsh Office's budget of £7 billion. The administration of policy in those matters devolved to the assembly is conducted by Assembly secretaries operating within a Cabinet structure. The Assembly was required by the 1998 Act to establish regional advisory committees to help integrate the geographical diversity of the country as well as to allay fears of South Wales domination. Whilst the powers of the Assembly are modest, they are not insignificant (Laffin and Thomas 2000, pp. 573–5).

Sceptics argue, however, that the lack of primary legislative power will result in the worst of both worlds. The Assembly will be dependent on legislation passed at Westminster which will not necessarily reflect local priorities. Hopes in Wales of independent action may be frustrated. The Assembly might come to be seen as a 'permanent supplicant in Whitehall, leading to continuous tension between Cardiff and London' (Hazell and Sinclair 1999, p. 165). This could happen. But the force of the argument presupposes a 'settled will' and a coherent agenda which the Assembly has yet to prove. It may be that the Assembly will create tension with London in order to foster that agenda. That too is uncertain. Those sympathetic to a vibrant, self-confident Wales would probably ill-serve the nation by making grievance the basis of policy (see Laffin et al. 2000; McAllister 2000b, pp. 603–4). Wales now can aspire to realise the vision of Glanmor Williams. That is not all it can do, but it is possibly the best that it can do.

Karl Mannheim once thought that Britain had 'a peculiar genius for working out in practice the correlation of principles which seem to be logically opposed to each other' (cited in Kent 1998, p. 29). That is the sort of quality required to answer effectively the Candido question. It is impossible to say whether that genius is sufficiently active in modern British politics and, even if it were, whether it can cope with the two truths of the constitutional and national peoples. The wager of all those opposed to the break-up of Britain is that it is and that it can. Nationalists look forward to their truth emerging victorious. Indeed, for the moment, sceptics can justifiably argue that the real crux of the Candido question has not yet been addressed. What will the answer be if and when the Conservatives achieve office at Westminster? So far there has been only one truth, that of New Labour in office in Scotland, Wales and Westminster (Northern Ireland remains a place apart). The real test is yet to come. That outcome will be decided as much by English attitudes as by anything else. Another question now presents itself. Where does England stand today?

8 Missing England

Vernon Bogdanor observed that England is hardly mentioned in devolution legislation though it is probably the key to the success of the whole enterprise (1999, p. 264). Indeed, it was Enoch Powell who once said that at the heart of the devolution question was neither Scotland nor Wales but the question of England (Heffer 1998, p. 746). Bogdanor thought this absence was a consequence of 'the poverty of much of English constitutional thought in the previous century' (1979, p. 38). Partly this poverty had to do with the genteel absentmindedness which smoothed the governance of Britain. Partly it had to do with the self-confident character of Englishness. The question of English identity today is bound up with the new complexity of British governance and with the new uncertainty of Englishness.

Jeremy Paxman, for instance, began his portrait of a people with the line: 'Once upon a time the English knew who they were' (1998, p. 1). Because they knew who they were they felt no obligation to devote a lot of energy to the question of identity. Paxman's conclusion was that today the English can no longer avoid that question. They now live in agonising and uncertain times. 'England,' he asserted, 'scarcely exists as a country.' A revived self-consciousness would not only be of psychic value, but would serve a utilitarian purpose: 'Those countries which do best in the world – the ones that are safe and prosperous – have a coherent sense of their own culture' (1998, p. 23). Paxman had grasped the significance of an important political trend. The knowledge economy, the global market, the communications revolution – however one tries to capture the distinctiveness of the present – have transformed the relationship between culture and politics. This trend, noted in Chapters 6 and 7, has already affected the currents of national sentiment and self-confidence in Scotland and Wales. In the communications revolution, 'the most vital sense of national identity is the individual awareness of the country of the mind'. The sense that England is missing the opportunity to secure a powerful and distinctive territory amongst the competing countries of the mind gives Paxman's study its urgency.

What his book explores is national anxiety. This is not new. The extent of periodic English anxiety has matched the sense of English superiority: the *Dreadnought* crisis and naval supremacy; the Boer War and imperial might; the devaluation of sterling and financial pre-eminence. Greatness, and anxiety about greatness, are inseparable. Whereas these anxiety attacks were predominantly concerned with external security, the current one may be concerned with inner certitude (or the lack of it). It is difficult to get a proper perspective on such matters. This has to do with a cult of historic self-esteem and its opposite, a cult of self-denigration. For every argument which claims that England's history reveals an exceptional virtue, there is an argument which claims it reveals an exceptional vice. It is a view of the world captured succinctly by Geoffrey Elton. On the one hand, English history 'most convincingly demonstrated how man should order his existence on earth'. On the other hand, it demonstrated exactly the opposite. These were two sides of the same exceptionalist medal worn proudly by English ideologues. The first sort, termed by Elton the 'Froude complex', was the belief that England was somehow peculiarly blessed in God's creation. The second, 'the *New Statesman* complex', was assured that everything was for the worst in that benighted country. (It would be fairer to the contemporary sophistication of the *New Statesman* to call that complex today 'the *Guardian* complex'.) The hallmark of this latter complex, observed Elton in a tone reminiscent of E.P. Thompson's criticism of Nairn, was an admiration of all things French. Both complexes shared the belief that the English and their history were exemplary for good or ill (1991, pp. 110–11). Elton was making a simple plea for balance, a plea that has had little noticeable effect in recent ideological exchanges.

Paxman's concern about the vacancy of English identity is not new either. In his survey of the ideas of nationhood in English poetry before 1900, John Lucas thought that to be English meant not to be English at all, that the romantic rejection of industrial, urban England was a rejection of what was real about the country (1990, p. 9). Imagining England often meant not imagining it at all (Lucas 1990, p. 205). The radical criticism of the prevailing literary imagery of Englishness as stubbornly rural and reactionary is a criticism which has been repeated of the prevailing political vision of England which remains stubbornly traditional and Conservative (Colls and Dodd 1986). Paxman's book is sufficiently attuned to what is distinctive about the present sense of English uncertainty and sufficiently attuned to what it has in common with others to be unpersuaded by that simple view. It is also clear about one thing. The realisation that one's country is no longer exceptional in the burdens it carries for and the gifts it bestows on civilisation should have one advantage. It should encourage a healthy scepticism of prophecies of doom. What, then, is the source of the English problem? 'The English,' according to Paxman, 'put their faith in institutions' (1998, p. 17). Nationalism was a British thing. It is the present crisis of institutions which is the crisis of Britishness. And the crisis of Britishness is the crisis of Englishness. That is the specific juncture where the present concern with English nationhood can be found.

ENGLISHNESS AND BRITISHNESS

The American cultural historian Gerald Newman once ran a computerised search through abstracts of more than 80,000 articles on all aspects of history and literature. It was designed to register articles on English or British nationalism. The result was meagre: it produced only two obscure essays. Newman judged that either England was so unlike the rest of the world that it had avoided entirely the ideology of nationalism, which he thought unlikely; or that those who have written on English history and politics have been victims of a myth of English exceptionalism, which he thought probable (1987, pp. xviii–xix). Newman concluded that there must be a coherent tradition of English nationalism. He discovered it in the rejection of French cultural hegemony after 1789. Newman's literary criticism was persuasive. His political analysis was less so. What he ignored was an English tradition which stressed the importance of institutional authority, rather than cultural integrity, as the basis of national identity.

In a series of essays on the subject, Bernard Crick provided a more nuanced view. He repeated the perplexing theme of Newman. Library catalogues show an abundance of texts on Irish, Scottish and Welsh nationalism but very few on England and Englishness. Why should this be so? Crick's answer is politically more subtle than Newman's and historically more satisfying than some commentators, such as Nairn and his followers, who argue that England's peculiar sense of nationhood is the result of transgressing some law of historical development. He proposed that for 'the English to have developed a strident literature of English nationalism, such as arose, often under official patronage, elsewhere in Europe, and in Ireland and Scotland, eventually in Wales, would have been divisive'. The strategy of English politicians was to develop a Briitsh nationalism and to make that the official ideology of government (Crick 1990, pp. 98–9). A strong sense of English nationality was fully compatible with a lack of self-conscious English nationalism. That may go some way towards explaining Hugh Seton-Watson's categorical claim that English nationalism never existed (1977, p. 34). The clue was already there in Hans Kohn's seminal study of the genesis of English nationalism in the seventeenth century. Kohn argued that England was the first country with a popularly based national consciousness. It became so deeply ingrained in the English mind that it became both natural and, like the air one breathes, taken for granted. Nineteenth-century English philosophers thought it unnecessary to meditate upon nationalism for it did not disturb the serenity of the constitutional people (Kohn 1940, pp. 92–3). This was a view later developed in some depth by Liah Greenfeld (1993, pp. 86–7). Why was it, though, that the English have seemed for the most part 'unthinking' in their Britishness in the way that, for instance, the Scots have never been (Rose 1982, p. 62)? What made this deeply ingrained national identity so compatible with the artefact of Britishness?

Lord Rosebery, a Scot, thought it understandable that when the English spoke of 'Britain' they really meant 'England'. It was a case of 'notable self-possession'. By this he implied that England's constitutionalism had accommodated within it the other nations of Britain and, without undue pressure, had absorbed them into its own consciousness (Grainger 1986, pp. 52–3). Englishness was not an official mobilisation; nor did it seek to convert. Ireland, once more, was the exception. Grainger's is one of the most suggestive accounts of this English 'presumption' and one full of important insights. The dominance of England within the Union had elements of design and imposition. But its dominance was mainly a consequence of being so powerfully present. English superiority tended not to be excessively nationalistic. Moreover, if there was some original, authentic England beneath its British constitutional capaciousness few appeared to know what it was. In a striking phrase, Grainger thought that England was 'a concrete reference' (1986, pp. 53–4). The concreteness of English experience, the massively self-confident sense of just being there, its constitution being its cultural form, may help to explain the supposed anti-intellectualism or philistinism of which radical critics have accused the English.

The twentieth century inherited that style. Ernest Barker believed that Englishness was defined by the good fortune of possessing the rule of law and representative government (Stapleton 1993, pp. 14–15). It was that tradition of law and representative government, a tradition more valuable than an ideology or a national purpose, which was defended with grace and intelligence by Michael Oakeshott. Nevertheless, Oakeshott often seemed at odds with the tendency of the modern world. In 1950, George Kitson Clark thought that 'the constitution which our forefathers so earnestly believed in, toasted after so many dinners, celebrated with such pompous oratory and called the palladium of their liberties, has been reformed out of all knowledge' (1950, p. 40). Most of this change had been necessary and for the best. But, like Oakeshott, he felt that the ideology of secular democracy and its corollary, the concentration of power, would have tremendous consequences for the English. Kitson-Clark reminded his readers that if the constitution faltered, the English had been English before they were British. In other words, there was an Englishness beyond the constitutional people. There was little evidence of what it was.

It is the diminishing authority of the old institutions which has provoked the current reassessment of the meaning of England. New Labour's constitutional reforms have been a major but not the only factor in this. As one literary critic detected, some of the drive towards reassessment has come from authors attempting to find and reclaim Kitson-Clark's Englishness before Britishness. The very act of naming England was an attempt to bring it back to non-British life (Cowley 1999, p. 29). There may be some exhilaration, especially amongst the literati, in throwing off the 'safety blanket' of Britishness in the pursuit of authentic England. There is also a degree of dangerous naivety. Radicals in politics have generally stressed the values of rationality. The pursuit of the authentic is not rationalism in politics, it is romanticism in politics. In the competition for the authentically national it is hard to believe that reason will always win out against the passions. The urgency of cultural Englishness has also been attributed to the widespread impatience with an enfeebled Conservative government under John Major. Those critical of *fin de siècle* Conservatism rejected what they saw as the retreat into mythological versions of England and Englishness. If that was the challenge facing those who wished to redefine English identity in a culturally diverse, non-Conservative and progressive way there were others who wished to throw off the security blanket of Britishness for precisely the opposite reasons. If the so-called Scottish national renaissance is built on a rejection of Conservative England and a questioning of British institutions, then this latter style of English nationalism has been driven by hostility to Scotland's new place in the Union and by opposition to the governance of New Labour. The most coherent exposition of this latter style is to be found in a recent book by Simon Heffer.

SIMON HEFFER'S ENGLAND

In *Nor Shall My Sword*, Heffer has provided one template for the rein-vention of England. Like Paxman, he argues that the English are suffering from a crisis of identity. For centuries they have been too self-conscious to assert their national identity. And since they have for generations been under intense cultural pressure to define their identity as British this was hardly surprising (1999, p. 38). Like Paxman, Heffer is acutely aware of the importance of refashioning and exploiting the cultural product of Englishness. Scottish nation-alists have understood the role which culture can play not only in instilling a sense of destiny, but also in defining the nation's place in global politics. The task for English nationalism is a democratic one, harnessing a distinctive culture to majority and not just to elitist taste. The Conservative populism of that view is quite explicit. It is connected to a commercial populism as well. This national culture would feed off London's international reputation as a market for fashion and culture. Heffer accepts that this may sound a little like a Tory version of Blair's Cool Britannia, but there are three obvious differences. First, it is all about England and not about Britain. Second, it is about fostering a 'conscious atavism' which would rescue the English tradition from the historyless vandals of Millbank Tower. Third, it would be beyond party. It would be consciousness-raising (1999, pp. 126–7).

The thrust of Heffer's argument is also liberationist in a manner designed to disorder conventional wisdom about the English imperial mentality. Facilitating Scotland's exit from the Union would be an act of non-imperialism. The opportunity would then arise for the English to strip away finally all those 'old relics of England as an imperial power'. It would mean a reassessment of the value of the Commonwealth and of England's subaltern relationship to the United States. This newfound independence would also have consequences for England's relations with the European Union whose socialist tendencies are, claimed Heffer, 'anathematical to the English spirit' (1999, pp. 121–4). There is a strong echo here of Enoch Powell, understandably so since Heffer was Powell's biographer. Powell's own view of England was a little reminiscent of the Baddiel and Skinner football anthem for Euro '96: 'Football's Coming Home'. England was coming home after its imperial excursion. And only in coming home to itself could England discover its authentic character. In this return to authentic, rooted Englishness Powell was prepared to say, paraphrasing the famous line from Kipling, that 'after all we know most of England who only England know'. Home from their distant wandering, the English come to find themselves as a nation once again (Heffer 1998, pp. 334–40). Though Powell remained a committed British Unionist, Heffer takes that homecoming one stage further. If for Powell the return was from empire and its illusions, for Heffer England must now return from Britishness and its malcontents, especially the Scots.

All that is solid in the 'concrete' identity of England's Britishness begins to melt into air. The United Kingdom is now thought to be an unreflective, sentimental affair. Sympathy for it is now perceived sharply as a form of indoctrination – sharply, because of the injustice which New Labour's constitutional changes have imposed on England. Heffer is not alone in such opinions. As the former Conservative Home Secretary, Kenneth Baker, put it, 'the Union which we have known for 300 years is over' (1998, p. 14). Neither modified nor reformed, it is over. Others have argued that under New Labour's constitutional arrangements there is provision for the Scots to be Scottish and the Welsh to be Welsh. Unfortunately, it seems that the English have to be forever British. It should no longer be assumed that they will continue to sacrifice their identity for the sake of Britain (Tong 1994, p. 16). There is some validity in the charge that New Labour's large majority at Westminster after the 1997 general election obscured the issue of Scottish and Welsh votes deciding English affairs. These 'inequitable practices', as Baker calls them, were acceptable as the price for British unity expressed in a single parliament. They have become unacceptable now that Scotland, Wales and Northern Ireland have their own parliament and assemblies. However, the rhetoric of the response in both cases seems disproportionate.

Nevertheless, the presumption which Grainger identified remains unchanged. It is presumed that the Union is an English possession. It is this attitude which leads to the disproportionate response. The English, suggests Heffer, are really the ones who have made Britain and Britishness. If the other parts of Britain now find that they are dispensable, the English should say good riddance to them (1998, pp. 14–15). This is the 'endism' of fatal anxiety which projects nationalist secession as the inevitable consequence of devolution. It *would* become inevitable if England decides that it is no longer interested in the Union, which is precisely the message to be found in Heffer's polemic. That the United Kingdom exists simply for the comfort and security of the English is implied here. Letting Scotland go would now be a smart move. England could thereby maximise the benefits of the British inheritance whilst minimising the financial costs. Under the new dispensation, Northern Ireland could be permitted to remain under the protection of the (English) Crown. Wales is anyway an 'English invention'. If the Welsh were confronted with the choice of throwing in their lot entirely with England or of opting for a Wales independent in Europe, then Heffer was certain what the choice would be. The Welsh would abandon their 'tinpot assembly' and take their place in running 'a country far richer, more significant and powerful than their own little princi- pality could ever be on its own' (Heffer 1998, p. 31). This is a good illustration of the old Tory belief that there are no authentically Con- servative Scotsmen, Irishmen or *genuine* Welshmen.

The concern which comes across most clearly is the prospect of English regionalism. The threat of a New Labour-imposed regional- ism is a convenient political rallying cry which, if properly managed, could secure the fortunes of the *English* Tory Party. Regionalism is, on the one hand, a badge of defeatism. It represents the last hope of those well-meaning, but ultimately appeasing, sentimentalists who wish to preserve the Union. On the other hand, English regionalism constitutes a plot by Scots-dominated New Labour to deny the legitimacy of the English nation. The proposal for regional assemblies has nothing to do with democratic equalisation within a reformed United Kingdom, and everything to do with 'the obsessive desire by much of the political class to eradicate the notion of nationhood' in England (Heffer 1998, p. 105). And always lurking in the background is the prospect of the European superstate, of which New Labour is the agent, and for whose bureaucrats English nationhood is anathema. The voice of Powellite populism conjures up a new patriotism. English regionalism is a New Labour, Celtic fringe, European plot and is the good cry of the English national cause. What would be the character of that nation if it were allowed to think only of itself?

Heffer is adamant that a newly independent England would have to think seriously about the difference between a society that happily tolerates various cultures and one that encourages multiculturalism. In the process of establishing English independence, multiculturalism would be a harmful distraction. The new state is not 'dear old, somewhat unsure-of-itself' Britain. It is England, *our* England. There could be no postmodern muddle about all cultures having equal weight. The object of state policy would be to encourage the English 'cultural continuum'. The majority would expect minorities to contribute to a flourishing of Englishness. It would be improper for those minorities to maintain a distance from it by demanding parity of cultural esteem. Diversity is acceptable so long as it does not challenge or violate 'legitimate English sensibilities' (1998, pp. 42–5). What is the point of having an independent national state if the indigenous is not given primacy? And if one is an English Conservative, what else would that indigenous be other than traditionalist in character? As Hobsbawm argued, nationalists will always have recourse to the ethnic thing. And that is not because of racism or a desire to oppress, but simply because that is what is thought to be just. Those who have pointed out the difficulties with that view and who have consistently confronted its unreasonableness in the face of the realities of modern British society could now face a new response (Parekh 1994a, p. 502). That was then and Britain. This is now and England.

Heffer's is one possible version of England. It shows clear signs of the Froude complex even if it believes that the virtuous energies of old England have been recently suppressed by a defeatist political leadership (Thatcher excepted). The object is to release those suppressed energies once more. Whilst Heffer's vision is a Conservative vision, it is not so in a conventional way. Ian Gilmour once wrote that though the concern of Toryism is with the preservation of the nation's unity and its institutions, in certain circumstances the Tory had no choice other than to be revolutionary (1977, p. 143). For Heffer, the unity and the institutions are no longer British. They are English. This is revolutionary, but revolutionary in a Conservative spirit, a revolution defended as a return to authentic England. Heffer's Froudean complex here shares some superficial similarities with other alternatives of the *New Statesman* complex. They are all revolutionary, but revolutionary in their own distinctive ways.

BILLY BRAGG'S ENGLAND

Richard Rose once captured the inspiration of contemporary radical Englishness. A frustrated radical, he argued, might proclaim that England hasn't become modern yet (1985, p. 32). That has been the consistent refrain of a broad alliance of constitutional reformers whose criticism of the Westminster model came to influence the policy of New Labour. Modernising England involved not only changing institutions but also changing historical consciousness 'from its present articulation in the dominant symbolism of the nation' to 'different expressions of cultural and historical identity' (Wright 1991, p. 26). What one detects is a feeling of historical claustrophobia, a Futurist disgust at the prospect of forever living in a stuffy constitutional museum (Porter 1993, p. 2). The transformation of England from an industrial and military power into a heritage theme park was a fate predicted by some critics and novelists (Bell 1995, p. 25). Even Thatcherism failed to dispel a national culture of the 'farewell tone' (Light 1991, p. 19). Some think New Labour has not gone far enough. The radical task is to go further, to transform England in a democratic and inclusive manner. This transformation would be based on a rediscovery of the country's radical tradition. It is the English, argued Robert Colls, who now need to redefine themselves. The inspiration would come from outside, from the example of the other nations of the Union (1998, p. 121).

One version of the *New Statesman* complex can be found in an essay by Richard Weight (1999, pp. 25–7). He discovered intimations of radical change in the course of the football World Cup in 1998. The most dramatic was the substitution of the flag of St. George for the Union Jack amongst England supporters. The patriotism symbolised by the cross of St. George was more inclusive because it 'lacks the historical baggage of the Union Jack and more clearly offers a right to belong to this country'. That is questionable. If, as Weight argues, Britishness is increasingly a foreign idea to most English people, then it is not necessarily good news for those who are not English of 'native stock' (Marr 2000, pp. 156–62). Equally, in drawing out the nationalist import of football partisanship, Weight would have done well to recall Jim Sillars' famous criticism of 'ninety-minute patriots'. In reappropriating the football supporter as a symbol of robust English nationalism, Weight inserted himself into an older tradition of patriotism. If Heffer's virtues are those of John Bull, Weight's are those of Ally Sloper F. O. M. and M. F. K. O. M. I. E. (Friend of Man and, appropriately enough for English football fans, the Most Frequently Kicked Out Man In Europe). Sloper's cartoon character had all the rumbustious irreverence associated with modern football culture (Mellini and Matthews 1987, p. 23). For Weight, a more decent sort of Sloperism, chauvinistic in football (especially against Scotland) but inclusive in its patriotism (there *will* be black in the flag of St. George) is the harbinger of an independent England. This England will not be the England of morris dancing. Nor will it be the England of racist skinheads. It will be a new popular England shorn of the Old Establishment. The solution to England's sense of dislocation and the solution to the democratic deficit in English political culture are the same: independence as a nation-state.

Like Heffer, Weight wants the English to take the initiative in dismantling Britain. Like Heffer, he is critical of the idea of regional assemblies. 'You cannot,' he argues logically, 'turn a nation into a collection of regions until you have first allowed it to become a nation again.' However, unlike Heffer, Weight wants independence within Europe to be the foundation of a modern England, where the Left would be the 'party of patriotism'. This might be the cure for what Peter Taylor termed England's 'post-hegemonic trauma' (1991, p. 154). Weight assumes, like Scottish and Welsh nationalists, that generational changes make English independence inevitable. His embrace of the vigour of nationalism implies that all attempts, like New Labour's, to patch up the British state are contemptible and ultimately decadent. It is a view he shares with Tom Nairn. The fertile principles of politics must breed separatism. Weight thinks he knows of a better England and in abandoning Britishness the English will come to know it too.

Another example of the *New Statesman* complex may be found in a number of articles by Billy Bragg. Bragg was rightly irritated by that element of the same complex which denigrated everything to do with Englishness (1995, p. 14). He thought that this attitude was not only misconceived but also politically counter-productive. Distancing the Left from Englishness merely conceded patriotism to the Right. It avoided thinking clearly about what was valuable in the English political tradition. Moreover, it precluded an intelligent engagement with the English question in post-devolution Britain. Rather than a healthy nationalism of the sort which Bragg assumes is the norm in Scotland, Wales and Ireland, England was stuck with 'the old sweaty sock of imperialism'. Like Weight, his real concern is with the politics of identity, the forging of an Englishness which reconciles the patriotism of the majority with the values of democracy and equality. Bragg too was impressed by his experiences of football, this time during Euro '96 in England. And again the cross of St. George appeared to be the harbinger of progressive change. It signalled the moment (again) to throw off 'the security blanket' of Britishness, to define the sort of England people wanted to live in and to make 'English an inclusive identity rather than an exclusive nationality' (1996, p. 15): a fine phrase. But is not Englishness under that blanket a much more inclusive identity (as Hobsbawm detected) than either Welshness or Scottishness?

Bragg's is a generous ideal, part of a long tradition of English radicalism. His patriotic rhetoric of solidarity is reminiscent of the best in that tradition, a tradition which worked for popular control of national destiny (Cunningham 1981, p. 9). And he is right to suggest that fighting for a nation's past is as important as transforming its present (Bragg 1997, p. 46). However, it is far from clear that the option of English nationalism is the proper route to take. Nor is it at all clear that that is the route Bragg wants to take. Security blankets also have their uses. To be impressed by the football fans in 1996 may again confuse ninety-minute patriotism with the political responsibilities of the real thing. In the rush not to be left behind in staking one's claim to patriotic territory one can confuse expressions of nationality with nationalism. If it is possible to redefine Englishness in a radical way, if identity and culture are malleable to political purposes, is it not also possible to redefine Englishness within Britishness? Some would say no and that the reason is Europe.

Stephen Haseler, for instance, has argued that Conservative Englishness has been too strongly secured in the old British state to be changed from within. Only the end of Britain will radicalise the English and liberate them from the thrall of Britishness. What will bring this about is not domestic endeavour but the European project (1996, pp. viii–ix). Haseler predicted that consciousness of being English, by which he meant a sense of superiority, will lose its hold on the popular imagination. Unlike Weight or Bragg, he favoured regionalism on the basis that regions are where the real and plural identities of England are to be found. As the structures of the British state melt in the heat of the European project, 'then the constrictions imposed by the straitjacket of UKanian nationality' will dissolve. Nairn's influence is apparent yet again. An Englishness that was once translated into Britishness is now translated into Europeanness. Germany is calling, not with threats of invasion but with a model of political association. Salvation must come from outside for the English are incapable of saving themselves. That would be a curious fate and it helps to explain the unpopularity of Haseler's sort of republicanism.

Weight, Bragg and Haseler give voice to a mood of identity-sickness. It is a sense of the nauseous quality of things as they are in England. That mood is best captured by the Russian word *skushno*. In *Memoirs of an Anti-Semite*, Gregor von Rezzori admitted that *skushno* was a difficult word to translate but suggested: 'a spiritual void that sucks you in like a vague but intensely urgent longing'. One finds in these radical critiques an intensity and an urgency, a longing to make clean lines, a longing for a grand political purpose. They claim that Englishness is a spiritual void and it is that void which their proposals are designed to fill. The sense of living amidst the ruins of traditional Britishness has made the critique all the more urgent. The fear is the fear of becoming historically superfluous, of being left behind, and in Haseler's case, of failing the test of European destiny. There is an interesting note here and it is the rising note of an English *Weltschmerz*.

THE GENTEEL TRADITION OF ENGLISHNESS

It is this note of *Weltschmerz* which the English genteel tradition has always refused to indulge. It presents itself as an alternative to both the Froude and *New Statesman* complexes. As Ernest Barker emphasised, *Weltschmerz* is not the English way (1947, p. 558). For Barker, that way was pragmatic adjustment to changing circumstances. The code of its politics was one of 'changing and moving with the times, and actively helping the times to change and move' (1945, p. 19). This was the compromise between precedent and progress which he thought characteristic of the history of England. This sort of benign adaptability would always regulate its relationships with the other nations of Britain (1928, p. 157). The English may not be very good at theory like the French, but they were generally good in practical matters. Their vice is the vice of piecemeal solutions. Their temper is what could be called one of 'wait and see' (1950, p. 7). There was, Barker believed, self-confidence in the wisdom of that approach which tended to make the English rather self-righteous. That self-righteousness has been being knocked out of them. The English nationalism which he thought was never reflective because it was so self-evident, so bound up as it was with Britishness, is obviously no longer so. Even faith in the practical abilities of the English has significantly diminished. Nevertheless, the lineage of the genteel tradition which Barker personified persists. For those who share Heffer's point of view, its persistence reveals an incorrigible disposition towards appeasement. For those who think like Haseler, its lack of imagination is crippling. For those who share neither of those positions, it reveals a worldly wisdom which, like Hobbesian logic, always seeks internal peace. In the newly devolved Britain, Barker's principle of neighbourliness – that quiet virtue which helps to regulate the popular passions and make of them a 'nation of the spirit' – may remain as the guiding light for England in its new relationships with Scotland, Wales and Northern Ireland (1919, pp. 144–5).

The tolerant quality of the genteel tradition when addressing the question of nationalism is best shown in the recent work of Bernard Crick. He diagnosed the reluctance of English intellectuals to embrace nationalism not only because of its potential subversion of Britishness, but also because of a folk memory of what happens when beliefs are taken 'too seriously' or are 'out of proportion' (1989, p. 33). Proportion had been assured by the old informal constitution which had cooled the passions of national identity amongst the peoples of Britain. However, Crick now thought that the old conventions had outlived their usefulness. It was time to formalise relationships within Britain for that is what devolution required. There remains much that is positive in the English political tradition, it just happens to be cramped by the dead wood of nostalgia. It was appropriate for English people to develop 'a self-confident and explicit national feeling' (1991, pp. 103–4). Crick's benign view of the expression of such nationalism – Scottish, Welsh or English – meant that he thought it would not threaten the stability of the United Kingdom.

The English variant needed to recall a tradition of citizenship that would take new pride in the differences between national and ethnic communities. In opposition to Hobsbawm, he thought the Left ought to abandon the 'mistaken zeal for their diminishment' (1995a, p. 180). The legislation establishing devolution would invite the English to think again about the character of Britain and celebrate 'a proud partnership of nations'. It could be thought of no longer as an extended English state. Celebrating national differences within a revised solidarity 'is true unionism; true nationalism, even' (1995b, p. 249). It is this sort of calm and self-conscious moderation, this level-headedness, this sang-froid (some might say, insouciance) about the prospects of constitutional change which is quintessentially liberal and, in an obvious way, so very English. It is the ballast of all that is best in liberal Englishness, which means that it is also what Conservatives take to be all that is worst in English liberalism – platitudinous, vague and politically unsound. However one judges it, it is a vital part of the inheritance of New Labour.

ENGLISH QUESTIONS

Englishness has been pervasive but not intrusive. Like the medieval ideal of self-government at the King's command, English identity was at once regionally proud and institutionally focused. G.M. Young wrote shortly after the Second World War, 'we may not have a demand for Home Rule in Northumbria or the East Midlands. We may very likely hear a claim for Regional Rights' in which the powers of the sovereign parliament would be delimited and possibly regional assemblies established. The result would be an infusion of a form of federalism into the constitution. He believed that the ancient powers of the counties and boroughs provided the scope for regional concentration, a concentration which would encourage a particular patriotism nesting within the larger security of Englishness. However, he was also conscious of the impact which the two world wars had had on the scope of modern government. To the tradition of local government had been added the administrative rationalism of central government because that was what the programme of social democratic equity required (1947, p. 111).

   The difficulty with English regionalism, in short, has been its intermediate and indeterminate position between the tradition of local government and the tradition of administrative rationalism. Local government has seen it as a threat and an unnecessary layer of interference between itself and Westminster. The idea that assemblies are required to democratise bureaucratic tiers of government at the regional level was once described by Brian Smith as sheer sophistry and politically misconceived (1977, p. 20). Devolution is either a way of catering for nationalism, in which case the answer is an English parliament; or it is about administrative efficiency, in which case regions may or may not be the best solution. If the latter, then Scotland and Wales would need to be regionalised as well. This was logical. As Smith himself acknowledged, it might not always be political. Regionalism might at some time be a convenient compromise for a government seeking to cater for nationalism in Scotland and Wales but without destabilising the United Kingdom. This is precisely the objective of New Labour's constitutional project.

The problem in these devolutionary times is that on the one hand, for all the recent concern about an identity crisis, England's sense of nationhood remains deeply ingrained. On the other hand, local allegiance is also deeply ingrained but in a manner which rarely means identification with a region – however it may be defined. Despite the claims in the 1980s that England in particular, as well as Britain as a whole, was a nation dividing; despite the historical and cultural evidence of a north-south divide; and despite hostility to the prevailing power of the Home Counties shown by other parts of the country, there is little evidence that any of this has had a significant impact on English political consciousness (Johnston and Pattie 1989). Peter Taylor's pioneering work in this field may have overestimated the degree of English 'regional' alienation (1993, p. 152). The problem for New Labour has been that of mobilising the support *of* the English for the prospect of regionalism *in* England. This is at least one case in which Freedland's rule of thumb does not apply. A simple top-down model of power would impose – as it did in France – a new regional structure upon the country. Since New Labour has made popular support a condition of moving to elected regional government – as it did in Northern Ireland, Scotland and Wales – then the obstacle is formidable. There is little popular demand for regional government, which is not to say that there is nothing distinctive about provincial England. There is no clear answer yet to the question whether the English want regional government. New Labour does not seem to believe they do (McQuail and Donnelly 1999, p. 281). Equally, this is not to say that there is no political interest in English regionalism. Nor is it to say that some of those who are interested do not feel the urgency of the matter of 'missing England'. Nor is it to argue that the intensity of frustration which has attended its advocacy is not sincerely felt (Mawson 1998, pp. 158–75).

John Tomaney, for instance, thought that New Labour's cautious approach to the question of England lacked coherence because it also lacked vision. He left open the possibility that the leadership was less than convinced of its merits (1999, p. 78). There could be no flowering of English provincial life, he felt, without the development of strong regional political cultures. Indeed, there was a very obvious Catch-22 in the government's proposals. It is hoped that an indirectly elected regional chamber composed of members of the relevant local government areas will foster the requisite local legitimacy to move on to the next stage of a directly elected regional assembly. To build that legitimacy a regional chamber requires to have significant responsibility and to exercise some authority. Yet in order to acquire responsibility and authority it needs to show that it has legitimacy. Catch-22. Tomaney thought that New Labour's approach was a recipe for inaction. There was some justification for his irritation since the signals coming from government have been mixed. This degree of confusion was dangerous as well as inconsistent because it might encourage a sense of grievance, especially in northern England, at the political benefits manifest in Scottish devolution. The outcome would likely be pressure for a separate English parliament at Westminster, giving advantage yet again to the southeast and to the Conservatives. Though the English reaction to devolution so far has been one of genteel indifference there were 'already enough ingredients available to brew constitutional destabilisation in the event of a change in the wider political conditions' (Tomaney 1999, p. 82). That sort of vague threat about a future crisis hardly counters the very real difficulties the New Labour government faces in the present. The English public may be unconvinced of the merits of regionalism not because of political apathy alone but because of a genuine concern about equality of public provision. For people in the poorer areas of the country, the possibilities of regional political initiatives in designated areas of competence may seem a poor exchange for national equity (Travers 1998, pp. xii–xiii).

In office, New Labour has already legislated for eight new Regional Development Agencies (RDAs), the 13 members of which are appointed by central government. Regional chambers have been established in each of the RDA areas but they are, as some commentators claim, 'simply a sounding board' (Hazell et al. 2000,

p. 251). The example of Scotland, Wales and Northern Ireland as well as pressure from Europe could stimulate regional consciousness and invigorate the political lobby for change, especially within the Labour Party at Westminster. Others believe that the proper example is no longer the sort of regionalism which informed the Minority Report of the Royal Commission on the Constitution a quarter of a century ago. Rather, the way forward is the option of directly elected mayors in England's large conurbations, an option less constitutionally disruptive and less threatening to either local government or to local identity. London, with its new mayor and elected assembly, may have set an example (Hawthorn 2000, pp. 28–30; see also Taylor 1997b).

The English question does need to be addressed – calmly and without hysteria or visionary excess. In a political culture which finds it bad form to confuse formal logic with politics or to substitute rationalism for what is convenient, the likelihood is that piecemeal change, as Barker identified it, will suffice unless the inconvenience of the situation becomes politically unsustainable. And there seems to be little evidence at the moment that the people of England do find the arrangements of New Labour's New Britain all that inconvenient. But one needs to add in the question of Europe. Hysteria and visionary excess have been the qualities recently associated with the politics of the European Union. The question of Europe has been the ghost haunting much of recent commentary on the question of Britain. That is the subject of the concluding chapter.

9 A European Conclusion?

In 1974 Lord Denning reasoned that the Treaty of Accession to the European Community was like an incoming tide: 'It flows into the estuaries and up the rivers. It cannot be held back' (cited in Mount 1993, p. 219). This inexorable course implied a neat historical irony. The notion of the Continent being isolated because of fog in the English Channel, with all its evocation of Britain's splendid isolation, was no longer imaginable. The waters of the Channel were now not a barrier to European influences but a current for them. What will be the ultimate effect of this European tide is still unclear. The debate, though, is marked by two polemically polar responses. There are those who welcome the integration of Britain into a dynamic European Union and are sincere in their convictions that the process is not only historically inevitable but also politically desirable. There are those whose hostility to that process remains undiminished and are sincere in their conviction that the process is both misconceived and politically undesirable. Both exaggerate and dramatise through the medium of Europe the issues which have defined the question of Britain itself: identity, sovereignty, self-government and legitimacy. Which pole one tends towards is not determined by any simple question of patriotism. What the former take to be a necessary enterprise to invest the country with new purpose and optimism, the latter take to be a threat to Britain's tradition of self-government. What the former take to be a narrative of opportunity and destiny, the latter take to be a narrative of defeatism and betrayal. In their very different ways both sides are serious about patriotism and each tend to see the other as scoundrels. How might these positions be understood?

IDENTITY

There is some truth in Kenneth Minogue's view that the attraction of European Union is a utopian one. Its appeal will remain 'for just so long as it remains incomplete; it has all the charm of potentiality' (1992, p. 27). Britishness, by contrast, appears to have exhausted its potential and its traditional expression is something of an embarrassment. This is the stuff of which mythologies are made. Indeed, it has been suggested that the main European myth today *is* the myth of European unity. The only problem is that there is no firm agreement on what constitutes that myth or even that unity (Puntscher Riekmann 1997, p. 60). However, there does exist a European narrative, and like most good stories it has its heroine and its villains. The heroine is 'Europa', though the boundaries of that motherland remain ill-defined. The villains are those conflicting national offspring whose violent struggles to seek mastery of her are now exhausted. The reconstruction of Europe has involved the spiritual revival of her peoples by way of ever closer union, a union which has finally suppressed the old instincts for national self-assertion and collective self-destruction (Keens-Soper 1989, p. 696). Unfortunately, there might be catch. Is the price for transcending fratricidal nationalism the creation of a European nationalism and a European super-state? (1989, pp. 700–1). Such an objective would be denied by supporters of the European Union. Nevertheless, the project itself is sufficiently ambiguous to make that outcome a credible one. The ambiguity opens it up to differing representations and misrepresentations.

This is to replay in a European Union context one of the questions raised about the British Union: whether a common identity is the prerequisite for a stable Union or whether the institutions of the European Union can engender a sufficient and sustainable sense of identity. Roger Eatwell thought that too little attention until now had been given to the construction of a common European identity. The present Union was run by technocrats who were ignorant of the importance of myth-making and by deal-making politicians who lacked visionary zeal (1997, p. 263). A rather different perspective is provided by Albert Weale. His emphasis is on the creative role of institutions. It would be around the institutional construction of democratic practices that a popular European identity would grow. Europe was less likely to be modelled on the nation-state. Rather, the nation-state could be profitably transformed into the model of the European Union. Weale's exposition revealed continuities with the genteel tradition of Ernest Barker. Like Barker, he thought that neighbourliness would be strengthened and enriched by seeing one's own locality as a part of a culturally diverse Europe. The stresses and strains of this mental adjustment might, he thought, be easier in Britain than elsewhere because of its experience of historic multinationality (Weale 1995, pp. 223–4). Despite all that has been written of the traditionalism and backwardness of Ukania, British political culture might actually lend itself to this task. It is something of which Conservative Eurosceptics have been all too aware and all too afraid (Bulpitt 1992, p. 274).

Some go so far as to argue that British history must be rewritten to foster the appropriate European identity and the British taught to see continental European history as their own (Haseler 1996, p. 185). 'When was Britain?' here intersects with 'What is Europe?' Haseler's sort of history is one which J.G.A. Pocock argued the British had always sought to avoid – at least in the colonising spirit in which Haseler defines it. The course of modern British history was a narrative which evaded being part of the continental story of 'Revolution and Counter-Revolution' (see Chapters 1 and 2). Revolution and Counter-Revolution was Franco-German history. But so too is the European Union a project of Franco-German history. Because the British experience had been outside that history a Haseler-style European vocation would require it to cease being 'British' history at all. What such a European history actually entailed was the subjugation of historic Britishness in the interests of the global market (Pocock 1999b, p. 136).

Critics fear that Pocock's judgement represents what is going on and also captures the defeatism of Britain's governing elites. Conservative Eurosceptics think that such an eventuality would represent the moment at which the British gave up on themselves (Steyn 2000, p. 21). Old Labour stalwarts like Peter Shore and Tony Benn also share that view. Austin Mitchell, for instance, thought that European Union meant the end of British nationhood: 'Nations can fail. They can abdicate and give up. They can be confused and divided. None before Britain has ever opted for all three at once' (1992, p. 141). Are these gross exaggerations? Probably, but then pro-Europeans are as much to blame as Eurosceptics. Their hectoring certainties and their prophecies of doom if Britain does not shape up to European requirements are as apocalyptically insistent as the apocalyptic arguments of their opponents.

SOVEREIGNTY

The historical importance of parliamentary sovereignty for the political purposes of the Conservative and Labour Parties was noted in Chapters 4 and 5. Of all the terms of traditional British usage, sovereignty has been the most contested in the debate about relations with Europe. The question of sovereignty is really a surrogate for a wider debate about the integrity of Britishness. This debate did not begin with Edward Heath's White Paper on accession in 1971 but it may be taken as a convenient starting point for reflection. That White Paper stated that there 'is no question of any erosion of essential national sovereignty'. What was involved was a pooling of sovereignty defined as 'a sharing and an enlargement of individual national sovereignties in the general interest'. However, this statement was profoundly ambivalent and contained a dichotomy which remains unresolved in British politics.

Pro-Europeans focus on the sharing of sovereignty. Anti-Europeans insist on the preservation of essential national sovereignty (Duff 1998, p. 36). This is a peculiar European version of the Candido question. Are these two truths which must coexist, as successive British governments have asserted? Or is it all one big lie, as anti-Europeans, especially leader writers on the *Daily Telegraph*, have consistently claimed? Can one ever define precisely when the boundary between pooling sovereignty and essential national sovereignty has been crossed? It was this very 'paradox of Europe' which was the subject of an address to The Bruges Group by the proprietor of the *Daily Telegraph*, Conrad Black. For Black, one of the most popular human impulses is to have your cake and eat it. He thought that this was the real political divide in contemporary Britain. Pro-Europeans were optimistic Don Antonios who believed you could have your cake and eat it. Sceptics thought that was one big lie (1992, p. 54). The prevailing problem was one of setting limits to European integration which would protect the constitutional integrity and rights of the British people from the European legislative tide. Was it ever possible, however, to conceive of such limits in an open-ended enterprise like European integration? That remains the question which Conservative Eurosceptics have themselves failed to answer convincingly (Buller 2000, p. 327).

From an opposite perspective Vernon Bogdanor has argued that the British problem with Europe is a party problem. There had been an historic failure to take constitutional arrangements seriously. The traditional British concept of sovereignty, he argued, was a myth, and strict adherence to it constituted 'a loss of constitutional and political imagination' (1988, p. 98). However, if constitutional arrangements are taken seriously, might that imply the need for greater barriers against the loss of essential sovereignty? Or would it involve acknowledging the rationality of sharing national sovereignty in the general European interest? Bogdanor advanced the latter course, but there is no good reason why one should not advance the former, as William Hague has done. For others, the resistant fact of British politics could be best surmounted by the 'innovative jurisprudence' of the European Court. Ian Loveland provided an interesting reinterpretation of the Glorious Revolution of 1688, bringing history into line with the requirements of a European vocation. He argued that the purpose of 1688 had been to create a consensual parliament to identify the national interest. Unfortunately, in the twentieth century the legislature had become an arena of conflict in which party interests dominated. Greater court activism to assert the consensual value of European law would not challenge parliamentary sovereignty but restore it to the original purpose (1996, p. 535; see also Harlow 2000).

None of this has persuaded those sceptics who continue to think that national sovereignty is far from being outmoded. In a logical exploration of the issue, Noel Malcolm decoded the 'myth of sovereignty' argument to imply that because interdependence means that no country can be absolutely powerful, sovereignty is obsolete (1996, p. 343). He thought this was nonsensical. It is a proposition which does not deter nationalist politicians in Scotland or Wales from seeking some of that obsolete sovereignty for themselves. They do so because sovereignty *is* still important (Chapter 3). Sovereignty, however compromised by interdependence (and it is always compromised by interdependence), is a government's claim to authority whether it be a British government or a separate Scottish government. Malcolm argued that the word 'power' has been confused with the concept of 'sovereign authority'. They are not the same and the neatest way of conveying the meaning of sovereignty is 'constitutional independence' (1996, p. 353). It is a universal definition which serves to distinguish a relatively autonomous region within a state from the sovereign state itself. The great fallacy of pro-European enthusiasts is their assertion that Britain has a unique problem with sovereignty because of its parliamentary traditions. For Malcolm, this was a worthless argument for the problem is the same in every case. Countries differ in how they are constituted, but this has nothing to do with the question of sovereignty (1996, pp. 357–8). In short, the idea of pooling sovereignty is a big lie.

Malcolm's was a subtle and valuable exercise in clarification but its distinction between authority and power might have been too sharp. One contrary judgement was that sovereignty was both a reality *and* a myth. Elie Lauterpacht proposed that within Europe the British state 'remains a sovereign state in international law and continues to be able to guide its future destiny within the limits that it has itself accepted' (1997 p. 149). Self-limitation is an act of sovereign authority. That, of course, is a judgement which Black and Malcolm would take to be a perfect illustration of pro-Europeans trying to have their cake and eat it.

It is a judgement, however, which corresponds well with Alan Milward's historically insightful work on European integration. Milward's story of integration has challenged both the hopes of federalism and the fears of nationalism. Defenders of national sovereignty, he thought, easily misrepresent the process of integration and confuse it with the story of the end of the state. The truth was rather different. Surrenders of sovereignty to 'Europe' have been so designed to leave almost all political power with the nation-state (Milward 2000, p. 435). States will make further surrenders of sovereignty only if they are compelled to in order to survive. It is not the abstract ideal of unity which is the strength of the European enterprise. It is, rather, the uncertainty of the nation-state's future in its quest to protect itself and to satisfy the demands of its citizens. The British case has one distinction. Whether the *British* state is the appropriate arrangement for articulating those interests and securing the necessary popular legitimacy, rather than a separate *Scottish* state or even *Welsh* state, is now open to question.

LEGITIMACY AND SELF-GOVERNMENT

This was the question William Wallace thought was now at the heart of British politics. After the end of the Cold War it was debatable, he thought, whether the British state could still maintain a coherent concept of the national interest or even whether a distinctively British response could be found at all on major European issues (1992, pp. 425–6). The British state is much less solid in its conception of itself and therefore less clear about what essential national sovereignty actually is. Interdependence and European institution-building have helped to transform the key relationship of the British Union, the relationship between Scotland and England.

The British Union for the Scots 'has become a question of weighing advantages and disadvantages rather than an essential condition of Scotland's future security and prosperity'. In the terms of Chapter 2, the contractual nature of the relationship between Scotland and England is clearer today than the traditional narrative of collective solidarity. Scottish independence would diminish the political and economic status of what remained of Britain and would also diminish its international standing. The idea of a Europe of the Regions, or in the case of both Scotland and Wales, a Europe of the Nations, has been adopted by nationalists as a way of subverting what remains of the solidarity of Britishness.

The benign model of post-Cold War politics which both the SNP and Plaid Cymru propose is one in which a tolerant European cosmopolitanism complements a resurgent civic nationalism (Chapters 6 and 7). Those attracted to the vision claim that the British state is too small to manage the challenges of modern interdependence and too large to cope effectively with the differing requirements of its constituent regions and nations. The former demands the transfer of authority and competence upwards to the European Union; the latter demands the transfer of power downwards to the regions and the nations. This is a charter not only for greater European unity but also for the rights of small nations. That formulation coincides with one influential view of European unity in which cultural nationhood, rather than statehood, complements a cosmopolitan political identity. It should be familiar to students of British politics because it is reminiscent of Ernest Barker's distinction between nationalisms of the first and second degree. It is for these reasons that the legitimacy of the British state has been called into question by European Union.

The solidarity of the British multinational state was based on military security, economic management and the provision of universal welfare. The national integrity of those services have been attenuated but they remain vital. Whether Scotland and Wales need the British state to secure their interests when bargaining at the European level has become a live issue. Those in favour of independence need to convince their own populations that the balance of advantage lies in undoing the solidarity of the Union in return for a larger but looser European contract (Wallace 1999, pp. 520–1). It is a risk and requires an optimistic view of the potential for European solidarity. Scottish and Welsh nationalists have shown imagination in localising Europe as a lever for greater autonomy. In both cases, the political challenge is to make independence or self-government within Europe appear something more than mere opportunism. Until quite recently opposition to European integration defined both parties. This was not unusual. The Labour Party until quite recently was also officially hostile and the European enthusiasm of the labour movement, like much else in contemporary British politics, had a lot to do with anti-Thatcherism. Ideologically, Plaid Cymru's modest and ambiguous regionalist vision may be more easily accommodated than the SNP's Europeanised version of independence (Lynch 1996). Scottish nationalism often appears in danger of desiring the end of the British connection in order to become a nation of the second degree, a state, only to become once again a nation of the first degree, a socio-cultural community within a united Europe. Or at least that is how the opponents of the SNP can present it.

As the devolved institutions develop their own identity so the potential for fractures in the perspectives of Edinburgh, Cardiff, Belfast and London become possible. Keith Robbins speculated that a future referendum on membership of the single European currency might be the occasion for an irreconcilable divergence. It could prove to be the case that a majority of the British constitutional people vote to retain the pound but that this majority is composed of English and Northern Irish (Unionist) voters. The majority of the Scots and possibly the Welsh national peoples might vote for the Euro. 'Were this situation to arise,' asked Robbins, 'how would foreign policy in a devolved Britain then be shaped? Could it be claimed, one way or another, that it was *British*?' (1998, p. 117).

It is the opposite worry which concerns English Eurosceptics. Jim Bulpitt, a member of the Bruges Group and, as he put it, 'a founder member of the English "Sod Off" school of Anglo-Scottish relations', was convinced that if the Europeanisation of British politics was to be avoided, especially a fateful commitment to economic and monetary union swung by Scottish votes, then Scotland had to be ditched from the Union (1992, pp. 271–2). There does exist a potential constituency for such a view. Bulpitt's anti-Europeanism, like Simon Heffer's, may be equated with a revived English nationalism.

The problem of legitimacy is not confined to Britishness. European integration creates its own problem. If much of the substance of state sovereignty has fallen away, national solidarity and the focus it provides for political accountability remains. There is an insufficient sense of European solidarity to make the breaking of British solidarity attractive to a critical mass of its citizens.

Whether that is ever possible remains to be seen. The making of Europe, as supporters as well as critics have agreed, has been an elite or top-down rather than a popular process. It, rather than Britain, is a good example of Jonathan Freedland's model (see Chapter 3). The idea of Europe has relied as much on a sense of inevitability as it has on public support. That contemporary nationalism in Scotland and Wales shares with European enthusiasts a faith in historical inevitability is one of those compatibilities of circumstance. And even if it were politically possible for the regions and nations to substitute a new contract with Europe for solidarity within Britain the evidence is far from clear that it would be economically desirable. Recent studies have shown how regional convergence within the European Union has been at a standstill for 20 years. Disparities have shown little inclination to erode (Armstrong 1998, p. 205). Differences of opinion about what regionalism actually means in the member states, as another study has argued, 'are enough by themselves to encourage scepticism about the feasibility of a "Europe of the Regions"'; but little evidence was found to sustain the thesis that a new regionalised Europe was emerging (Bomberg and Peterson 1998, p. 219). Solidarity must begin at home and the danger lies in ignoring the fact that it is the nation-state which has the resources and the commitment to affect economic opportunity and social cohesion. If central government were encouraged to think otherwise, the consequences for the regions and nations could be critical.

Of course, it can be said that this is not an argument for the British state but an argument for a democratic strengthening of the institutions of Europe and an argument in favour of a 'solidaristic' Europe. Despite the rational case for such a development the making of the case does not dispose of the problem. It merely displaces it. The question is whether the European Union is capable of enjoying the necessary legitimacy to affect directly and unmediatedly large sections of the population (Tsoukalis and Rhodes 1997, p. 36). Writers such as Malcolm believe it is impossible, though that belief may not ultimately dispel the European charm of potentiality for Scotland and perhaps Wales. If the recent trend in Europe, as John Redwood argued, is the desire of people to live in smaller countries and not mega-states, does that not also have important consequences for Britain? (1997, p. ix). The quest for political legitimacy, the complement of identity and sovereign authority, is unending. The intertwining of a European dimension with domestic matters simply puts that quest in sharp focus. When Andrew Schonfield

(1972) wrote of Britain and Europe, he used the phrase 'journey to an unknown destination'. The same phrase could equally describe recent constitutional changes in Britain. European Union and devolution are now part of the history of British politics, part of the dull routine of governance. They are no longer part of the novel of British politics which lends itself to speculative fantasy. Where the European and devolution journeys will lead is unknown. However, the Britishness of British politics remains solid. It is only speculative fantasy which suggests the inevitable end of British politics.

AFTER BRITAIN?

That has not prevented writers claiming that they do know the destination and claiming to have the proper route map and timetable. The title of Nairn's book, *After Britain* (2000a), implied that the fate of Britishness had already been decided, if not yet at the polls, then at the bar of history. Those who do not accept his premises, of course, find difficulty engaging with the arguments. The reason for this is simple. They can see no arguments, only assertion. *After Britain* is a political novel not political history. We are not yet after Britain. The idea of the national people has not yet displaced that of the constitutional people. The European contract has not yet displaced British solidarity.

Some of the critical literature on the condition of Britain which has been examined in this book often gives a different impression. It might appear that Britain is a country still living on the memory of imperial greatness, still living with the illusion that its political institutions remain the wonder of the world, still believing that its culture is uniquely privileged and that the world still looks to its politicians for leadership. This, critics have concluded, is sheer blindness to the condition of Britain and to the realities of the modern world. They point out that British greatness, along with the family silver, was sold off years ago. Britain is now an empty museum of former glories. It is an *ancien régime*. It has become a theme park of political nostalgia. Even the Millennium Dome, its contemporary project of modernisation, designed to confirm its renewed vigour and creativity, is a metaphor for the vacuity and decadence of modern Britishness. There seems to be a certain ecstasy in this gloom of decline, an ecstatic loathing common to elements on the Right as well as on the Left (Walden 2000).

However, one is tempted to think that these reflections are the flip-side of the fantasy which they attack. Who actually believes in that fantasy of greatness anyway? Jeremy Paxman is correct to raise a quizzical eyebrow at all of this (1998, pp. 264–5). Condemning the illusion of British greatness involves an unspoken pride in the contrary illusion that Britain's problems are somehow uniquely desperate, a sort of self-satisfaction in the thought of this grand decay. Once again Britain is unique, only this time uniquely benighted. Partly, of course, this is astute political calculation, no better exemplified than in the work of Nairn. Whether it be to promote the European Union or to encourage nationalist separatism or both, there is a lot of mileage to be had out of pressing the claim of the end of Britain. The fallacy, of course, is to believe that there was a period of British history which was – exclusively – the best of times and that, by contrast, Britain is now experiencing the worst of times. The truth is that every period is both the best of times and the worst of times, a lesson which should have been learnt from schoolbook Dickens. Confidence in the old narratives of Britishness has waned and the smug certainties of British providentialism have gone. Faith in its venerable institutions, so much a part of the genteel tradition, has crumbled. Pop internationalism, singing the demise of the capacity of multinational government in the face of globalisation, harmonises with pop nationalism, singing of the demise of the solidarity of the multinational state in the face of ethnic self-confidence. Yet it all seems rather overdone (Sally 2000, p. 252; Dearlove 2000, pp. 116–17). The electorate still votes over-whelmingly for parties that support the Union. The economic and social outlook of that electorate still supposes the continued solidarity of political Britishness. If this book does have a message it is that prophecies of doom are, at best, unhelpful. It cannot claim to have dispelled all illusions in the cause of realism. Politics does not lend itself to such neat contrasts. Ideologues always aim to remove ambiguity in the pursuit of certainty. Maybe the only job of the academic is to reinstate a degree of ambiguity, not for the sake of confusion, but for the sake of accuracy.

And so the ambiguous conclusion about Britishness presents itself. The charm of the nationalist alternative cannot be doubted. Nor can one ignore the complementary charm of an ever closer European Union. Yet the loss of British solidarity should not be lightly con-templated. In *After Britain*, Nairn made much of the analogy between Britain and the fall of the Habsburg Empire. Perhaps a Habsburgian reference is appropriate in this case. In his short story *The Bust of the Emperor*, Joseph Roth wrote that Austria-Hungary died not because of the arguments of those who wished to destroy it, but because of the ironic disbelief of those who should have believed in and supported it. Which leads one to conclude that Britain and Britishness will survive so long as people in Scotland, Wales, Northern Ireland, but especially England, continue to believe in it and support it. That is the democratic basis of modern Britain. Belief in Britain may have diminished, but it has not yet disappeared. Constitutional change intimates another chapter in history and not the end of the story.

References

Acton, J.E.E. (Lord) (1909) *The History Of Freedom and Other Essays*. London: Macmillan.

Alavi, H. (1997) 'Socialism: Long Dead, Now Buried', pp. 1901–7, *Economic and Political Weekly*, Vol. 32, No. 30.

Alexander, D. (1999) 'Judge it by its Deeds, not Words', p. 36, *New Statesman Scotland*, 5 July.

Alibhai-Brown, Y. (1998) 'Nations under a Groove', p. 47, *Marxism Today*, December.

—— (2000a) 'Muddled Leaders and the Future of the British National Identity', pp. 26–30, *Political Quarterly*, Vol. 71, No. 1.

—— (2000b) *Who Do We Think We Are?* Harmondsworth: Penguin Books.

Anderson, B. (1983) *Imagined Communities: Reflections on the Origins and Spread of Nationalism*. London: Verso.

Armstrong, H. (1998) 'What Future for Regional Policy in the UK?', pp. 200–14, *Political Quarterly*, Vol. 69, No. 3.

Ascherson, N. (1986) 'Ancient Britons and the Republican Dream', pp. 295–304, *Political Quarterly*, Vol. 57, No. 3.

—— (1999) 'Put Out More Flags', pp. 12–14, *New York Review of Books*, Vol. XLVI, No. 9.

Baker, K. (1998) 'Speaking for England', pp. 14–15, *Spectator*, 1 August.

Baldwin, S. (1926) *On England*. London: Philip Allan.

Balsom, D. (1990) 'Wales', pp. 8–23, in M. Watson (ed.) *Contemporary Minority Nationalism*. London: Routledge.

Balsom, D. and I. McAllister (1979) 'The Scottish and Welsh Devolution Referenda of 1979: Constitutional Change and Popular Choice', pp. 394–407, *Parliamentary Affairs*, Vol. 31, No. 3.

Balsom, D., P. Madgwick and D. Van Mechelen (1984) 'The Political Consequences of Welsh Identity', pp. 160–81, *Ethnic and Racial Studies*, Vol. 7, No. 1.

Barker, E. (1919) 'Nationality', pp. 135–45, *History*, Vol. 4.

—— (1927) *National Character and the Factors in its Formation*. London: Methuen.

—— (1945) *Essays on Government*. Oxford: The Clarendon Press.

—— (1947) *The Character of England*. Oxford: The Clarendon Press.

—— (1950) 'The English Character and Attitude Towards Life', pp. 6–9, *England*, September.

—— (1951a) *The Ideas and Ideals of the British Empire*. Cambridge: Cambridge University Press.

—— (1951b) *Principles of Social and Political Theory*. Oxford: The Clarendon Press.

Barker, R. (1992) 'Legitimacy in the United Kingdom: Scotland and the Poll Tax', pp. 521–33, *British Journal of Political Science*, Vol. 22, No. 4.

——— (1996) 'Political Ideas since 1945, or How Long was the Twentieth Century?', pp. 2–19, *Journal of Contemporary British History*, Vol. 10, No. 1.

Barnes, J. (1998) *Federal Britain. No Longer Unthinkable*. London: Centre for Policy Studies.

Barnett, A. (1997) *This Time: Our Constitutional Revolution*. London: Vintage.

——— (1998) 'All Power to the Citizens', pp. 44–6, *Marxism Today*, Nov./Dec.

——— (1999) 'Please Stop Patronising Us', pp. 25–7, *New Statesman*, 28 June.

——— (2000) 'Corporate Populism and Partyless Democracy', pp. 80–9, *New Left Review* (2nd Series), No. 3.

Barnett, C. (1986) *The Audit of War. The Illusion and Reality of Britain as a Great Nation*. London: Pan Books.

Baucom, I. (1999) *Out of Place: Englishness, Empire, and the Locations of Identity*. Princeton, NJ: Princeton University Press.

Beckett, J.C. (1966) *The Making of Modern Ireland 1603–1923*. London: Faber and Faber.

Bell, I.A. (1995) 'To See Ourselves: Travel Narratives and National Identity in Contemporary Britain', pp. 6–26, in I.A. Bell (ed.) *Peripheral Visions: Images of Nationhood in Contemporary British Fiction*. Cardiff: University of Wales Press.

Beloff, M. (1974) 'Empires and Nations', pp. 411–29, *Government and Opposition*, Vol. 9, No. 4.

——— (1999) 'Empire Reconsidered', pp. 13–26, *The Journal of Imperial and Commonwealth History*, Vol. XXVII, No. 2.

Berrington, H. (1998) 'Britain in the Nineties: The Politics of Paradox', pp. 1–27, *West European Politics*, Vol. 21, No. 1.

Bew, P., P. Gibbon and H. Patterson (1995) *Northern Ireland 1921–1994: Political Forces and Social Classes*. London: Serif.

Bianchi, T. (1995) 'Aztecs in Treodrhiwgwair: Recent fictions in Wales', pp. 44–76, in I. A.Bell (ed.) *Peripheral Visions*. Cardiff: University of Wales Press.

Billig, M. (1995) *Banal Nationalism*. London: Sage.

Black, C. (1992) 'Conservatism and the Paradox of Europe', pp. 54–71, in P. Robertson (ed.) *Reshaping Europe in the Twenty-First Century*. Basingstoke: Macmillan, in association with The Bruges Group.

Blair, T. (1995) *Let Us Face the Future*. London: Fabian Society.

Blake, R. (1985) *The Conservative Party from Peel to Thatcher*. London: Methuen.

Bogdanor, V. (1979) 'The English Constitution and Devolution', pp. 36–49, *Political Quarterly*, Vol. 50, No. 1.

——— (1980) 'Devolution', pp. 50–75, in Z. Layton-Henry (ed), *Conservative Party Politics*. London: Macmillan.

——— (1988) 'Britain and Europe: the Myth of Sovereignty', pp. 81–99, in R. Holme and M. Elliott (eds) *Time for a New Constitution*. Basingstoke: Macmillan.

——— (1996) 'The Monarchy and the Constitution', pp. 407–23, *Parliamentary Affairs*, Vol. 49, No. 3.

——— (1999a) 'Devolution: Decentralisation or Disintegration?', pp. 185–95, *The Political Quarterly*, Vol. 70, No. 2.

—— (1999b) *Devolution in the United Kingdom*. Oxford: Oxford University Press.

Bomberg, E. and Peterson, J. (1998) 'European Union Decision Making: the Role of Sub-national Authorities', pp. 219–35, *Political Studies*, Vol. XLVI, No. 2.

Bonney, N. (1978) 'The Scottish Assembly: A Proving Ground for Parliamentary Reform?', pp. 191–9, *Political Quarterly*, Vol. 49, No. 2.

Bosanquet, B. (1910) *The Philosophical Theory of the State*, 2nd edition. London: Macmillan.

Boutmy, E. (1904) *The English People: A Study of Their Political Psychology*. London: T. Fisher Unwin.

Boyce, D.G. (1975) 'Dicey, Kilbrandon and Devolution', pp. 280–92, *Political Quarterly*, Vol. 46, No. 2.

Bradbury, J. (1997) 'The Blair Government's White Papers on British Devolution: A Review of *Scotland's Parliament* and *A Voice for Wales*', pp. 115–33, *Regional and Federal Studies*, Vol. 7, No. 3.

—— (1998) 'The Devolution Debate in Wales: The Politics of a Developing Union State?', pp. 120–39, *Regional and Federal Studies* Vol. 8, No. 1.

Bradley, J.M. (1997) 'Political, Religious and Cultural Identities: The Undercurrents of Scottish Football', pp. 25–32, *Politics* Vol. 17, No. 1.

Bragg, B. (1995) 'Looking for a New England', p. 14, *New Statesman*, 17 March.

—— (1996) 'I am Looking for a *New* England', pp. 14–15, *New Statesman*, 26 July.

—— (1997) 'Diary', pp. 45–6, *New Statesman*, 13 June.

Brand, J. (1978) *The National Movement in Scotland*. London: Routledge and Kegan Paul.

—— (1979) 'From Scotland with Love', pp. 169–82, in I. Kramnick (ed.) *Is Britain Dying? Perspectives on the Current Crisis*. Ithaca, NY: Cornell University Press.

—— (1987) 'National Consciousness and Voting in Scotland', pp. 334–48, *Ethnic and Racial Studies*, Vol. 10, No. 3.

—— (1990) 'Scotland', pp. 24–37, in M. Watson (ed.) *Contemporary Minority Nationalism*. London: Routledge.

—— (1993) 'Scotland and the Politics of Devolution: A Patchy Past, a Hazy Future', pp. 38–48, *Parliamentary Affairs*, Vol. 46, No. 1.

—— J. Mitchell and P. Surridge (1994) 'Social Constituency and Ideological Profile: Scottish Nationalism in the 1990s', pp. 616–29, *Political Studies*, Vol. XLII.

Brown, A. (1998) 'Asymmetrical Devolution: The Scottish Case', pp. 215–23, *Political Quarterly*, Vol. 69, No. 3.

Brown, A. (2000) 'Designing the Scottish Parliament', pp. 542–56, *Parliamentary Affairs*, Vol. 53, No. 3.

Brown, A., D. McCrone and L. Paterson (1996) *Politics and Society in Scotland*. Basingstoke: Macmillan.

Brown, G. (1997) 'Outward Bound', *Spectator*, 8 November.

—— (2000) 'Why the Party Still Needs its Soul', pp. 21–3, *New Statesman*, 23 February.

Brubaker, R. (1998) 'Myths and Misconceptions in the Study of Nationalism', pp. 272–306, in J.A. Hall (ed.) *The State of the Nation: Ernest Gellner and the Theory of Nationalism*. Cambridge: Cambridge University Press.

Buckler, S. and D.P. Dolowitz (2000) 'New Labour's Ideology: A Reply to Michael Freeden', pp. 102–9, *The Political Quarterly*, Vol. 71, No. 1.

Buller, J. (2000) 'Understanding Contemporary Conservative Euro-scepticism: Statecraft and the Problem of Governing Autonomy', pp. 319–27, *Political Quarterly*, Vol. 71, No. 3.

Bulpitt, J. (1983) *Territory and Power in the United Kingdom. An Interpretation*. Manchester: Manchester University Press.

—— (1991) 'The Conservative Party in Britain: A Preliminary Paradoxical Portrait'. Paper presented to the PSA Annual Conference, Lancaster.

—— (1992) 'Conservative Leaders and the "Euro-Ratchet": Five Doses of Scepticism', pp. 258–75, *Political Quarterly*, Vol. 63, No. 3.

Buruma, I. (1999) *Voltaire's Coconuts or Anglomania in Europe*. London: Weidenfeld and Nicolson.

Butler, D. and D. Stokes (1974) *Political Change in Britain: The Evolution of Electoral Choice*, 2nd edition. London: Macmillan.

Campbell, J. (2000) 'The Appeal of the Dual', p. 31, *Times Literary Supplement*, 21 January.

Canavan, D. (1989) 'Sovereignty of the People', pp. 70–8, in O.D. Edwards (ed.) *A Claim of Right for Scotland*. Edinburgh: Polygon.

Cannadine, D. (1987) 'British History: Past, Present – and Future?', pp. 169–92, *Past and Present*, Vol. 116.

Cannon, J. (1986) 'The Survival Of The British Monarchy', pp. 143–65, *Transactions of the Royal Historical Society* (fifth series), Vol. 36.

Canovan, M. (1990) 'On Being Economical with the Truth: Some Liberal Reflections', pp. 5–19, *Political Studies*, Vol. XXXVIII.

—— (1996) *Nationhood and Political Theory*. Cheltenham: Edward Elgar.

—— (1999) 'Trust the People! Populism and the Two Faces of Democracy', pp. 2–17, *Political Studies*, Vol. XLVII.

Carter, M. (1999) 'Ball, Bosanquet and the Legacy of T.H. Green', pp. 674–94, *History of Political Thought*, Vol. XX, No. 4.

Clark, A. (1999) *The Tories. Conservatives and the Nation State 1922–1997*. London: Phoenix.

Clark, J.C.D. (1990a) 'National Identity, State Formation and Patriotism: The Role of History in the Public Mind', pp. 95–103, *History Workshop*, Vol. 29.

—— (1990b) 'A History of Britain: A Composite State in a Europe des Patries?', pp. 32–49, in J.C.D. Clark (ed.) *Ideas and Politics in Modern Britain*. London: Macmillan.

—— (1997) 'The Strange Death of British History? Reflections on Anglo-American Scholarship', pp. 787–809, *Historical Journal*, Vol. 40.

—— (2000) 'Protestantism, Nationalism, and National Identity, 1660–1832', pp. 249–76, *Historical Journal*, Vol. 43, No. 1.

Cohen, N. (2000) 'I've Seen Revolt, and it will be Welsh', pp. 9–10, *New Statesman*, 7 February.

Colley, L. (1992) *Britons: Forging the Nation 1707–1837*. London: Pimlico.

—— (1999) 'This Country is not so Special', pp. 27–9, *New Statesman and Society*, 3 May.

—— (2000) 'Mongrels Looking for a Kennel', pp. 6–7, *Times Literary Supplement*, 10 March.

Colls, R. (1998) 'The Constitution of the English', pp. 97–128, *History Workshop Journal*, Vol. 46.

Colls, R. and P. Dodd (1986) *Englishness: Politics and Culture 1880–1920*. London: Croom Helm.

Conservative Party (1977) *The Campaign Guide*. London: Conservative Research Department.

Coogan, T.P. (1995) *The Troubles: Ireland's Ordeal 1966–1995 and the Search for Peace*. London: Hutchinson.

Cosgrove, P. (1992) *The Strange Death of Socialist Britain*. London: Constable.

Cowley, J. (1999) 'A Search for Identity in the Shock of the New', pp. 28–9, *New Statesman*, 24 May.

Crick, B. (1968) *The Reform of Parliament*, 2nd edition. London: Weidenfeld and Nicolson.

—— (1988) 'Sovereignty, Centralism and Devolution', pp. 57–81, in R. Holme and M. Elliott (eds) *1688–1988: Time for a New Constitution*. Basingstoke: Macmillan.

—— (1989) 'An Englishman Considers His Passport', pp. 23–34, in N. Evans (ed.) *National Identity in the British Isles*. Cardiff: Centre for Welsh Studies Coleg Harlech.

—— (1990) *Political Thought and Polemics*. Edinburgh: Edinburgh University Press.

—— (1991) 'The English and the British', pp. 90–105, in B. Crick (ed.) *National Identities: The Constitution of the United Kingdom*. Oxford: Blackwell.

—— (1992) 'On Scottish Nationalism', pp. 385–96, *Government and Opposition*, Vol. 23, No. 3.

—— (1995a) 'The Sense of Identity of the Indigenous British', pp. 167–82, in B. Parekh (ed.) *British National Identity in a European Context: New Community* special issue, Vol. 21, No. 2.

—— (1995b) 'Ambushes and Advances: The Scottish Act 1998', pp. 237–49, *Political Quarterly*, Vol. 66, No. 4.

Cross, P.R. (1988) 'British History: Past, Present – and Future? Comment', pp. 171–83, *Past and Present*, Vol. 119.

Crozier, M. (ed.) (1990) *Cultural Traditions in Northern Ireland: Varieties of Britishness*. Belfast: Institute of Irish Studies.

Cunningham, H. (1981) 'The Language of Patriotism, 1750–1914', pp. 8–33, *History Workshop Journal*, Vol. 12, Autumn.

Curtice, J. (1999) 'Is Scotland a Nation and Wales not?', pp. 119–48, in B. Taylor and K. Thomson (eds) *Scotland and Wales: Nations Again?* Cardiff: University of Wales Press.

Dangerfield, D. (1936) *The Strange Death of Liberal England*. London: Constable.

Darwin, J.G. (1986) 'The Fear of Falling: British Politics and Imperial Decline since 1900', pp. 27–43, *Transactions of the Royal Historical Society* (fifth series) Vol. 36.

Davies, N. (1999) *The Isles: A History*. London: Macmillan.

Davies, R. (1995a) 'The Governor General', p. 39, *Parliamentary Brief*, June.

—— (1995b) 'Change Must Serve Wales – Not Rule It', *Western Mail*, 17 January.

Dearlove, J. (2000) 'Globalisation and the Study of British Politics', pp. 111–18, *Politics*, Vol. 20, No. 2.

Denver, D. (1998) 'The British Electorate in the 1990s', pp. 197–217, *West European Politics*, Vol. 21, No. 1.

Devine, T. M. (1999) *The Scottish Nation 1700–2000*. Harmondsworth: Allen Lane.

Dewar, D. (1998) 'Bonding over the Border', pp. 18–19, *Spectator*, 21 November.

—— (1999) 'Forged in the White Heat of Devolution', p. 58, *New Statesman Scotland*, 27 September.

Dicey, A. V. and R.S. Rait (1920) *Thoughts on the Union between England and Scotland*. London: Macmillan.

Drucker, H.M. (1977) 'Devolution and Corporatism', pp. 178–93, *Government and Opposition*, Vol. 12, No. 2.

—— (1979) *Doctrine and Ethos in the Labour Party*. London: George Allen and Unwin.

Duff, A. (1998) 'Britain and Europe: The Different Relationship', pp. 34–46, in M. Westlake (ed.) *The European Union beyond Amsterdam: New Concepts of European Integration*. London: Routledge.

Eatwell, R. (1997) 'Conclusion: Part Two – Reflections on Nationalism and the Future of Europe', pp. 252–69, in R. Eatwell (ed.) *European Political Cultures: Conflict or Convergence?* London: Routledge.

Edwards, O.D. (ed.) (1989) *A Claim of Right for Scotland*. Edinburgh: Polygon.

Elliott, G. (1993) *Labourism and the English Genius: The Strange Death of Labour England?* London: Verso.

Elton, G.R. (1991) *Return to Essentials: Some Reflections on the Present State of Historical Study*. Cambridge: Cambridge University Press.

Evans, G. and D. Trystan (1999) 'Why was 1997 Different?', pp. 95–118, in B. Taylor and K. Thomson (eds) *Scotland and Wales: Nations Again?* Cardiff: University of Wales Press.

Evans, M. (1999) 'The Constitution under New Labour', in G.R. Taylor (ed.) *The Impact of New Labour*. Basingstoke: Macmillan.

Evans, N. (1988) 'British History: Past, Present – and Future? Comment', pp. 194–203, *Past and Present*, Vol. 119.

Featherstone, M., S. Lash and R. Robertson (eds) (1995) *Global Modernities*. London: Sage.

Findlay, R. (1996) 'Scottish Conservatism and Unionism since 1918', pp. 111–27, in M. Francis and I. Zweiniger-Bargielowska (eds) *The Conservatives and British Society, 1880–1990*. Cardiff: University of Wales Press.

Foote, G. (1997) *The Labour Party's Political Thought: A History*, 3rd edition. Basingstoke: Macmillan.

Francis, M. and I. Zweiniger-Bargielowska (eds) (1996) *The Conservatives and British Society, 1880–1990*. Cardiff: University of Wales Press.

Freeden, M. (1999) 'The Ideology of New Labour', pp. 42–52, *Political Quarterly*, Vol. 70, No. 1.

Freedland, J. (1998) *Bringing Home the Revolution: How Britain Can Live the American Dream*. London: Fourth Estate.

Fry, M. (1999) review of D. Seawright's *An Important Matter of Principle: The Decline of the Scottish Conservative and Unionist Party*, pp. 467–9, *Political Quarterly*, Vol. 70, No. 4.

Gamble, A. (1974) *The Conservative Nation*. London: Routledge and Kegan Paul.

—— (1989) *The Free Economy and the Strong State*. London: Macmillan.

Garnett, M. and Lord Gilmour (1996) 'Thatcherism and the Conservative Tradition', pp. 78–95, in M. Francis and I. Zweiniger-Bargielowska (eds) *The Conservatives and British Society, 1880–1990*. Cardiff: University of Wales Press.

Geekie, J. and R. Levy (1989) 'Devolution and the Tartanisation of the Labour Party', pp. 399–412, *Parliamentary Affairs*, Vol. 42, No. 3.

Gellner, E. (1994) *Encounters with Nationalism*. Oxford: Blackwell.

—— (1995) 'Introduction', pp. 1–7, in S. Periwal (ed.) *Notions of Nationalism*. Budapest: Central European University Press.

—— (1998) *Language and Solitude: Wittgenstein, Malinowski and the Habsburg Dilemma*. Cambridge: Cambridge University Press.

Giddens, A. (1994) *Beyond Left and Right: The Future of Radical Politics*. London: Polity Press.

Gilmour, I. (1977) *Inside Right: A Study of Conservatism*. London: Hutchinson.

—— (1993) *Dancing with Dogma. Britain under Thatcherism*. London: Pocket Books.

Gilroy, P. (1990) 'Nation, History and Ethnic Absolutism', pp. 114–120, *History Workshop*. Vol. 30.

Goodall, D. (1993) 'The Irish Question', Headmaster's Lecture given at Ampleforth College, November 1992, pp. 126–35, *Ampleforth Journal*, Vol. XLVII, No. 1.

Goulbourne, H. (1991) *Ethnicity and Nationalism in post-Imperial Britain*. Cambridge: Cambridge University Press.

Gould, P. (1998) *The Unfinished Revolution: How the Modernisers Saved the Labour Party*. London: Little, Brown and Company.

Gove, M. (1999) 'Nothing Wrong with Michael', pp. 14–15, *Spectator*, 18 September.

Grainger, J. H. (1986) *Patriotisms: Britain 1900–1939*. London: Routledge and Kegan Paul.

Gray, J. (1996) *After Social Democracy: Politics, Capitalism and the Common Life*. London: Demos.

—— (1998) 'A Strained Rebirth of Liberal Britain', pp. 28–9, *New Statesman*, 21 August.

Greenfeld, L. (1993) *Nationalism: Five Roads to Modernity*. Cambridge, Mass.: Harvard University Press.

Gwynn, S. (1924) *Ireland*. London: Ernest Benn.

Hague, W. (1999) 'Identity and the British Way'. Text of speech to Centre of Policy Studies, 19 January.

Hailsham, Q. (1978) *The Dilemma of Democracy*. London: Collins.

Hain, P. (1999) 'Meet Blair, the Libertarian Socialist', pp. 25–6, *New Statesman*, 12 March.

Harlow, C. (2000) 'Disposing of Dicey: From Legal Autonomy to Constitutional Discourse?', pp. 356–69, *Political Studies*, Vol. 48.

Harris, J. (1994) 'Political Thought and the State', pp. 15–29, in S.J.D. Green and R.C. Whiting (eds) *The Boundaries of the State in Modern Britain*. Cambridge: Cambridge Univerity Press.

—— (1992) 'Political Thought and the Welfare State 1870–1949: An Intellectual Framework for British Social Policy', pp. 116–41, *Past and Present*, Vol. 135.

Harvie, C. (2000) 'The Moment of British Nationalism, 1939–1970', pp. 328–40, *Political Quarterly*, Vol. 71, no. 3.

Haseler, S. (1990) 'Britain's Ancien Régime', pp. 415–26, *Parliamentary Affairs*, Vol. 43, No. 4.

—— (1996) *The English Tribe: Identity, Nation and Europe*. Basingstoke: Macmillan.

Hassan, G. (1994) 'Parachuting into Berkshire: Inside the Scottish Tories', pp. 13–16, *Cencrastus*, Vol. 47, Spring.

—— (1998) 'Labour Adrift in Tartan Water', pp. 25–6, *New Statesman*, 27 March.

Hastings, A. (1997) *The Construction of Nationhood: Ethnicity, Religion and Nationalism*. Cambridge: Cambridge University Press.

Hawthorn, D (2000) 'Yes, We Have No Greater Authority', pp. 28–30, *London Review of Books*, 13 April.

Hazell, R, M. Russell, B. Seyd and D. Sinclair (2000) 'The British Constitution in 1998–99: The Continuing Revolution', pp. 242–62, *Parliamentary Affairs*, Vol. 53, No. 2.

—— and D. Sinclair (1999) 'The British Constitution in 1997–98: Labour's Constitutional Revolution', pp. 161–78, *Parliamentary Affairs*, Vol. 52, No. 2.

Heath, A. et al. (1999) 'British National Sentiment', pp. 155–77, *British Journal of Political Science*, Vol. 29, No. 1.

—— and B. Taylor (1999) 'Were the Welsh and Scottish Referendums Second-order Elections?', pp. 149–68, in B. Taylor and K. Thomson (eds) *Scotland and Wales: Nations Again?* Cardiff: University of Wales Press.

Heffer, S. (1998) *Like The Roman: The Life of Enoch Powell* London: Phoenix.

—— (1999) *Nor Shall My Sword: The Reinvention of England*. London: Weidenfeld and Nicolson.

Hennessey, T. (1997) *A History of Northern Ireland 1920–1996*. Basingstoke: Macmillan.

Hitchens, P. (1999) *The Abolition of Britain: The British Cultural Revolution from Lady Chatterley to Tony Blair*. London: Quartet Books.

Hobsbawm, E. (1977) 'Some Reflections on "The Break-up of Britain"', pp. 3–24, *New Left Review*, Vol. 105, September/October.

—— (1989) *Politics for a Rational Left: Political Writing 1977–1988*. London: Verso.

—— (1990) *Nations and Nationalism since 1780: Programme, Myth, Reality*. Cambridge: Cambridge University Press.

—— (1991) 'Dangerous Exit from a Stormy World', pp. 16–17, *New Statesman*, 8 November.

—— (1992) 'Ethnicity and Nationalism in Europe Today', pp. 3–8, *Anthropology Today*, Vol. 8, No. 1.

—— (1993) *Nations and Nationalism since 1780: Programme, Myth, Reality*, revised edition. Cambridge: Cambridge University Press.

—— (1995) *Age of Extremes. The Short Twentieth Century 1914–1991*. London: Abacus.

—— (1996) 'Identity Politics and the Left', pp. 38–47, *New Left Review*, Vol. 217, May/June.

Holtham, G. and E. Barrett (1996) 'The Head and the Heart: Devolution and Wales', pp. 72–94, in S. Tindale (ed.) *The State and the Nations: The Politics of Devolution*. London: Institute of Public Policy Research.

Hopkins, A.G. (1999) 'Back to the Future: From National History to Imperial History', pp. 198–244, *Past and Present*, Vol. 164.

Howe, S. (1989) 'Labour Patriotism 1939–83', pp. 127–39, in R. Samuel (ed.) *Patriotism: The Making and Unmaking of British National Identity*. London: Routledge.

Howell, D. (1997) 'The Best and the Worst of Times: Rise of New Labour', pp. 1697–1704, *Economic and Political Weekly*, 12 July.

Ingle, S. (2000) 'The Political Scene in 1999', pp. 275–89, *Parliamentary Affairs*, Vol. 53, No. 2.

Institute for Public Policy Research (1991) *The Constitution of the United Kingdom*. London: Institute for Public Policy Research.

Jacques, M. and F. Mulhern (1981) *The Forward March of Labour Halted?* London: NLB in association with *Marxism Today*.

Jahn, D. and M. Henn (2000) 'The "New" Rhetoric of New Labour in Comparative Perspective: A Three-Country Discourse Analysis', pp. 26–46, *West European Politics*, Vol. 23, No. 1.

James, A. (1999) 'The Practice of Sovereign Statehood in Contemporary International Society', pp. 457–74, *Political Studies*, Vol. XLVII.

Jarvie, G and G. Walker (eds.) (1994) *Scottish Sport in the Making of the Nation. Ninety-Minute Patriots?* London: Leicester University Press.

Johnson, N. (2000) 'Then and Now: the British Constitution', pp. 118–31, *Political Studies*, Vol. 48.

Johnson, R.W. (1985). *Politics of Recession*. London: Macmillan.

Johnston, R.J. and C.J. Pattie (1989) 'A Nation Dividing: Economic Well-Being, Voter Response and the Changing Electoral Geography of Great Britain', pp. 37–57, *Parliamentary Affairs*, Vol. 42, No. 1.

Jones, J.B. (1984) 'Labour Party Doctrine and Devolution: the Welsh Experience', *Ethnic and Racial Studies*, Vol. 7, 1.

—— (1999a) 'Devout Defender of the Union: John Major and Devolution', pp. 126–45, in P. Dorey (ed.) *The Major Premiership: Politics and Policies under John Major, 1990–97*. London: Macmillan.

—— (1999b) 'The First Welsh National Assembly Election', pp. 323–32, *Government and Opposition*, Vol. 34, No. 3.

—— and M. Keating (1982) 'The British Labour Party: Centralisation and Devolution', pp. 177–201, in P. Madgwick and R. Rose (eds) *The Territorial Dimension in United Kingdom Politics*. London: Macmillan.

—— and M. Keating (1985) *Labour and the British State*. Oxford: The Clarendon Press.

Jones, P. (1998) 'Scotland's Next Step', pp. 268–74, in L. Patterson, *A Diverse Assembly: The Debate on a Scottish Parliament*. Edinburgh: Edinburgh University Press.

Joyce, P. (1999) *Realignment of the Left? A History of the Relationship between the Liberal Democrat and Labour Parties*. Basingstoke: Macmillan.

Kane, P. (1999) 'From Braveheart to Cosmo-Scotia', p. 28, *New Statesman*, 19 March.

Kavanagh, D. (1985) 'Whatever Happened to Consensus Politics?', pp. 529–46, *Political Studies*, Vol. XXXIII.

Kearney, H. (1989) *Britain: A History of Four Nations*. Cambridge: Cambridge Univerity Press.

—— (2000) 'The Importance of Being British', pp. 15–26, *Political Quarterly*, Vol. 71, No. 1.

Keating, M. (1996) *Nations against the State: The New Politics of Nationalism in Quebec, Catalonia and Scotland*. Basingstoke: Macmillan.

—— (1998) 'What's Wrong with Asymmetrical Government?', pp. 195–218, *Regional and Federal Studies*, Vol. 8, No. 1.

—— and Jones, B. (1991) 'Scotland and Wales: Peripheral Assertion and European Integration', pp. 311–24, *Parliamentary Affairs*, Vol. 44, No. 3.

Keens-Soper, M. (1989) 'The Liberal State and Nationalism in Post-War Europe', pp. 689–703, *History of European Ideas*, Vol. 10, No. 6.

Kellas, J. G. (1990) 'The Constitutional Options for Scotland', pp. 426–34, *Parliamentary Affairs*, Vol. 43, No. 4.

—— (1991) 'The Scottish and Welsh Offices as Territorial Managers', pp. 87–100, *Regional Politics and Policy*, Vol. 1, No. 1.

—— (1995) 'A Decision Best Made by Trusting the People', *Parliamentary Brief*, February.

Kelly, E. (1999) '"Stands Scotland Where it Did?" An Essay in Ethnicity and Internationalism', pp. 83–99, *Scottish Affairs*, Vol. 26, Winter.

Kennedy, D. (1988) *The Widening Gulf: Northern Attitudes to the Independent Irish State 1919–49*. Belfast: The Blackstaff Press.

Kennedy, S. (1998) 'New Labour and the Reorganization of British Politics', pp. 14–26, *Monthly Review*. Vol. 49, No. 9.

Kent, J. (1998) 'William Temple, the Church of England and British National Identity', pp. 19–35, in R. Weight and A. Beach (eds) *The Right to Belong: Citizenship and National Identity in Britain, 1930–1960*. London: I.B. Taurus.

Kidd, C. (1993) *Subverting Scotland's Past: Scottish Whig Historians and the Creation of an Anglo-British Identity*. Cambridge: Cambridge University Press.

—— (1996) 'North Britishness and the Nature of Eighteenth-century British Patriotisms', pp. 361–83, *Historical Journal*, Vol. 39, No. 2.

Kitson-Clark, G. (1950) *The English Inheritance: An Historical Essay*. London: S.C.M Press.

Kohn, H. (1940) 'The Genesis and Character of English Nationalism', pp. 69–94, *Journal of the History of Ideas*, Vol. 1, No. 1.

Laborde, C. (2000) 'The Concept of the State in British and French Political Thought', pp. 540–57, *Political Studies*, Vol. 48.

Laffin, M. and A. Thomas (2000) 'Designing the National Assembly for Wales', pp. 557–76, *Parliamentary Affairs*, Vol. 53, No. 3.

—— and A. Webb (2000) 'Intergovernmental Relations after Devolution: The National Assembly for Wales', pp. 223–33, *Political Quarterly*, Vol. 71, No. 2.

Lamont, W. (1988) 'British History: Past, Present – and Future? Comment', pp. 183–94, *Past and Present*, Vol. 119.

Laski, H.J. (1939) *The Danger of Being a Gentleman and Other Essays*. London: George Allen and Unwin.

Lauterpacht, E. (1997) 'Sovereignty – Myth or Reality', pp. 137–50, *International Affairs*, Vol. 73, No. 1.

Lawrence, R.J. (1965) *The Government of Northern Ireland*. Oxford: The Clarendon Press.

Leadbeater, C. (1999) *Living on Thin Air: The New Economy*. London: Viking.

Leicester, G. (1999a) 'Scottish and Welsh Devolution', pp. 251–63, in R. Blackburn and R. Plant (eds) *Constitutional Reform: The Labour Government's Constitutional Agenda*. London: Longman.

—— (1999b) 'From Muddle and Mess, a New Politics', pp. 32–4, *New Statesman Scotland*, 6 September.

Leonard, M. (1997) *Britain^TM: Renewing our Identity*. London: Demos.

—— (1998) 'It's Not Just Ice-cream', pp. 15–16, *New Statesman*, 3 July.

Letwin, S. (1992) *The Anatomy of Thatcherism*. London: Fontana.

Levy, R. (1992) 'The Scottish Constitutional Convention, Nationalism and the Union', pp. 222–34, *Government and Opposition*, Vol. 27, No. 2.

Light, A. (1991) *Forever England: Feminity, Literature and Conservatism Between the Wars*. London: Routledge.

Lloyd, J. (1997) 'What's the Story?', pp. 37–8, *New Statesman*, 8 August.

—— (1998) 'The New Tory Federalists', pp. 18–19, *New Statesman*, 20 February.

—— (1999) 'The Tories Should Ditch the Union', p. 31, *New Statesman*, 5 March.

—— (2000) 'A Culture War Rages in Scotland', pp. 11–12, *New Statesman*, 27 March.

Loveland, I. (1996) 'Parliamentary Sovereignty and the European Community: The Unfinished Revolution?', pp. 517–35, *Parliamentary Affairs*, Vol. 49, No. 4.

Lucas, J. (1990) *England and Englishness*. London: The Hogarth Press.

Lynch, P. (1995) 'From Red to Green: The Political Strategy of Plaid Cymru in the 1980s and 1990s', pp. 197–210, *Regional and Federal Studies*, Vol. 5, No. 2.

—— (1996) *Minority Nationalism and European Integration*. Cardiff: University of Wales Press.

—— (1999) *The Politics of Nationhood: Sovereignty, Britishness and Conservative Politics*. London: Macmillan.

—— (2000) 'The Conservative Party and Nationhood', pp. 59–68, *Political Quarterly*, Vol. 71, No. 1.

McAllister, L. (1998) 'The Perils of Community as a Construct for the Political Ideology of Welsh Nationalism', pp. 497–517, *Government and Opposition*, Vol. 33, No. 4.

—— (1999) 'The Road to Cardiff Bay: The Process of Establishing the National Assembly for Wales', pp. 634–48, *Parliamentary Affairs*, Vol. 52, No. 4.

—— (2000a) 'Changing the Landscape? The Wider Political Lessons from Recent Elections in Wales', pp. 211–22, *Political Quarterly*, Vol. 71, No. 2.

—— (2000b) 'The New Politics in Wales: Rhetoric or Reality', pp. 591–604, *Parliamentary Affairs*, Vol. 53, No. 3.

McCormick, J. and W. Alexander (1996) 'Firm Foundations: Securing the Scottish Parliament', pp. 99–166, in S. Tindale (ed.) *The State and the Nations: The Politics of Devolution*. London: Institute of Public Policy Research.

MacCormick, N. (1996) 'Liberalism, Nationalism and the post-Sovereign State', pp. 553–67, *Political Studies*, Vol. XLIV.

McCrone, D. (1984) 'Explaining Nationalism: The Scottish Experience', pp. 129–37, *Ethnic and Racial Studies*, Vol. 7, No. 1.

—— (1992) *Understanding Scotland: The Sociology of a Stateless Nation*. London: Routledge.

—— (1998) *The Sociology of Nationalism: Tomorrow's Ancestors*. London: Routledge.

—— (1999) 'History and National Identity', pp. 97–101, *Scottish Affairs*, Vol. 27, Spring.

McMillan, J. (1996) 'Scotland's Quiet Nationalism', pp. 75–84, in R. Caplan and J. Feffer (eds.) *Europe's New Nationalism: States and Minorities in Conflict*. Oxford: Oxford University Press.

—— (1999) 'Remind Me Who I Am Again...', pp. 30–3, *New Statesman Scotland*, 5 July.

McQuail, P. and K. Donnelly (1999) 'English Regional Government', pp. 264–81, in R. Blackburn and R. Plant (eds) *Constitutional Reform: The Labour Government's Constitutional Reform Agenda*. London: Longman.

Mair, P. (2000) 'Partyless Democracy', pp. 21–37, *New Left Review* (2nd series), Vol. 1, Mar./Apr.

Major, J. (1999) *John Major. The Autobiography*. London: HarperCollins.

—— (2000) 'You Can't Win on the Right, William', pp. 10–11, *Spectator*, 1 January.

Malcolm, N. (1996) 'Sense on Sovereignty', pp. 342–67, in M. Holmes (ed.) *The Eurosceptical Reader*. Basingstoke: Macmillan.

Mandelson, P. and R. Liddle (1996) *The Blair Revolution: Can New Labour Deliver?* London: Faber and Faber.

Mansfield Jr., W.H. (1983) 'The Forms and Formalities of Liberty', pp. 121–31, *The Public Interest*, Vol. 70.

—— (1987) 'Constitutional Government: The Soul of Modern Democracy', pp. 53–64, *The Public Interest*, Vol. 86.

Marquand, D. (1993) 'The Twilight of the British State? Henry Dubb versus Sceptred Awe', pp. 210–21, *Political Quarterly*, Vol. 64, No. 2.

—— (1995) 'After Whig Imperialism: Can There be a New British Identity?', in B. Parekh (ed.) *British National Identity in a European Context, New Community* special issue, Vol. 21, No. 2.

—— (1997) *The New Reckoning: Capitalism, States and Citizens*. London: Polity Press.

—— (2000) 'Democracy in Britain', pp. 268–76, *Political Quarterly*, Vol. 71, No. 3.

Marr, A. (1992) *The Battle for Scotland*. Harmondsworth: Penguin Books.

—— (1998) 'Stuff the Hope and Glory', pp. 25–7, *New Statesman*, 27 November.

—— (2000) *The Day Britain Died*. London: Profile Books.

Marshall, P.J. (1994) 'Imperial Britain', pp. 379–94, *The Journal of Imperial and Commonwealth History*, Vol. 23, No. 3.

Martin, I. (1998) 'Why Alex Salmond Wants to Lose', pp. 17–20, *Spectator*, 5 December.

Mawson, J. (1998) 'English Regionalism and New Labour', pp. 158–75, *Regional and Federal Studies*, Vol. 8, No. 1.

Mellini, P. and R.T. Matthews (1987) 'John Bull's Family Arises', pp. 17–23, *History Today*, May.

Miller, B., J. Brand and M. Jordan (1981) 'Government without a Mandate: Its Causes and Consequences for the Conservative Party in Scotland', pp. 203–13, *Political Quarterly*, Vol. 52, No. 2.

Miller, D. (1995) *On Nationality*. Oxford: The Clarendon Press.

Miller, W.L. (1983) 'The De-nationalisation of British Politics: The Re-emergence of the Periphery', pp. 103–29, *West European Politics*, Vol. 6, No. 4.

—— (1998) 'The Periphery and its Paradoxes', pp. 167–96, *West European Politics*, Vol. 21, No. 1.

—— (1999) 'Modified Rapture All Round: The First Elections to the Scottish Parliament', pp. 299–322, *Government and Opposition*, Vol. 34, No. 3.

Milne, K. (1998) 'New SNP, new Scotland', p. 20, *New Statesman*, 15 May.

—— (1999) 'Scotland: the "Fundies" Keep Quiet', pp. 23–4, *New Statesman*, 19 April.

Milward, A.S. (2000) *The European Rescue of the Nation-State*, 2nd edition. London: Routledge.

Minogue, K. (1992) 'Transcending the European State', pp. 22–34, in P. Robertson (ed.) *Reshaping Europe in the Twenty-First Century*. Basingstoke: Macmillan, in association with The Bruges Group.

Mitchell, A. (1992) 'Nationhood: The End of the Affair', pp. 122–42, *Political Quarterly*, Vol. 63, No. 2.

Mitchell, G.J. (1999) *Making Peace*. New York: Alfred A. Knopf.

Mitchell, J. (1990) *Conservatives and the Union: A Study of Conservative Party Attitudes to Scotland*. Edinburgh: Edinburgh University Press.

—— (1996) 'Conservatives and the Changing Meaning of Union', pp. 30–44, *Regional and Federal Studies*, Vol. 6, No. 1.

—— (1998) 'The Evolution of Devolution: Labour's Home Rule Strategy in Opposition', pp. 479–97, *Government and Opposition*, Vol. 33, No. 4.

—— (1999) 'The Creation of the Scottish Parliament: Journey without End', pp. 649–65, *Parliamentary Affairs*, Vol. 52, No. 4.

—— (2000) 'New Parliament, New Politics in Scotland', pp. 605–21, *Parliamentary Affairs*, Vol. 53, No. 3.

Modood, T. (1992) *Not Easy Being British: Colour, Culture and Citizenship*. Stoke: Trentham Books.

Moffat, A. (1999) 'The Midwife of Devolution', p. 35, *New Statesman*, 18 October.

—— (2000) 'The Importance of Thinking Local', p. 35, *New Statesman Scotland*, 10 January.

Morgan, K.O. (1970) *Wales in British Politics 1868–1922*. Cardiff: The University of Wales Press.

—— (1996) 'Welsh Nationalism', pp. 291–304, in W. R. Louis (ed.) *Adventures with Britannia: Personalities, Politics, and Culture in Britain*. Austin: University of Texas Press.

—— (1999) 'Welsh Devolution: The Past and the Future', pp. 199–220, in B. Taylor and K. Thomson (eds.) *Scotland and Wales: Nations Again?* Cardiff: University of Wales Press.

Morrill, J. and B. Bradshaw (eds.) (1996) *The British Problem, c. 1534–1707; State Formation in the British archipelago*. London: Macmillan.

Mount, F. (1993) *The British Constitution Now*. London: Mandarin.

Nairn, T. (1977) *The Break-Up of Britain: Crisis and Neo-Nationalism*. London: NLB.

—— (1981) *The Break-Up of Britain: Crisis and Neo-Nationalism*, 2nd edition. London: Verso.

—— (1988) *The Enchanted Glass: Britain and its Monarchy*. London: Radius.

—— (1989) 'Britain's Royal Romance', pp. 72–86, in R. Samuel (ed.) *Patriotism: The Making and Unmaking of British National Identity*, vol. 3. London: Routledge.

—— (1997) *Faces of Nationalism: Janus Revisited* London: Verso.

—— (2000a) *After Britain*. London: Granta.

—— (2000b) 'Ukania under Blair', pp. 69–104, *New Left Review* (2nd Series), Vol. 1.

Naughtie, J. (1989) 'Labour 1979–1988', pp. 156–77, in I. Donnachie, C. Harvie and I.S. Wood (eds) *Forward! Labour Politics in Scotland 1888–1988*. Edinburgh: Polygon.

Neil, A. (1998) 'Scotland the Self-Deluded', pp. 11–12, *Spectator*, 15 August.

Newman, G. (1987) *The Rise of English Nationalism: A Cultural History 1740–1830*. London: Weidenfeld and Nicolson.

Nicholas, S. (1996) 'The Construction of a National Identity: Stanley Baldwin, "Englishness" and the Mass Media in Inter-War Britain', pp. 127–47, in M. Francis and I. Zweiniger-Bargielowska (eds) *The Conservatives and British Society, 1880–1990*. Cardiff: University of Wales Press.

—— (1998) 'From John Bull to John Citizen: Images of National Identity and Citizenship on the Wartime BBC', pp. 36–58, in R. Weight and A. Beach (eds) *The Right to Belong: Citizenship and National Identity in Britain, 1930–1960*. London: I.B. Taurus.

Norton, P. (1989) 'The Glorious Revolution of 1688 and 1689: Its Continuing Relevance', pp. 135–48, *Parliamentary Affairs*, Vol. 42, No. 2.

Oakeshott, M. (1948) 'Contemporary British Politics', pp. 468–81, *Cambridge Journal*, Vol. 1, No. 8.

—— (1975) *On Human Conduct*. Oxford: Clarendon Press.

—— (1991) *Rationalism in Politics and Other Essays*. Indianapolis: The Liberty Press.

O'Hear, A. (1998) 'Diana, Queen of Hearts', pp. 183–90, in D. Anderson and P. Mullen (eds) *Faking It. The Sentimentalisation of Modern Society*. Harmondsworth: Penguin Books.

O'Neill, M. (2000) 'Great Britain: From Dicey to Devolution', pp. 69–96, *Parliamentary Affairs*, Vol. 53, No. 1.

Osmond, J. (1988) *The Divided Kingdom*. London: Constable.

—— (1989) 'Educating the English', pp. 140–9, in O.D. Edwards (ed.) *A Claim of Right for Scotland*. Edinburgh: Polygon.

—— (1995) 'The Contradictions of Welsh Politics', pp. 31–47, *Scottish Affairs*, Vol. 11.

—— (1998) *The National Assembly Agenda*. Cardiff: Institute of Welsh Affairs.

Owens, D.E. (1985) Review of J. Osmond (ed.) *The National Question Again. Welsh Political Identity in the 1980s*, pp. 159–62, *Anglo-Welsh Review*, Vol. 81.

Parekh, B. (1994a) 'Discourses on National Identity', pp. 492–504, *Political Studies*, Vol. XLII.

—— (1994b) 'National Identity and the Ontological Regeneration of Britain', pp. 93–108, in P. Gilbert and P. Gregory (eds) *Nations, Cultures and Markets*. Aldershot: Avebury.

—— (2000) 'Defining British Identity', pp. 4–15, *Political Quarterly*, Vol. 71, No. 1.

Partridge, S. (1999) *The British Union State: Imperial Hangover or Flexible Citizens' Home?* London: The Catalyst Trust.

Paterson, L. (1993) 'Scottishness', pp. 1–4, *Scottish Affairs*, Vol. 4.

—— (1995) *The Autonomy of Modern Scotland*. Edinburgh: Edinburgh University Press.

—— (1998) 'Scottish Home Rule: Radical Break or Pragmatic Adjustment', pp. 53–67, *Regional and Federal Studies*, Vol. 8, No. 1.

—— and R. Wyn Jones (1999) 'Does Civil Society Drive Constitutional Change?', pp. 169–98, in B. Taylor and K. Thomson (eds) *Scotland and Wales: Nations Again?* Cardiff: University of Wales Press.

——, A. Brown and D. McCrone (1992) 'Constitutional Crisis: The Causes and Consequences of the 1992 Scottish General Election Result', pp. 627–39, *Parliamentary Affairs*, Vol. 45, No. 4.

Paxman, J. (1998) *The English: A Portrait of a People*. London: Michael Joseph.

Pinto-Duschinsky, M. (1967) *The Political Thought of Lord Salisbury 1854–1868*. London: Constable.

Plant, R. (1999) 'Crosland, Equality and New Labour', pp. 19–35, in J. Leonard (ed.) *Crosland and New Labour*. Basingstoke: Macmillan.

Pocock, J.G.A. (1975) 'British History: A Plea for a New Subject', pp. 601–28 *Journal of Modern History*, Vol. 47.

—— (1997) 'What Do We Mean by Europe?', pp. 12–29, *Wilson Quarterly*, Winter.

—— (1999a) 'The New British History in Atlantic Perspective. An Antipodean Commentary', pp. 491–500, *The American Historical Review*, Vol. 104.

—— (1999b) 'Enlightenment and Counter-Enlightenment, Revolution and Counter-Revolution: A Eurosceptical Enquiry', pp. 125–39, *History of Political Thought*, Vol. XX.

Pollard, S. (1999) 'Letter from London', pp. 161–4, *Partisan Review*, Vol. 66, No. 1.

Porter, R. (1993) 'Introduction', pp. 1–11, in R. Porter (ed.) *Myths of the English*. London: Polity Press.

Primoratz, I. (1994) 'The Word "Liberty" on the Chains of The Galley-Slaves: Bosanquet's Theory of the General Will', pp. 249–67, *History of Political Thought*, Vol. XV, No. 2.

Prosser, T. (1996) 'Understanding the British Constitution', pp. 473–88, *Political Studies*, Vol. XLIV.

Pugh, M. (1988) 'Popular Conservatism in Britain: Continuity and Change, 1880–1987', pp. 254–82, *Journal of British Studies*, Vol. 27.

Puntscher Riekmann, S. (1997) 'The Myth of European Unity', pp. 60–71, in G. Hosking and G. Schopflin (eds) *Myths and Nationhood*. London: Hurst and Company.

Radice, G. (1992) *Southern Discomfort*. London: Fabian Society.

Redwood, J. (1995) 'Labour Dream – a Nightmare', *Western Mail*, 18 January.

—— (1997) *Our Currency, Our Country. The Dangers of European Monetary Union*. Harmondsworth: Penguin Books.

—— (1999) *The Death of Britain?: The UK's Constitutional Crisis*. Basingstoke: Macmillan.

Richards, S. (1999) 'The NS Interview: Gordon Brown', pp. 18–19, *New Statesman*, 19 April.

Rifkind, M. (1998) 'Scotland, Britain and Europe: A New United Kingdom for a New Century', pp. 78–89, *Scottish Affairs*, Vol. 25.

Robbins, K. (1981) 'History, the History Association and the "National Past"', pp. 412–25, *History*, Vol. 66.

—— (1983) 'How Historians Can Construct a United Kingdom', pp. 3–4, *History Today*, December.

—— (1984) 'Core and Periphery in Modern British History', pp. 274–97, *Proceedings of the British Academy*, Vol. LXX.

—— (1995) 'An Imperial and Multinational Polity, 1832–1922', pp. 244–54, in A. Grant and K. Stringer, *Uniting the Kingdom?: The Making of British History*. London: Routledge.

—— (1998a) *Great Britain: Identities, Institutions and the Idea of Britishness*. Harlow: Longman.

—— (1998b) 'Britain and Europe: Devolution and Foreign Policy', pp. 105–18, *International Affairs*, Vol. 74, No. 1.

—— (1999) pp. 185–8, in G. Lucy and E. McClure (eds) *Cool Britannia? What Britishness Means to Me*. Lurgan: The Ulster Society.

Rose, B. and G. Ross (1994) 'Socialism's Past, New Social Democracy, and Socialism's Futures', pp. 439–69, *Social Science History*, Vol. 18, No. 3.

Rose, K. (1999) 'Don't Depend on Mr Blair, Ma'am', pp. 42–4, *Spectator*, 20 March.

Rose, N. (1999) 'Inventiveness in Politics', pp. 467–95, *Economy and Society*, Vol. 28, No. 3.

Rose, R. (1975) *The Future of Scottish Politics: A Dynamic Analysis*. Edinburgh: Scottish Academic Press.

—— (1982) *Understanding the United Kingdom: The Territorial Dimension in Government*. London: Longman.

—— (1985) *Politics in England: Persistence and Change*, 4th edition. London: Faber and Faber.

Roth, J. (1988) *Hotel Savoy*. London: Picador Classics.

Rowan, B. (1995) *Behaind The Lines: The Story of the IRA and Loyalist Ceasefires*. Belfast: The Blackstaff Press.

Royal Commission on the Constitution 1969–1973 (1973) *Report*, vol. 1. Cmnd. 5460. London: HMSO.

Ryan, A. (1997) 'New Labour – New Start', pp. 13–16, *Dissent*, Vol. 44, No. 3.

Saeed, A. et al. (1999) 'New Ethnic and National Questions in Scotland: Post-British Identities among Glasgow Pakistani Teenagers', pp. 821–44, *Ethnic and Racial Studies*, Vol. 22, No. 5.

Sally, R. (2000) 'Globalization and Policy Response: Three Perspectives', pp. 237–53, *Government and Opposition*, Vol. 35, No. 2.

Samuel, R. (1990) 'Grand Narratives', pp. 120–33, *History Workshop*, Vol. 29.

—— (1995) 'British Dimensions: "Four Nations History"', pp. iii–xxii, *History Workshop*, Vol. 40.

Sanders, D. (1996) 'New Labour, New Machiavelli: A Cynic's Guide to Economic Policy', pp. 290–302, *The Political Quarterly*, Vol. 67, No. 4.

Santayana, G. (1998) *The Genteel Tradition at Bay*. Lincoln and London: The University of Nebraska Press.

Sassoon, D. (1994) 'Social Democracy and the Europe of Tomorrow', pp. 94–101, *Dissent*, Vol. 41, No. 1.

Savage, J. (1996) 'Celtic Pride', p. 38, *Art Forum*, Vol. 35, No. 2.

Schochet, G.J. (1993), 'Why Should History Matter? Political Theory and the History of Discourse', pp. 321–57, in J.G.A. Pocock (ed.) *The Varieties of British Political Thought, 1500–1800*. Cambridge: Cambridge University Press.

Schonfield, A. (1972) *Europe: Journey to an Unknown Destination*. Baltimore: Penguin Books.

Schwarzmantel, J. (1991) *Socialism and the Idea of the Nation*. London: Harvester Wheatsheaf.

Scott, A. (ed.) (1997) *The Limits of Globalization: Cases and Arguments*. London: Routledge.

Scott, P. (1990) *Knowledge and Nation*. Edinburgh: Edinburgh University Press.

Scottish Constitutional Convention (1995) *Scotland's Parliament. Scotland's Right*. Edinburgh: Scottish Constitutional Convention.

Scruton, R. (1990) 'In Defence of the Nation', pp. 53–87, in J.C.D. Clark (ed.) *Ideas and Politics in Modern Britain*. London: Macmillan.

Seawright, D. and J. Curtice (1995) 'The Decline of the Scottish Conservative and Unionist Party 1950–92: Religion, Ideology or Economics?', pp. 319–42, *Contemporary Record*, Vol. 9, No. 2.

Seldon, A. (1997) *Major: A Political Life*. London: Phoenix.

—— and S. Ball (eds) (1994) *Conservative Century. The Conservative Party since 1900*. Oxford: Oxford University Press.

Seton-Watson, H. (1977) *Nations and States: An Enquiry into the Origins of Nations and the Politics of Nationalism*. London: Methuen.

Sharpe, L.J. (1985) 'Devolution and Celtic Nationalism in the UK', pp. 82–101, *West European Politics*, Vol. 8, No. 3.

Simon, S. (1999a) 'The Prime Minister Most in the Middle', pp. 11–12, *Spectator*, 23 January.

—— (1999b) 'Trimble: a Moses, not a Judas', p. 30, *Daily Telegraph*, 29 November.

Sinclair, T. (1970), 'The Position of Ulster', pp. 169–81, in S. Rosenbaum (ed.) *Against Home Rule*. Port Washington: The Kennikat Press.

Smart, I.M. (1980) 'The Political Ideas of the Scottish Covenanters, 1638–88', pp. 167–93, *History of Political Thought*, Vol. 1, No. 2.

Smith, A.D. (1990) 'Towards a Global Culture?', pp. 171–91, *Theory, Culture, and Society*, Vol. 7.

—— (1992) 'Chosen Peoples: Why Ethnic Groups Survive', pp. 436–56, *Ethnic and Racial Studies*, Vol. 15, No. 3.

—— (1995) *Nations and Nationalism in a Global Era*. Oxford: Polity Press.

—— (1996) 'Culture, Community and Territory: The Politics of Ethnicity and Nationalism', pp. 445–58, *International Affairs*, Vol. 72, No. 3.

—— (1998) *Nationalism and Modernism: A Critical Survey of Recent Theories of Nations and Nationalism*. London: Routledge.

Smith, B. (1977) 'Confusions in Regionalism', pp. 14–29, *Political Quarterly*, Vol. 48, No. 1.

Smith, C. (1996) *New Questions for Socialism*. London: Fabian Society.

Snicker, J. (1998) 'Strategies of Autonomist Agencies in Wales', pp. 140–58, *Regional and Federal Studies*, Vol. 8, No. 1.

Stapleton, J. (1993) *Law and State in English Political Thought since Dicey*. Durham Research Papers in Politics, No. 5.

—— (1994) *Englishness and the Study of Politics: The Social and Political Thought of Ernest Barker*. Cambridge: Cambridge University Press.

—— (1995) 'Dicey and His Legacy', pp. 234–56, *History of Political Thought*, Vol. XVI, No. 2.

Stargardt, N. (1998) 'Beyond the Liberal Idea of the State', pp. 22–36, in G. Cubitt (ed.) *Imagining Nations*. Manchester: Manchester University Press.

Steyn, M. (2000) 'Making Foreigners of Us All', pp. 20–1, *Spectator*, 1 January.

Studlar, D.T. and I. McAllister (1988) 'Nationalism in Scotland and Wales: A Post-industrial Phenomenon', pp. 48–62, *Ethnic and Racial Studies*, Vol. 11, No. 1.

Surridge, P. and D. McCrone (1999) 'The 1997 Scottish Referendum Vote', pp. 41–64, in B. Taylor and K. Thomson (eds) *Scotland and Wales: Nations Again?* Cardiff: University of Wales Press.

Taylor, A.J.P. (1977) *Essays in English History*. London: Book Club Associates.

Taylor, B., J. Curtice and K. Thomson (1999) 'Introduction and Conclusions', pp. xxiii–xlii, in B. Taylor and K. Thomson (eds) *Scotland and Wales: Nations Again?* Cardiff: University of Wales Press.

Taylor, P.J. (1991) 'The English and their Englishness: "A Curiously Mysteriously, Elusive and Little Understood People"', pp. 146–61, *Scottish Geographical Magazine*, Vol. 107, No. 3.

—— (1993) 'The Meaning of the North: England's "Foreign Country" Within?', pp. 136–55, *Political Geography*, Vol. 12, No. 2.

—— (1997a) 'Geographical Correctness', pp. 425–30, *Progress in Human Geography*, Vol. 21, No. 3.

—— (1997b) 'Is the United Kingdom big enough for both London and England?', pp. 766–70, *Environment and Planning A*, Vol. 29, No. 5.

Thatcher, M. (1989) *The Revival of Britain. Speeches on Home and European Affairs 1975–1988* (compiled by Alistair B. Cooke). London: Aurum Press.

—— (1993) *The Downing Street Years*. London: HarperCollins.

Thompson, E.P. (1963) *The Making of the English Working Class*. London: Gollancz.

—— (1978) *The Poverty of Theory and Other Essays*. London: The Merlin Press.

—— (1993) 'The Making of a Ruling Class', pp. 377–382, *Dissent*, Vol. 40, No. 3.

Thompson, H. (1997) 'The Nation-State and International Capital Flows in Historical Perspective', pp. 84–113, *Government and Opposition*, Vol. 32, No. 1.

Tilly, C. (1994) 'States and Nationalism in Europe 1492–1992, pp. 131–46, *Theory and Society*, Vol. 23.

Tindale, S. (1996) 'Introduction: The State and the Nations', pp. 1–12, in S. Tindale (ed.) *The State and the Nations: The Politics of Devolution*. London: Institute of Public Policy Research.

Tomaney, J. (1999) 'New Labour and the English Question', pp. 75–82, *Political Quarterly*, Vol. 70, No. 1.

Tomlinson, B.R. (1982) 'The Contraction of England: National Decline and Loss of Empire', pp. 58–73, *The Journal of Imperial and Commonwealth History*, Vol. XI, No. 1.

Tomlinson, J. (1998) 'Reconstructing Britain: Labour in Power 1945–1951', pp. 77–102, in N. Tiratsoo (ed.) *From Blitz to Blair: A New History of Britain since 1939*. London: Phoenix.

Tong, R. (1994) 'The English Dimension', pp. 14–17, *The Salisbury Review*, September.

Travers, T. (1998) 'The Freedom to be More Unequal', pp. xii–xii, *New Statesman* (special supplement), 26 June.

Trosset, C. (1993) *Welshness Performed: Welsh Concepts of Person and Society*. Tucson: University of Arizona Press.

Tsoukalis, L. and Rhodes, M. (1997) 'Economic Integration and the Nation-State', pp. 19–36, in M. Rhodes, P. Heywood and V. Wright (eds) *Developments in West European Politics*. Basingstoke: Macmillan.

Vincent, J. (1990) *Disraeli*. Oxford: Oxford University Press.

Vincenzi, C. (1998) *Crown Powers, Subjects and Citizens*. London: Pinter.

von Rezzori, G. (1983) *Memoirs of an Anti-Semite*. London: Picador.

Walden, G. (2000) *The New Elites: Making a Career in the Masses*. Harmondsworth: Penguin Books.

Wallace, W. (1990) 'Cry Havoc', pp. 16–17, *New Statesman*, 9 November.

—— (1992) 'British Foreign Policy after the Cold War', pp. 423–42, *International Affairs*, Vol. 68, No. 3.

—— (1999) 'The Sharing of Sovereignty: the European Paradox', pp. 503–21, *Political Studies*, Vol. XLVII, special issue.

Ward, P. (1998) *Red Flag and Union Jack: Englishness, Patriotism and the British Left, 1881–1924*. Rochester: Boydell Press.

Watson, G. (1973) *The English Ideology: Studies in the Language of Victorian Politics*. London: Allen Lane.

Weale, A. (1995) 'From Little England to Democratic Europe?', pp. 215–25, in B. Parekh (ed.) *British National Identity in a European Context, New Community* special issue, Vol. 21, No. 2.

Weight, R. (1999) 'Raise St George's Standard High', pp. 25–6, *New Statesman*, 8 January.

—— and A. Beach (1998) 'Introduction', pp. 1–19, in R. Weight and A. Beach (eds) *The Right to Belong: Citizenship and National Identity in Britain, 1930–1960*. London: I.B. Taurus.

Weir, R. (1999) 'The Scottish and Irish Unions: The Victoran View in Retrospect', pp. 56–66, in S.J. Connolly (ed.) *Kingdoms United? Great Britain and Ireland since 1500*. Dublin: The Four Courts Press.

Wheatcroft, G. (1999) 'Forging Our History', pp. 57–8, *New Statesman and Society*, 13 December.

Wigley, D. (1995) 'Quangos, Europe and Tory Rule Force New Ideas', *Western Mail*, 6 January.

Williams, C.H. (1982) 'Separatism and the Mobilization of Welsh National Identity', pp. 145–202, in C.H. Williams (ed.) *National Separatism*. Cardiff: University of Wales Press.

Williams, D. (1977) *A History of Modern Wales*, 2nd edition. London: John Murray.

Williams, E. (1989) 'The Dynamics of Welsh Identity', pp. 46–59, in N. Evans (ed.) *National Identity in the British Isles*. Cardiff: Centre for Welsh Studies Coleg Harlech.

Williams, Glanmor (1979) *Religion, Language, and Nationality in Wales*. Cardiff: University of Wales Press.

Williams, Gwyn (1991) *When Was Wales?* Harmondsworth: Penguin Books.

Williams, T. (1997) *The Patriot Game: Reflections on Language, Devolution and the Break-up of Britain*, vol. 1 Cardiff: Tynant Books.

Worsthorne, P. (1999) 'Only a Federal Europe Can Stop the Abolition of Britain', p. 27, *Spectator*, 4 September.

Wright, A. (1990) 'British Socialists and the British Constitution', pp. 322–41, *Parliamentary Affairs*, Vol. 43, No. 3.

Wright, P. (1991) *On Living in an Old Country. The National Past in Contemporary Britain*, 2nd edition. London: Verso.

Wyn Jones, R. and B. Lewis (1999) 'The Welsh Devolution Referendum', pp. 37–46, *Politics*, Vol. 19, No. 1.

—— and D. Trystan (1999) 'The 1997 Welsh Referendum Vote', pp. 65–94, in B. Taylor and K. Thomson (eds) *Scotland and Wales: Nations Again?* Cardiff: University of Wales Press.

Young, G.M. (1947) 'Government', pp. 85–111, in E. Barker (ed.) *The Character of England*. Oxford: The Clarendon Press.

Young, H. (2000) 'Little More than an Extension of France', pp. 18–20, *The London Review of Books*, 6 January.

Žižek , S. (1994) 'Identity and its Vicissitudes: Hegel's "Logic of Essence" as a Theory of Ideology', pp. 40–75, in E. Laclau (ed.) *The Making of Political Identities*. London: Verso.

—— (1997) 'Multiculturalism, or, the Cultural Logic of Multinational Capitalism', pp. 28–51, *New Left Review*, Vol. 225 Sept./Oct.

—— (2000) 'Why We All Love to Hate Haider', pp. 37–47, *New Left Review* (2nd series), Vol. 1.

Index